Policy Analysis and Economics

Recent Economic Thought Series

Editor: Warren J. Samuels
Michigan State University
East Lansing, Michigan, U.S.A.

Policy Analysis and Economics

Developments, Tensions, Prospects

Edited by
David L. Weimer

Kluwer Academic Publishers
Boston / Dordrecht / London

Distributors for North America:
Kluwer Academic Publishers
101 Philip Drive
Assinippi Park
Norwell, Massachusetts 02061 USA

Distributors for all other countries:
Kluwer Academic Publishers Group
Distribution Centre
Post Office Box 322
3300 AH Dordrecht, THE NETHERLANDS

Library of Congress Cataloging-in-Publication Data

Policy analysis and economics: developments, tensions, prospects/
    [edited by] David L. Weimer.
        p.   cm.—(Recent economic thought series)
    Includes bibliographical references and index.
    ISBN 0−7923−9154−3
    1. Policy sciences.   2. Economics.   I. Weimer, David Leo.
II. Series.
H97.P637   1991
338.9—dc20   91−3197
                                                                CIP

Printed on acid-free paper.

Printed in the United States of America

Contents

Contributing Authors

Amitai Etzioni
University Professor
Gelman Library, Room 714
George Washington University
Washington, D.C. 20052

Howard Frant
College of Business and Public Administration
453 B Harvill Building
University of Arizona
Tucson, Arizona 85721

W. Lee Hansen
Department of Economics
1180 Observatory Drive
University of Wisconsin
Madison, Wisconsin 53706

Alphonse G. Holtmann
Department of Economics
P.O. Box 248126
University of Miami
Coral Gables, Florida 33124

George Horwich
Department of Economics
Krannert Building

Purdue University
West Lafayette, Indiana 47907

Hank Jenkins-Smith
Department of Political Science
University of New Mexico
Albuquerque, New Mexico 87106

Robert H. Nelson
Office of Policy Analysis
U.S. Department of the Interior
18th and C Streets N.W.
Washington, D.C. 20240

John Pomery
Department of Economics
Krannert Building
Purdue University
West Lafayette, Indiana 47907

W. Kip Viscusi
Department of Economics
Duke University
Durham, North Carolina 27706

David L. Weimer
Public Policy Analysis Program
University of Rochester
Rochester, New York 14627

Preface

Long before policy analysis emerged as a separate profession with its own graduate schools, economists offered advice about government policies. Positive economics provides the tools for predicting the impacts of proposed policies; normative economics, especially welfare theory, offers a framework for valuing the impacts of policies in terms of efficiency and simple notions of equity. With the expansion of economic theory into ever wider fields of human behavior, it is no wonder that economists have prominence as teachers and practitioners of policy analysis. Indeed, many economists see policy analysis as essentially applied economics. Though other social scientists might object to this somewhat parochial view, economics and policy analysis share much in commom in terms of development and prospects. The purpose of this volume is to trace these interrelationships and explore the tensions that they create.

Tensions arise for several reasons. Changes in the discipline of economics affect the findings, methods, and personnel offered to policy analysis. For example, on the one hand, the "new institutional economics" appears to be extending the influence of economists to questions involving nonmarket oranizations, while on the other hand, the apparently growing emphasis within the economics profession on creating rather than empirically testing theory suggests that fewer of the best young scholars will be drawn to policy-relevant research. Within the schools of policy analysis, the drift toward public management may reduce the demand for traditional economic training. These changes may complicate the long-standing debate among policy analysts over the adequacy of the self-interest paradigm for predicting behavior and the appropriateness of welfare economics as a normative foundation for public policy.

Economists as Policy Analysts

The Progressive Movement, which emphasized the separation of technical expertise from politics, opened the door for the participation of economists in the formulation and evaluation of federal policy. In chapter 1, Robert H. Nelson traces the changing role of economists in policy-making from this early involvement to the present. He notes the spread of economists from agencies such as the Treasury Department, the Council of Economic Advisers, and the Federal Reserve, which deal directly with economic issues, to all the major units of the federal government. Either in terms of job classification or self-identification, the economists in federal executive agencies now number in the thousands. Add to these the economists serving the legislative branch in the Congressional Budget Office, the Congressional Research Service, and committee staffs, as well as the growing number of economists in "think tanks" and consulting firms who contribute research and analysis to the policy process, and one might conclude that economic analysis now makes an important contribution to public policy.

Though Nelson points to these numbers as a rough measure of the influence of economic analysis on federal policy, he notes several factors that have limited, and are likely to continue to limit, the effectiveness of economists as policy analysts.

First, as economists move beyond the traditional concerns of economic policy, they often must compete more directly with other sorts of expertise. At the Environmental Protection Agency, for instance, physical scientists have a claim to expertise about the substance of policy and lawyers have a claim to expertise about the policy-making process. Nelson notes that the limited influence of economists in this area is not only indicated by the rejection of effluent taxes, markets in pollution rights, and other policy instruments commonly advanced by economists but also by congressional prohibitions in some circumstances against the use of benefit-cost analysis, the primary technique of applied economic analysis. One might speculate that the prospects for the increased influence of economists in such substantive policy areas may be as much a function of the penetration of economics into the curriculum of the competing professions as it is a function of the direct participation of economists.

Second, the increasingly theoretical orientation of graduate training in economics does not sufficiently encourage the development of the practical skills most useful in policy analysis. Graduates with fields in public finance may never have been asked to do a benefit-cost analysis; those with fields in econometrics may know much about asymptotic theory but little about the nuts-and-bolts of collecting and using data; few graduates in any fields have experience explaining economic concepts in nontechnical terms. Nelson worries that, if trends continue, graduate programs in economics may no longer be a primary source of policy analysts. (In chapter 9, W. Lee Hansen considers the match between graduate education in economics and policy research of various kinds.)

Third, economists often have little perparation for dealing with the ambiguity of goals found in most areas of public policy. On the one hand, taking the concept of economic efficiency from welfare economics as the only goal of public policy puts the economist at odds with the distributional goals that loom so large in politics. On the other hand, it is naive to think that the political process can routinely provide sufficiently clear goals and their relative weights so that policy analysis can be viewed as an optimization problem. Nelson argues that economists, and other experts, are likely to enjoy even less professional authority in the future so that to be influential they will have to address the full range of values held by participants in the policy process.

Welfare Economics as a Normative Foundation for Policy Analysis

Efficiency informs normative economic analysis. In chapter 2, Hank Jenkins-Smith discusses the evolution of this value from its utilitarian foundations to its development in welfare economic theory as Pareto efficiency and in application as potential Pareto efficiency. He notes the recurring criticisms of these concepts as the normative basis for policy analysis: Accepting preferences as given ignores the possible role of education and public discourse in shaping values; defining social value only in terms of the preferences of individuals slights socially desirable processes such as democratic choice; Pareto efficiency as a theoretical concept takes the initial endowment as a given; use of the potential Pareto criterion as a practical rule does not guarantee that adopted policies will actually leave everyone better off; and intangible costs and benefits tend to be excluded in application of the potential Pareto criterion.

In addition to these criticisms, which have been discussed extensively in the policy literature, Jenkins-Smith identifies two others that are likely to be the focus of future debate. One criticism is the issue of standing in benefit-cost analysis. Whose preferences count? Economists usually measure costs and benefits in terms of national polities. But should willingness to pay be aggregated for citizens, residents, illegal aliens, or criminals?

How should the preferences of future generations be counted? Economists have given little attention to resolving these questions of practical importance to policy analysis.

The second criticism concerns the inadequacy of welfare economics as a framework for evaluating alternative institutional arrangements. Changes in technology and tastes may create opportunities for increasing aggregate welfare through the alteration of the system of entitlements, rights, and obligations. Jenkins-Smith reviews the arguments made by Daniel W. Bromley that proper evaluation of such "institutional transactions" demands a broader concept of social welfare than Pareto efficiency. Bromley argues that some reference must be made to a social welfare function for the determination of social efficiency. Jenkins-Smith worries that Bromley's approach might leave economic analysis so indeterminate as to make it ineffective.

In chapter 3, Alphonse G. Holtmann considers the development of the concept of the social welfare function in modern welfare economics. He focuses on the question: What can economists contribute to the discussion of distributional issues in public policy? Although it is unrealistic to expect the political system to provide economists with social welfare functions for evaluating policies with both efficiency and distributional effects, economists may be able to make a contribution by determining what form the social welfare function would have to take to justify the selection of one policy rather than another. They can also contribute by moving discussion beyond consideration of only the static consequences of policies to such dynamic topics as econonic growth and intergenerational equity.

Holtmann is optimistic that positive economics can play an increasing role in informing public policy. The greater availability of data and increasing computing power make distributional analysis more feasible. Further, as economic theory advances it should permit better predictions of the effects of alternative policies.

Economics as a Positive Basis for Policy Analysis

The belief in the adequacy of positive economics is not universally shared, however. In chapter 4, Amitai Etzioni challenges the basic assumption of neoclassical economics that individuals act in their own self-interest. He does not wish to replace the self-interest assumption but rather to expand behavioral motivations to include moral and social considerations. So, for example, he rejects explanations of altruism in terms of self-interest as reductionist and uninformative. He argues that concerns about what one ought to do not only explain altruistic acts but also the much more common obedience to laws, observance of conventions, and general respect for others that make society civil.

Accepting the positive proposition that moral and social considerations do affect behavior in important ways has important normative implications. Public policies should not just be evaluated in terms of the material incentives they provide, but also in terms of their contributions to personal and social norms that promote socially desirable behavior. In other words, preferences should not be taken as given, and the nature of social relationships should not be ignored.

The major problem with the socioeconomic approach to policy analysis advocated by Etzioni is our relative inability to predict behavior in terms of noneconomic variables that can be manipulated by government. If socioeconomics is to replace neoclassical economics as the dominant paradigm for policy analysis, it must provide a theory that offers better predictions of the consequences of policy alternatives. Until a track record develops, it is likely to serve largely as an important reminder that self-interest does not explain all policy relevant behavior.

Even this role is hindered by a lack of theory. Consider, for example, Etzioni's critique of educational choice and educational vouchers. His criticisms fall largely within the standard economic framework: Parents face an informational asymmetry in evaluating schools, and wealthier parents enjoy a larger choice set. Yet one might be inclined to make socio-economic arguments in favor of parental choice and vouchers: They invigorate the desirable social norm of parental involvement in education, and they increase the opportunity for parents to express a demand for moral education consistent with their beliefs.

Less fundamental, but nevertheless policy-relevant, challenges can be made to positive economics. In chapter 5, W. Kip Viscusi considers decision making under uncertainty, a topic in positive economics especially important to public policy in the areas of health, safety, and environment. Despite the considerable success of the expected utility model in predicting behavior in situations of uncertainty, accumulating evidence from laboratory experiments and observation of insurance markets brings its adequacy into question. It is not just that people sometimes deviate from the predictions of the expected utility model, but that they often seem to do so in systematic ways such as overestimating very small risks and underestimating relatively larger ones. Obviously, a theory that can encompass these behaviors without forfeiting the successes of expected utility theory is very desirable for predicting the consequences of public policies.

Viscusi rejects prospect theory, which allows the utility of lotteries to depend on functions of the probabilities and utilities of prizes, because it can accommodate almost any patterns of behavior and thus offers few predictions. Instead, he proposes what he calls "prospective reference theory," which is based on Baysian updating of information about probabilities. Individuals hold beliefs about the probabilities of future events. As they discover more information, they update their beliefs, moving closer, but not necessarily all the way, to beliefs consistent with the new information. Viscusi argues that prospective reference theory explains most of the documented anomalies in risk behavior while preserving the expected utility framework as a basis of ex ante prediction.

Critics of the neoclassical paradigm have also argued that it largely ignores the problem of institutional design. The view that market competition weeds out less efficient forms of organization has made the problem of institutional design seem unimportant to many economists until recently. Of course, the limited competition faced by most government organizations should have attracted attention to the problem of nonmarket supply, but the dominant tradition in public finance, the field of most direct relevance, was to focus on market failures as justifications for government rather than the more general question of appropriate institutional design. In recent years, however, several intellectual streams have coalesced into what has become known as the new institutional eonomics. In chapter 6, Howard Frant outlines these intellectual streams and considers the relevance of the new institutional economics for policy analysis.

One stream takes the transaction as the basic unit of analysis. Beginning with Ronald Coase in the 1930s, a small number of economists have attempted to understand the choice between production and contracting in terms of the minimization of transaction costs. The work of Oliver Williamson, for example, points to opportunism, asset specificity, and bounded rationality as important attributes of the contracting process.

The second stream considers the problem of agency: How can contracts between principals and agents be structured so as to minimize the sum of discretionary and monitoring costs? Frant notes that it shares with the transaction cost framework a central concern with opportunism. Nevertheless, because it posits self-interested behavior and explicitly models asymmetric information, it has been much more readily accepted by economists than the transaction cost framework.

The new institutional economics that is taking shape seems to be encompassing these streams within a game theoretic framework. It is likely to interest more economists in a number of questions cutting across substantive areas of public policy. Frant points to a better understanding of privatization and the functioning of the nonprofit sector as areas where economists are just starting to make policy-relevant contributions. More generally, he sees the new institutional economics as expanding the range of policy instruments commonly considered by economists to include changes in institutional structures as well as changes within existing structures.

Applications: Macroeconomics and Trade Theory

The relationship between economics and public policy exhibits different trends in different areas of application. Economists have played, and will continue to play, a dominant role in the area of macroeconomics. In the area of trade policy, however, the weakening of the apparent professional consensus in support of free trade may make economists relatively less influential in the future than they have been in the past.

In chapter 7, George Horwich traces the development of macroeconomic theory and its influence on public policy from the Great Depression to the current debate over the significance of the federal budget deficit. He argues that, just as the comparative statics of supply and demand provide a powerful framework for micropolicy, comparative statics with appropriately defined aggregate supply and aggregate demand can play a similar role in macropolicy.

It is only relatively recently, however, that aggregate supply has received serious treatment from macroeconomists involved in policy debates. The Keynesian system, which focuses attention on the problems created by inadequate aggregate demand, served as the basis for the large-scale macroeconomic models that became major analytical tools in the federal agencies during the 1970s. It is not surprising that these models did not deal well with the oil price shocks of that decade—economic shocks having their primary effects through shifts in aggregate supply. The Council of Economic Advisers, though less bound to any particular model, also viewed the oil price shocks as having adverse effects largely through reductions in aggregate demand. Indeed, CEA at various times supported petroleum price controls, strongly rejected by most microeconomists, because they might limit the transfer of funds to oil companies and a subsequent reduction in aggregate demand.

A major macroeconomic controversy continues to surround the implications of the apparently large federal deficits of the 1980s. Horwich sees this controversy continuing. He argues that resolution demands fundamental changes in the way the deficit is measured.

Overall, the story that Horwich tells is one of relatively slow shifts in macroeconomic policy. Nevertheless, despite considerable controversy over the relevant theory, economists usually play a central role in the policy process. Aside from the fact that the substance of the macropolicy falls squarely within the purview of economics, one can speculate that the diffuse costs and benefits of macropolicy leave economists less constrained by the competition of organized interests within the political process.

In the case of trade policy, however, costs and benefits tend to be concentrated for industries so that they have an incentive to seek various forms of protection from the government. Until recently, a near consensus among economists in favor of free trade has provided a strong conceptual bulwark to blunt somewhat the concentrated interests seeking protectionism. The new trade theory, which starts from the perspective of imperfect competition, has begun to break the consensus among economists for free trade as a first "rule of thumb."

In chapter 8, John Pomery reviews the growing controversy among trade theorists over the free trade prescription. Even economists who start from the assumption of competitive world markets have long admitted the possibility that in some circumstances, such as when an importer has monopsony power or domestic markets are distorted, protective measures can be welfare enhancing. But the new trade theory admits many more possibilities. Critics charge, however, that its conclusions are too sensitive to small changes in assumptions for it to be a reliable guide for public policy. They also fear that the very breakdown of near consensus among economists will clear the way for special interests to secure protections.

After clarifying the issues in this ongoing debate, Pomery turns in his last sections to several fundamental questions in the philosophy of science that are relevant not only to trade theory but more generally to other areas of economic theory with policy implications. Indeed, the questions he raises provide the broadest conceptual framework for the topic of this volume and therefore deserve consideration even from those readers not specifically interested in trade theory.

Pomery suggests that a conflict in theoretical perspectives underlies the debate. Just as Newtonian and quantum mechanics each have validity in certain circumstances, so too might the competitive perspective of the old trade theory and game theoretic perspective of the new trade theory. If each has validity in some circumstances, more and better empirical evidence will be unlikely to resolve the debate. A clearer specification of both what is inside and outside of each perspective is needed for deciding which is appropriate for informing any particular policy issue.

Making perspectives more comprehensive may not necessarily be the best approach for policy purposes. Pomery notes, for example, the conceptual puzzle that arises in interpreting models that endogenously predict trade policy for each country based on strategic interaction among governments and domestic interest groups. If such models describe and predict well, by what means would one expect an exogenous policy recommendation to have any effect? Pomery points out that endogenizing political behavior and information acquisition push potential leverage points on policy to areas such as ideology, ideas, and institutions.

Economics Training and Policy Analysis

In the final chapter of the volume, W. Lee Hansen considers the prospects for policy research remaining a major concern of economists. He notes factors that suggest the declining importance of policy research for the academic economists who train and influence the coming generations of economists. Recent years have witnessed less availability of funding for empirical policy research. The very proliferation of economists within government has reduced the demand by agencies for economics faculty as consultants and visitors, thus weakening the attraction of policy research and reducing the opportunity for policy experience. Perhaps of greatest significance, however, is the apparent mismatch between the knowledge and skills emphasized in the most highly ranked doctoral programs in economics and the skills most useful to practicing policy researchers and analysts.

Hansen draws on recent findings of the American Economic Association's Commission on Graduate Education in Economics to characterize doctoral training and its applicability for policy practitioners. A majority of current faculty believe that knowledge of theory is, and should be, emphasized. A majority of surveyed Ph.D.s from the 1977–1978 cohort report that, even though theory was emphasized in their own doctoral training, the emphasis in their current jobs, both academic and nonacademic, is on application, The apparent mismatch is even more striking with respect to skills. Whereas the educational experience emphasizes analytics and mathematics, practitioners point to the importance of communication skills and critical judgment in their current jobs.

How important is the mismatch? On the one hand, the continued demand for economists as policy analysts suggests that the knowledge and skills currently emphasized in doctoral training have intrinsic value, provide a good foundation for acquiring the more immediately useful skills, or at least signal the ability to be analytical. Indeed, formal training in most professions emphasizes theory over practice so as to provide as solid foundation for self-learning. Further, the graduates of public policy schools serve as good substitutes for economists in situations where the more practical skills take precedence. On the other hand, if the trend away from policy research in graduate programs continues, even fewer students with an interest in policy will be recruited, possibly leading to a poor correspondence between the interests of new Ph.D.s and the jobs that many will inevitably take outside of academia. Hansen notes that this trend, along with the reduced opportunity for academic economists to gain policy experience, suggests that public policy schools will find it more difficult to recruit appropriate economists for their faculties in the future, thus perhaps threatening the quality of their products.

Economics and economists now make essential contributions to policy analysis. It is inconceivable that economics will not continue to be one of the foundations of policy analysis. The declining involvement of academic economists in policy research may be but a temporary phenomenon. Yet it might signal a more significant trend toward a sharp division of labor between the faculty of economics departments who speak mainly to other academic economists about puzzles within the body of economic theory and economists in professional schools, government, and think-tanks who speak mainly to issues of public policy. Such a division of labor need not concern either economists or policy analysts as long as the division is not so complete as to preclude intellectual exchange.

David L. Weimer
University of Rochester

Policy Analysis and Economics

1 ECONOMISTS AS POLICY ANALYSTS: HISTORICAL OVERVIEW

Robert H. Nelson

1. Introduction

Through the mid-nineteenth century a major task of American colleges was to train students for the ministry; they read Adam Smith and other economists in their study of moral philosophy. In the late nineteenth century, however, higher education acquired a new mission (Bledstein, 1976; Buck, 1965). In the future the university would be the training ground for a scientific elite to manage American society. The social sciences were required along with many other specialized disciplines to provide the technical knowledge to serve this purpose. The role of the economist as policy analyst took shape in this era.

The underlying belief motivating these changes was that social and individual behavior obeyed scientific laws that were discoverable and usable, much as in the realm of physical science. If a correct scientific understanding of the laws that controlled social and individual behavior could be achieved, it would be possible to build a new and better society—one reflecting the improvements that physical science was generating in the physical world. It was the heyday of faith in human progress based on scientific knowledge—hence, the characterization of the "progressive" era (Waldo, 1984).

1

The creation of the American Economic Association (AEA) in 1885 reflected these beliefs (Coats, 1960; Farmer, 1975; Rader, 1966). The first AEA statement of principles indicated the existence of "a vast number of social problems, whose solution requires the united efforts, each in its own sphere, of the church, of the state, and of science" (Ely, 1977: 140). Richard Ely, the founding father of the AEA, was also a leading member of the social gospel movement who sought to improve the conditions of the poor, to create a more equal distribution of income, and to serve other progressive causes, all based on a scientific analysis of American society. Improvements in the condition of American labor, for example, depended on assembling facts and figures relating to the actual condition of labor and then applying this scientific knowledge to develop a program of social reform. Moreover, Ely was no academic recluse; he wrote widely, including popular books and magazine articles and took his case for progressive reforms directly to the American public. His efforts were so successful that a later historian would find that Ely had exerted "a pervasive influence on [American] social thought and the course of social reform both during the 80's and 90's and during subsequent periods of reform" (Fine, 1964: 238).

Ely's activism and explicit grounding of his efforts in an ethical set of convictions, however, generated unease among many of his fellow economists. Frequently, they did not share Ely's particular convictions and in any case saw a conflict between the objectivity that economic science was seeking and the enlisting of economics in a particular reform movement. By 1892 pressures of fellow economists drove Ely out as secretary (chief administrative officer) of the AEA. There was increasing acceptance among American economists that a sharper dichotomy should be maintained between scientific and political activities.

2. The Progressive Model

The scientific-political dichotomy would be central to the governing theories of the American progressive movement of the early twentieth century. According to progressive writers, government should be divided into two distinct domains, one of politics and a second of technical expertise (Goodnow, 1967). Politics would be characterized by subjective considerations involving social values, ethical beliefs, and other matters unsuitable for scientific determination. Taking such factors into account, political leadership would set the overall social goals. Then, in the second domain of expertise, decisions would be made to implement these goals, based on objective knowledge derived from scientific research. Much of the routine administration of government was believed by progressives to be the proper responsibility of professional experts. In such matters special interests and other political influences should be strictly excluded.

Economists had a critical role in the progressive vision because they were the keepers of the particular field of expert knowledge concerned with material growth and production. Indeed, the diminishing of material scarcity was critical to progressive thinking because it would reduce conflict over possession of material goods—and ultimately, many hoped, such conflict would become unnecessary and irrelevant. The striving for greater possessions and riches in the past had been the source of much of the wars, hatreds, and other human misbehavior in history. If modern progress now seemed to offer the possibility of material abundance, the future might hold a new heavenly condition on earth, a kind of secular salvation of humankind. The economics profession would become a leading priesthood guiding the way.

Such a vision appeared in the writings of the professional economist who achieved the greatest visibility in the progressive era. A leading historian of progressivism describes Thorstein Veblen as having had "the most brilliant mind of his time" (Wiebe, 1967: 153). If outside the professional mainstream and unique in many respects, Veblen was nevertheless associated closely with the institutional school of economics, which also included John R. Commons, John Wesley Mitchell, and a number of other American economists. This school contended with neoclassical economists for supremacy in American economics during the first two decades of this century but then receded sharply in numbers and influence (Dorfman, 1959).

Veblen portrayed in graphic form many of the themes that were characteristic of progressive thought. The management of an increasingly complex society required "a core of highly trained and specially gifted experts, of diverse and various kinds," who would constitute the "indispensable General Staff of the industrial system." They would be possessed of "technological knowledge" of a character that was "exactly specialized, endlessly detailed, reaching out into all domains of empirical fact." Even in business, Veblen believed, technically trained engineers should be given final control of enterprises because they were not "in any degree benefited by any supervision or interference on the side of the owners" and thus should operate "unhampered by commercial considerations and reservations" (Veblen, 1965: 68–70).

Although progressive thinking developed the foundations for the creation of the American welfare state in the twentieth century, and for the role that economists would play in administering it, only the first steps were taken in the progressive era itself. Agencies such as the Civil Service Commission (1883), Bureau of Labor Statistics (1884), Interstate Commerce Commission (1887), Forest Service (1905), Food and Drug Administration (1906), Federal Reserve Bank (1913), Federal Trade Commission (1914), and Bureau of the Budget (1922) paved the way for what would later in the century become an even greater proliferation of federal agencies and responsibilities. Initially, the role of economists in the new progressive agencies was limited. Professional foresters, for example, dominated the new Forest Service, which had few ecomomists and did little economic analysis (Nelson, 1985). And professionals in the field of public administration held sway at the Bureau of the Budget. At the Federal Reserve System, however, economics professionals played a major role from the beginning.

Within cabinet agencies, the Bureau of Agricultural Economics, created in 1922 to advise the secretary of Agriculture, became a leading center for economic research and policy study. This office may well have been the first of the many policy "shops" that are found now in virtually every federal agency (Barber, 1981, 1985). In the 1920s and 1930s economists in government exerted probably more influence over agricultural policy than over any other area of federal policy. The efforts of government economists laid the groundwork for new American farm policies of the 1930s. Some, such as E. J. Working, Mordecai Ezekiel, and Frederick Waugh, were also prominent leaders in American agricultural economics and contributed significantly in broader professional fields such as the development of statistical methods and econometrics in the United States (Fox, 1986).

3. The Spread of Economists in Government

The depression of the 1930s, and then to even a greater degree the demands of World War II, brought economists in growing numbers to the federal government (Stein, 1986). Many economists participated individually in developing legislation for and administering New Deal programs. A Federal Reserve economist, Lauchlin Currie, did much in the 1930s to introduce Keynesian ideas into Washington policy debates. During the later New Deal, economists also began asserting a greater institutional and formal presence in government. Two of the most important current economic staffs were created in 1938, the Office of Tax Analysis of the Treasury Department and the economic staff of the Antitrust Division of the Justice Department. The Office of Tax Analysis in the 1940s consisted of around 25 economists and at one time or another included a number of leading future members of the American economics profession —among them, E. Cary Brown, Richard Goode, Milton Friedman, C. Lowell Harriss, Walter Heller, Joseph Pechman, Nancy Ruggles, and Carl Shoup. Paul Samuelson served for a time as a consultant.

Another important development during the New Deal years was the government's assuming of responsibility for assembling and publishing national income statistics (Duncan and Shelton, 1978). Initially, this effort was privately undertaken by the National Bureau of Economic Research (NBER) under the leadership of John Wesley Mitchell. Founded in 1919 by Mitchell, the NBER worked during the 1920s to solve theoretical and practical problems of national income accounting. In the early 1930s, Simon Kuznets, an NBER employee on loan to the Commerce Department, spearheaded the publication of the first comprehensive national income estimates of the federal government. The Bureau of Economic Analysis in the Commerce Department, which is today responsible for GNP, national income, and other basic economic statistics, traces its origins to these developments in the early 1930s.

World War II gave a further large boost to the employment of government economists, as federal planners assumed control over many economic tasks. Economists were required to assist in economic planning and coordination to meet military production requirements, to impose price controls, to collect new taxes, to supply allies, and to study enemy economic capabilities. During the war years the number of economists in the State Department, for example, increased from about 100 to about 400 and the Bureau of Economic Analysis was created, in 1944.

The visibility of government economists rose still further with the enactment of the Employment Act of 1946, creating the Council of Economic Advisers (CEA) (Flash, 1965). The council consists of a chairman, who reports directly to the President, and two other council members. They are assisted by a small staff of 15 to 20 economists, typically recruited from leading universities for temporary stays in government. The CEA was given the role of promoting high employment with stable prices and otherwise overseeing the macroeconomic management of the U.S. economy. Influenced by newly spreading Keynesian ideas, and desiring to avoid any repetition of the depression years, Congress accepted that the government could in principle manage scientifically the future overall directions of the American economy. This new charge to American economists involved an abandonment of earlier laissez-faire views of a self-regulating economic system; instead, the members of the American economics profession and the expert knowledge they possessed were now to be responsible for assuring a happy national macroeconomic result.

4. Economists and Politics: An Uneasy Relationship

The agencies in which economists served and the expectations of economists themselves were generally based on progressive political theories and writings. Yet, as more economists entered government service, they often found their experiences at odds with progressive formulations. Other social science and professional experts often had similar experiences. Historian Barry Karl (1963: 222) writes of the 1930s that "some of those who had considered their mission to Washington a new step forward in the relations between government and the academic community left with the feeling that they had, in part at least, been subjected to a political trick." It turned out that democratic politicians were much less respectful of the boundaries of professional expertise than the experts coming into government had been led to expect. Indeed, many concluded that "political elites only use social science for ends that still fit into the jungle politics [that] science was supposed to be eliminating" (Seidelman, 1985: 148).

As the focal point for the activities of economists in government, the Council of Economic Advisers would offer important lessons for economists concerning the relationship of economic professionals with the political process. The first CEA chairman, Edwin Nourse, sought to adhere closely to the progressive model (Nourse, 1953). The CEA should supply the President and other top political leaders of the executive branch with data on economic trends, possible danger signs in the economy, alternative economic policy measures, and other important economic information. Reviewing the menu of options developed by his economic advisers, the President would then make a choice that in part reflected social values (e.g., the pain caused by unemployment versus the harm of inflation), his own political aims, and other subjective factors. Nourse went so far in adhering to this view as to decline even to participate in some key policy discussions that he regarded as having an excessively political content.

Nourse was rewarded for his loyalty to progressive prescriptions with a reputation for ineffectiveness and weakness. His successors would not make the same mistake. Leon Keyserling, and all subsequent CEA chairmen, have found the maintenance of a strict dichotomy of politics and economic expertise to be unworkable. For one thing, economic policymaking raises political and value concerns that frequently seem to be inextricably interwoven with the economic elements. To advocate an economic policy effectively, therefore, also requires advocating the political and value consequences. Economists in government could not credibly suggest to political leaders that noneconomic matters were outside their domain but were the responsibility of someone else. Successful advocacy of sound economic policies depended on the ability to package economic policies with political, administrative, legal, and other attractive features. In choosing an economic policy measure, a government economist might well be compelled to pick second-best economic answers because they had superior political prospects.

The CEA achieved perhaps its greatest influence under the chairmanship of Walter Heller in the 1960s. Heller successfully promoted the "Kennedy tax cut," which helped to spur rapid economic growth in the mid-1960s and raised the public reputation of government economists to new heights. Heller was a skillful player in the internal politics of the Kennedy administration and also was adept at public persuasion, especially using the medium of television. (He would eventually appear on "Meet the Press" 12 times, a frequency exceeded by only three other public figures.) Heller later explained that "the detached, Olympian, take-it-or-leave-it approach to presidential economic advice—the dream of the logical positivist—simply does not accord with the demands of relevance and realism." Instead, the economic adviser in government "presses the case for some measures and against others" (Heller, 1967: 15). This approach may involve pointing out not only economic consequences but also "political hazards." As Gardner Ackley, Heller's successor as CEA chairman, put it, "If his economic adviser refrains from advice on the gut questions of policy, the President should and will get another" (Ackley, 1966: 176).

Not only the three CEA members but the professional staff as well found that in practice a direct involvement with politics was common place and perhaps inevitable. Reflecting on his experiences on the CEA staff in 1963–1964, Burton Weisbrod observed that almost every staff member became in part an "amateur political strategist." They would "think about how we could get this thing through that group, who would accept what, and what kind of friends and allies you needed to do what" (Allen, 1977: 67–68). The choice of topics, the factors taken as given, and the policy solutions proposed could all be significantly influenced by political, administrative, and other noneconomic considerations.

5. The Demise of the Progressive Model

The experiences of economists mirrored changing views among political scientists and other students of American government in the years following World War II. Dwight Waldo, for example, wrote in 1948 that "either as a description of the facts or a scheme of reform, any simple division of government into politics-and-administration is inadequate." Instead, "the governing process is a 'seamless web of discretion and action'" (Waldo, 1984: 128). Another leading political scientist, David Truman (1951), portrayed American politics in terms of interest-group pressures exerted throughout the affairs of government; special interests could not be confined to a domain of politics. Indeed, by the late 1960s Theodore Lowi would conclude that many students of government saw no alternative to, and were now defending the legitimacy of, a governing system of "interest-group liberalism" (Lowi, 1969: 68). The proper goal of American politics was to incorporate all the affected interests into the decision-making process; the social acceptability and legitimacy of government decisions depended on achieving a satisfactory compromise among all the parties.

In one of the most famous social science articles of the post-war era, Charles Lindblom (1959) wrote of government as "the science of 'muddling through.'" Contrary to progressive expectations for comprehensive planning and rational decision making, government seldom was able to set clear goals and frequently failed to evaluate systematically the alternative courses of action. Democratic political preferences and social values could seldom be established in advance to guide administrative and other expect decisions. Instead, the values themselves were an outcome of the muddling process, typically revealed only after the fact. Lindblom found that "pluralism" best described the practices of American government, a pluralism of interest-group pressures, conflicting ideologies, bureaucratic incentives, and still other inputs.

In such a process economists became yet another voice pressing their case, although in this instance the objective was not to establish an interest-group agenda but to advance particular economic policies and more generally an economic way of thinking. Thus, commenting on his experiences as director of the Bureau of the Budget in the mid-1960s, Charles Schultze observed that "political values permeate every aspect of the decision-making process in the majority of federal domestic programs. There is no simple division of labor in which the politicians 'achieve' consensus on an agreed-on set of objectives while the 'analysts' design and evaluate—from efficiency and effectiveness criteria—alternative means of achieving these objectives" (Schultze, 1968: 2–3). Schultze saw the necessity for economists to enter directly and energetically into the pluralistic processes by which decisions were made in American government. They would function not as disinterested technicians but as active advocates for an economic point of view, the official spokespersons in internal government debate for more efficient programs and policies. As Schultze now concluded, the proper role of economists in government would be to serve as "partisan efficiency advocates" (Schultze, 1968: 101).

In the mid-1960s Schultze was taking action to put his views into practice not only at the Bureau of the Budget (BOB) but more broadly throughout government by means of the Planning, Programming, and Budgeting System (PPBS). When BOB was founded in 1922, its efforts were grounded in the precepts of scientific administration, taught at leading American universities in professional schools of public administration (Berman, 1979). The emphasis was on achieving greater efficiency through a better understanding of the proper span of control, personnel policies, and other administrative mechanics. In the 1960s, however, BOB shifted its emphasis to an economic understanding of efficiency, reflected in the preparation of benefit-cost studies, the undertaking of cost-effectiveness analyses, and generally the use of economic methods and tools. The first director of BOB in the Kennedy administration was an economist, Kermit Gordon. Including Gordon, four of the past nine directors have been economists.

This ascendancy of economic thinking and professional economists at the budget office reflected a governmentwide trend in the 1960s and 1970s. Economists began to analyze and recommend policy in fields where they had previously had little input. Partly for this reason, the number of economists in government, which had already grown rapidly after World War II, continued its rate of increase in this period.

Statistics on the numbers of economists in government are derived in several ways. For one set of calculations, the Office of Personnel Management (OPM) (1987) compiles data on the numbers of federal employees who occupy positions formally classified "economist." By this standard, the number of federal economists totaled 2,221 in 1947 and rose by 57 percent to reach 3,480 in 1961. Over the next 16 years it rose another 52 percent, yielding 5,298 economists in 1977. However, growth slowed considerably in the next decade, with OPM reporting 5,748 federal economists in 1987. These economists represented 0.4 percent of all federal civilian employment in 1987. The State Department had the largest number (1,167), followed by the Labor Department (1,069), Agriculture Department (837), Commerce Department (516), Department of the Treasury (306), and Department of the Army (301). Women represented 22 percent of federal economists in 1987; 65 percent of federal economists worked in the Washington, D.C. area; and 18 percent had a Ph.D.

Another source of data on the number of federal economists is the National Science Foundation (NSF, 1988). The NSF survey is not based on formal job classifications but reflects self-identification of job status. It thus includes many who work on policy analysis, program planning, policy evaluation, and other such tasks yet who consider themselves economists.

For 1986 NSF estimated that there were 12,800 federal economists, more than twice the number identified by OPM. According to NSF, federal economists represented about 8 percent of the economics profession nationwide. About 35 percent were engaged in "reporting [of economic data], statistical work, and computing"; 28 percent in "management/ administration"; 27 percent in "research and development"; and the remaining 10 percent in other duties.

The post–World War II rise of the American welfare state thus stimulated a demand for the skills of many economists in government, performing a wide range of tasks. Many were engaged in the generation of economic statistics, production of economic reports, and other activities that did not routinely bring them into direct contact with top policy-makers. Other economists served as close advisers to high-level officials and in some cases assumed top political positions themselves. Initially, economists were concentrated in agencies with specific economic responsibilities. However, an important development since the 1960s has been the use of economic analysis and the spread of policy analysts into many fields where they previously had had little involvement.

6. The Old and the New Policy Economics

Economists were traditionally found in important policy-making positions in areas where the economics profession had a long research interest and where the objective of the government agency tended to be narrowly economic. Thus in addition to the Council of Economic Advisers, the agencies in which economists had the largest institutional presence over the years were the Treasury, Department of Commerce, and Federal Reserve. The Department of Agriculture and the Department of Labor also traditionally included large numbers of economists in statistical and economic research departments, although their impact on policy was less assured and was often considerably diluted by strong interest-group pressures, competing professional groups, and the diverse viewpoints found in these agencies. In the 1960s, however, economists began to move outside of traditional domains to take on whole new fields. It was the beginning of a period that in the social sciences has since been characterized as exhibiting a pervasive "economic imperialism," challenging the basic methods and outlooks of other fields of social science inquiry (Radnitzky and Bernholz, 1987). There were related developments within government as well, as economists in new policy fields challenged other professional groups for their traditional dominance.

The formal introduction of economic and systems analysis in the early 1960s in the Defense Department opened one major new policy area in which economists had previously made a limited contribution. The development of the Planning, Programming, and Budgeting System (PPBS) in the mid-1960s was modeled after Defense Department efforts. Although PPBS was dismantled early in the Nixon administration, its goals and purposes survived in a less formal and more incremental way. In the 1970s offices of policy analysis, program planning, and similar designations were created throughout the federal government (Meltsner, 1976).

Although there were predecessor offices in many cases, the new offices tended to give a greater emphasis to, and to ground their thinking in, economics (Nelson, 1989; Wildavsky, 1979: 407–419). By means of such offices, economic approaches to policy issues obtained an institutional base in diverse agencies such as the Department of Housing and Urban Development; the Department of Health, Education and Welfare; the Environmental Protection Agency; the Department of Transportation; and ultimately almost every major federal agency. The creation of the Congressional Budget Office in 1974 similarly gave the Congress a much increased capability to obtain its own independent sources of economic analysis.

The new agencies in which economics was now being applied often differed in a number of respects from the traditional economic agencies. Frequently the new agencies had to confront value questions more explicitly and in ways that did not arise, for instance, in designing a price index to measure inflation. Economists might propose vouchers as a means of using the market mechanism to improve American education, but such a proposal would inevitably be challenged as undermining the sense of national unity promoted by a common system of public education. The very legitimacy of a market approach and method thus was an issue in the education field. Similarly, health policy operated in a setting in which a market allocation of access to health care was increasingly rejected; within a bureaucratic system of health care, rationing access according to economic calculations of benefits and costs was also widely unacceptable. In the environmental field Congress in some cases expressly prohibited federal agencies from even considering benefits and costs in deciding allowable pollution levels and in making other environmental policy decisions.

In these new arenas for the application of economic ideas, economists also frequently encountered other professional groups with their own long-standing policy preferences, administrative approaches, and world views. Doctors, educators, foresters, military officers, environmental scientists, and other professionals—to say nothing of the lawyers found everywhere—often clashed with economists. Noneconomists, for example, often proclaimed a standard of maximum physical output at the highest quality as the proper social goal. In the Forest Service, professional foresters stated that maximizing the physical volume of wood was the appropriate output objective for timber harvest policy in the national forests. Foresters, like noneconomics professionals in most fields, often strongly opposed introducing discount rates, applying benefit-cost tests, and using other economic methods. In some cases, remarkable as it was to economists first encountering these fields, noneconomics professionals were even reluctant to enter explicitly the costs of production into their calculations with respect to socially appropriate output levels.

The role of interest groups was often greater in policy-making outside traditional economic agencies. When the Federal Reserve adopts a monetary policy, or the Council of Economic Advisers recommends a fiscal policy, the impacts tend to fall over broad areas of the American economy. Because of the breadth of the impacts, the President and other high-level officials often become involved. Although tax policy has traditionally been filled with special-interest provisions, the enactment of the Tax Reform Act of 1986 demonstrated that in this area as well strong presidential and other high-level leadership could overcome the many demands for special tax treatment. The federal agencies responsible for collection of economic statistics have been successful over the years in defending their activities from interest-group pressures. By contrast, when the Corps of Engineers decides whether to build a dam in a particular county, or when the Bureau of Land Management decides whether to increase fees for grazing cattle on public land, special-interest pressures are frequently decisive. In such areas intensely interested parties have well-developed skills and a long record of success in obtaining their particular needs from government.

In the newer agencies all these factors tended to impose on economists a less secure status and greater obstacles to exerting a policy impact. Confronted with direct challenges to their influence and sometimes to their very presence, economists have had to try to develop skills over a wider range. Economists in the newer agencies were more likely to see themselves in terms of policy "entrepreneurs." They have had to "sell" more effective policies in their agencies, exhibiting an entrepreneurial resourcefulness and frame of mind (Leman and Nelson, 1981).

Economists in the newer agencies have also been pressed in recent years to defend explicitly the way of thinking that is implicit in the application of economic analysis (Rhoads, 1985). Such a defense takes economists well beyond the realms of economic or even political analysis, into the domains of philosophy and cultural analysis. To argue that an economic approach is an appropriate way of thinking is to make a claim with respect to core assumptions and values on which society is based. In short, one of the newer roles of a government economist might be said to be that of "ideological combatant," recognizing that by ideology is meant a perspective or way of thinking about the world such as economics represents.

In the new agencies the educational backgrounds of those who applied economic tools often differed from those in the traditional economic agencies. In the latter a graduate degree in economics, often a Ph.D., has frequently been expected. In the new policy and program evaluation offices, however, there is much greater variety, reflecting the wider range of skills sought. In many cases staff members have degrees from public policy schools whose intent has been to provide a basis not only for effective economic analysis but also for the adoption and implementation of this analysis in the policy arena. Other practitioners of the new policy economics may not have formal training in either economics or public policy. In the newer agencies there is less confidence that any one form of education or type of knowledge is uniquely suited or even necessary to being an effective policy economist.

7. The Impact of Policy Economists

The introduction of policy economists in most Washington agencies has by now generated a considerable literature concerning their impact and contribution to policy formulation (Nelson, 1987). On the whole, the reports are mixed. Policy economists have failed to realize the high expectations of the 1960s, when at least some proponents expected that the spreading use of economic analysis would sharply increase the overall rationality and efficiency of government. Yet, there have been some major successes and many minor triumphs.

The deregulation of several key industries and tax reform, two of the most important policy developments of the past 15 years, were significantly attributable to the efforts of government economists. The foundations for deregulation were laid in a series of economic studies—many sponsored by the Brookings Institution and later the American Enterprise Institute— from 1960 onward. By the mid-1970s the political climate had shifted to the point where deregulatory measures were becoming feasible. In the late 1970s two professional economists, Alfred Kahn and Darius Gaskins, became chairmen of the Civil Aeronautics Board and the Interstate Commerce Commission, respectively. In these positions they led successful efforts to enact legislation significantly deregulating the American transportation industry. They were assisted by many other government economists in less visible staff positions. Economists also played important roles in the deregulation of the communications and energy industries. Reviewing these developments, Martha Derthick and Paul Quirk (1985: 246) conclude that "if economists had not made the case for pro-competitive deregulation, it would not have occurred—at least on the scale the nation has witnessed."

As director of the economic studies program at Brookings, Joseph Pechman was a key figure in supporting the groundwork not only for deregulation but also for tax reform. Economists had long criticized the tax system for setting high marginal rates and then undermining these rates through numerous loopholes. The consequence was both to offend a widely held American sense of equity and to seriously distort the efficiency of national investment. In 1977 David Bradford, a Princeton economist then serving as director of the Office of Tax Analysis in the Treasury Department, organized the writing of the *Blueprints for Basic Tax Reform*, which stimulated considerable discussion of basic changes in tax law. In 1984 another economist in the Office of Tax Analysis, Eugene Steuerle, organized the preparation of a comprehensive proposal for tax reform. Many political compromises later, much of this effort survived in the historic Tax Reform Act of 1986 (Minarek, 1989).

There have also been areas in which government economists have been less successful. Since at least the early 1970s, many government and other economists have argued that U.S. environmental policies should rely less on command-and-control methods and more on market incentives. Most economists initially favored taxes on pollution, but in recent years a number have seen equal or greater merit (and political feasibility) in a system of marketable permits to pollute. Although 1990 legislation to amend the Clean Air Act includes a market permit system, the use of the market mechanism for environmental purposes has on the whole made little headway. Economists have generally had a peripheral role in the development of environmental policy over the past quarter century. Their proposals to apply benefit-cost tests to the development of regulatory rules, for instance, have not met much greater success than their proposals to use the market mechanism (Anderson and Ostro, 1983).

The problems of the savings and loan industry illustrate a failure of another type among policy economists. In this case few economists recognized the ingredients brewing for a national economic loss of huge magnitude or forcefully took the argument for remedial actions to the public and political leadership. Although a handful of economists were in the field and had an understanding of the problems, these economists tended to see their obligations in a limited professional context. It was enough to write articles or books making the information, and a professional diagnosis of it, available to policy-makers. It was not necessary—or perhaps even compatible with professional norms—to became a public crusader for savings and loan reform in the way that an Alfred Kahn had done with respect to the deregulation of key industries.

In the defense area, where there were such high expectations for economic analysis in the 1960s, the results have fallen well short. A number of weapons systems have, however, been altered or canceled, based at least partly on economic arguments. Reviewing the three decades over which the use of economic and systems analysis has become institutionalized within the Defense Department, Peter deLeon (1987: 122, 124) found that "in many instances, one can plausibly argue that analysis has played a substantial, beneficial role in defense policy-making." Yet, there have also been many failures, partly because "the key to successful policy analysis and formulation is the definition of objectives. Yet, . . . there is nothing resembling agreement on this central issue, either in terms of ends or means." As have economists working in areas of domestic policy, deLeon (124–125) concludes that in the future "defense analysts must explicitly incorporate the social and political aspects of policy into the defense decision-making calculus" and that "defense analysts are being forced to incorporate contexts, assumptions, and approaches well beyond the system analysis techniques once thought to be the cardkeys to policy-making chambers."

In the 1960s a number of economists began to argue forcefully that controlled experiments were required to resolve key issues that underlay policy developments in areas such as welfare, health, education, and housing. With strong support from economists serving in government policy offices, a series of major social experiments were undertaken, eventually receiving more than $1 billion (1983 dollars) in federal funds (Greenberg and Robins, 1986: 357–360). These experiments yielded estimates superior to those that had been available concerning matters such as the impact of a negative income tax on work effort. Yet, different analysts often achieved different statistical results, and a "litany of problems" clouded the overall reliability (Haveman, 1987: 193).

Haveman (175–199) suggests that on balance the social experiments exerted a constructive influence on policy-making. Greenberg and Robins (1986: 351) are somewhat less enthusiastic, concluding that "the lessons provided so far by previous social experiments are not especially encouraging." One problem was that "the researchers have sometimes appeared to be more concerned with methodological issues than with policy issues," an orientation promoted by the disinclination of professional journals to publish articles that "merely report results using standard evaluation techniques." Partly for this reason, the level of researcher communication with the ostensible beneficiaries of their efforts, the "government agencies, Congress, the administration and the general public" has generally been poor and "has sometimes been nonexistent" (346–347). Contrary to many initial expectations, the overall effect of social experiments tended to dampen enthusiasm of political leaders for social policy reforms; by raising complex questions, and then providing answers that were inconclusive or cast doubt on proposed solutions, policy-makers were more likely to shy away from bold departures.

A systematic examination of the experiences of a range of economists serving at high policy-making positions in government was undertaken by William Allen (1977). From 1972 to 1976 Allen taped interviews with about 60 economists who had had such experience. Typical of many responses, W. Lee Hansen, who had worked on the staff of the Council of Economic Advisers, saw the role of the policy economist as "just good-common-sense economics. . . . The kind of basic analytical framework that we all sort of got in Econ 101. . . . Simple supply and demand and benefit-cost. . . . If you can just keep these things in your mind, plus if you are open to seeing how they might have to be modified in the light of institutional constraints and considerations, then, I think that's the game really" (Allen, 1977: 70–71).

Summing up the overall sense of the many economists interviewed, Allen offered a pessimistic assessment of the influence of high-level economists in the normal course of events:

> In speaking with economists who are or have been in government, one obtains a picture and gains an impression which is sobering. The government economist typically is not a highly independent researcher and analyst, free first to pick many of his subjects and entirely free to broadcast generally the results of his labors. He is a member of an organization, commonly devoting the bulk of his time to topics specified from on high—the specification often being enunciated only a few days (or, indeed, hours) before the deadline; conscious of a prevailing orientation and purpose on the part of these administrative superiors who constitute his main audience; conscious, also, that the decisionmakers he is more or less directly advising are themselves subject to constraints of worldly realism and political feasibility—along with innocence in the area of economic analysis; bringing to his task an accumulated intellectual capital which, even if impressive at the outset of his government work, may not thereafter be greatly enlarged or even well maintained; having more or less available a corpus of theory and an arsenal of techniques which, for all their elegance, refinement, and

academic glamor, are often too time-consuming for purposes of shooting from the hip and too esoteric for the data, the colleagues, and the audience; and having little reason to suppose that his work has significant impact in the making of policy, being largely confined to support of programs and procedures determined earlier and by others and for which he may have only modest sympathy. [pp. 86–87]

8. The Future of Policy Economics

In the current period there are trends both favorable and unfavorable to the future role and influence of policy economists in government decision making (Rivlin, 1987; Pechman, 1989). For the past 15 years energy policy, deregulation, tax reform, and deficit reduction—all in significant degree economic issues—have been at the center of national policy debates. Indeed, economists have had the opportunity to play visible and important roles in these national debates. Economics has become the leading currency of Washington policy discussion. Even when political factors may be the driving force, proponents of policy initiatives are today commonly expected to show how these initiatives will contribute to higher incomes and the growth of U.S. economic productivity. Thus, current proponents of major reforms in the U.S. education system frequently argue that these reforms are needed to improve international economic competitiveness and to make the best possible investment in the future of the nation.

Although conflicts in the Middle East still seem to follow older patterns, the waning of the cold war suggests that the international politics of military alliances will receive declining attention in the future, while international economic relations (and environmental relations) may become more important. Recent events in communist nations, including the virtual renunciation of communist economic organization in Eastern Europe, have focused the attention of the world on the problems of establishing a market economy and generally building a satisfactory economic system. The leading message of the economics profession for many years, the efficiency of using the market mechanism, has now become the message of political leaders all over the world. Numerous economists are being consulted and their services sought for tasks that may be critical to the future peace and well-being of the world.

Other trends, however, suggest a less promising future for policy economists. The reputation of economists with the American public has eroded sharply since the high point of the mid-1960s. Predictive and other failures have diminished public confidence in the scientific qualities of economic knowledge. The tendency of economists to divide among themselves and seemingly to quarrel endlessly over so many policy matters is perhaps even more damaging to the scientific prestige of economists. If such erosion in its scientific status continues for long, difficult questions concerning the legitimacy and proper role of economics in government may be raised.

The forces buffeting the economics profession are symptomatic of developments affecting all American professions in recent years. The past 20 years has seen a sharp decline in public confidence in experts and in almost any type of professional who makes claims to special authority based on expertise. Experts are seen as commonly asserting much more knowledge than they actually possess. Experts are accused of often failing to maintain objectivity and neutrality; instead, they offer value-laden conclusions, even while presenting these conclusions in many cases as scientific truths. Thus not only economists but lawyers, doctors, psychologists, foresters, and many other professionals have been facing a growing public distrust.

The future world in which policy economics operates will seemingly be a world in which economists, and other professionals as well, will have to persuade top officials, not by asking these officials to trust their professional authority, but by persuading in the language and in the manner of argument that are the daily fare of ordinary government debate and public discussion. The persuasive skills called for will involve the ability to draw convincing historical analogies; to take diverse events and integrate them into a big picture; to show that economic policy proposals make sense from political, moral, legal, philosophical, and other perspectives; to find simple statistics and data that effectively make a point; and to convert broad policy principles into feasible short-term measures that over time will serve to implement these principles.

This exercise will be much closer to art than to science (Wildavsky, 1979). The need for all these and other skills will impose new demands and pressures on the educational institutions responsible for training the policy economists of the future. What will be needed will be graduates who have at least some command of many disciplines and who have the ability to see connections and to tie diverse strands together. In a way it will be a return to an emphasis on the liberal arts, requiring a reversal of the trend to specialization that has marked university life for many years—indeed, since the progressive era. The challenge will be, as higher education once saw its mission, to instill and support the qualities of judgment, resourcefulness, commitment, and the capacity to grasp the larger dimensions of political and economic issues.

Meeting this challenge, to be sure, will not be easy. Indeed, recent trends in economics education at the graduate level seem, if anything, to be moving in the opposite direction, toward specialization and emphasis on mathematical and statistic skills over breadth of knowledge. In the worst case, the result could be a group of economics professionals who are suited only for teaching other professionals in the nuances of a self-contained system. If the economics profession is itself unable to supply the need for policy-relevant economic advice, society will undoubtedly look elsewhere —perhaps to public policy schools, but there are a number of other possible sources. Both the economics profession and the quality of economic advice might eventually prove to be the worse for this result.

References

Ackley, Gardner, "The Contribution of Economists to Policy Formation," *The Journal of Finance* 21:2 (May 1966), 169–177.

Allen, William R., "Economics, Economists, and Economic Policy: Modern American Experiences," *History of Political Economy* 9:1 (Spring 1977), 48–88.

Anderson, Robert C., and Ostro, Bart, "Benefits Analysis and Air Quality Standards," *Natural Resources Journal* 23:3 (July 1983), 565–575.

Barber, William J., *From New Era to New Deal: Herbert Hoover, the Economists and American Economic Policy, 1921–1933* (New York: Cambridge University Press, 1985).

———, "The United States: Economists in a Pluralist Society," in A. W. Coats, ed., *Economists in Government: An International Comparative Study* (Durham, N.C.: Duke University Press, 1981).

Berman, Larry, *The Office of Management and Budget and the Presidency, 1921–1979* (Princeton: Princeton University Press, 1979).

Bledstein, Burton J., *The Culture of Professionalism: The Middle Class and the Development of Higher Education in America* (New York: Norton, 1976).

Buck, Paul, *Social Sciences at Harvard: From Inculcation to the Open Mind* (Cambridge: Harvard University Press, 1965).

Coats, A. W., "The First Two Decades of the American Economic Association," *American Economic Review* 50:4 (September 1960), 555–574.

deLeon, Peter, "The Influence of Analysis on U.S. Defense Policy," *Policy Sciences* 20:2 (1987), 105–128.

Derthick, Martha, and Quirk, Paul J., *The Politics of Deregulation* (Washington, D.C.: The Brookings Institution, 1985).

Dorfman, Joseph, *The Economic Mind in American Civilization: Volumes IV and V, 1918–1933* (New York: Viking, 1959).

Duncan, Joseph W., and Shelton, William C., *Revolution in United States Government Statistics, 1926–1976* (Washington, D.C.: Government Printing Office, 1978).

Ely, Richard T., *Ground Under Our Feet: An Autobiography* (New York: Arno Press, 1977; first ed. 1938).

Farmer, Mary O., *Advocacy and Objectivity: A Crisis in the Professionalization of American Social Science, 1865–1905* (Lexington: University of Kentucky Press, 1975).

Fine, Sidney, *Laissez-Faire and the General Welfare State: A Study of Conflict in American Thought, 1865–1901* (Ann Arbor: University of Michigan Press, 1964).

Flash, Edward S., Jr., *Economic Advice and Presidential Leadership: The Council of Economic Advisors* (New York: Columbia University Press, 1965).

Fox, Karl A., "Agricultural Economists as World Leaders in Applied Econometrics, 1917–1933," *American Journal of Agricultural Economics* 68:2 (May 1986), 381–386.

Goodnow, Frank J., *Politics and Administration: A Study in Government* (New York: Russell and Russell, 1967; first ed. 1900).

Greenberg, David H., and Robins, Philip K., "The Changing Role of Social Experiments in Policy Analysis," *Journal of Policy Analysis and Management* 5:2 (Winter 1986), 340–362.

Haveman, Robert H., *Poverty Policy and Poverty Research: The Great Society and the Social Sciences* (Madison: University of Wisconsin Press, 1987).

Heller, Walter W., *New Dimensions of Political Economy* (New York: Norton, 1967).

Karl, Barry Dean, *Executive Reorganization and Reform in the New Deal: 1932–1940* (Cambridge, Mass.: Harvard University Press, 1963).

Leman, Christopher K., and Nelson, Robert H., "Ten Commandments for Policy Economists," *Journal of Policy Analysis and Management* 1:1 (Fall 1981), 97–117.

Lindblom, Charles E., "The Science of 'Muddling Through,'" *Public Administration Review* 19:2 (Spring 1959), 79–88.

Lowi, Theodore J., *The End of Liberalism: Ideology, Policy and the Crisis of Public Authority* (New York: W. W. Norton, 1969).

Meltsner, Arnold J., *Policy Analysts in the Bureaucracy* (Berkeley: University of California Press, 1976).

Minarek, Joseph J., "How Tax Reform Came About," in David Colander and A. W. Coats, eds., *The Spread of Economic Ideas* (New York: Cambridge University Press, 1989).

National Science Foundation, *Profiles-Economics: Human Resources and Funding*, special report NSF 88–333 (Washington, D.C.: November 1988).

Nelson, Robert H., "The Office of Policy Analysis in the Department of the Interior," *Journal of Policy Analysis and Management* 8:3 (Summer 1989), 395–410.

———, "The Economics Profession and the Making of Public Policy," *Journal of Economic Literature* 25:1 (March 1987), 49–91.

———, "Mythology Instead of Analysis: The Story of Public Forest Management," in Robert T. Deacon and Bruce M. Johnson, eds., *Forestlands: Public and Private* (San Francisco: Pacific Institute for Public Policy Research, 1985).

Nourse, Edwin G., *Economics in the Public Service: Administrative Aspects of the Employment Act* (New York: Harcourt Brace, 1953).

Office of Personnel Management, *Occupations of Federal White-Collar and Blue-Collar Workers*, Pamphlet 56–20, September 30, 1987.

Pechman, Joseph A., "The United States," in Joseph A. Pechman, ed., *The Role of the Economist in Government: An International Perspective* (New York: New York University Press, 1989).

Rader, Benjamin G., *The Academic Mind and Reform: The Influence of Richard T. Ely in American Life* (Lexington: University of Kentucky Press, 1966).

Radnitzky, Gerard, and Bernholz, Peter, *Economic Imperialism: The Economic Method Applied Outside the Field of Economics* (New York: Paragon House, 1987).

Rhoads, Steven E., *The Economist's View of the World: Government, Markets, and Public Policy* (New York: Cambridge University Press, 1985).

Rivlin, Alice M., "Economics and the Political Process," *The Amercian Economic Review* 77:1 (March 1987), 1–10.

Schultze, Charles L., *The Politics and Economics of Public Spending* (Washington, D.C.: Brookings Institution, 1968).

Seidelman, Raymond, *Disenchanted Realists: Political Science and the American Crisis, 1884–1984* (Albany: State University of New York Press, 1985).

Stein, Herbert, "The Washington Economics Industry," *American Economic Review* 76:2 (May 1986), 1–9.

Truman, David B., *The Governmental Process: Political Interests and Public Opinion* (New York: Alfred A. Knopf, 1951).

Veblen, Thorstein, *The Engineers and the Price System* (New York: Augustus M. Kelley, 1965; first ed. 1921).

Waldo, Dwight, *The Administrative State: A Study of the Political Theory of American Public Administration* (New York: Holmes and Meier, 1984; first ed. 1948).

Wiebe, Robert H., *The Search for Order, 1877–1920* (New York: Hill and Wang, 1967).

Wildavsky, Aaron, *Speaking Truth to Power: The Art and Craft of Policy Analysis* (Boston: Little Brown, 1979).

2 CONTINUING CONTROVERSIES IN POLICY ANALYSIS

Hank Jenkins-Smith

1. Introduction

Contemporary public policy analysis is built on a foundation of principles at the heart of welfare economics: Analysts are typically trained to rely on aggregation of individual preferences to specify social value, generally in terms of economic surplus. While there are indeed other foundations of policy analysis and there are numerous challenges to the primacy of welfare economics (Kelman, 1981; DeLeon, 1989; Brown, 1991), the dominant paradigm for public policy remains deeply imbedded in the concepts and principles of microeconomics and the primacy it places on efficiency (Jenkins-Smith, 1990).

Despite their continuing prominence in the foundations of policy analysis, controversy over welfare economic principles has been both vigorous and sustained. Furthermore, the critiques of the welfare economic bases of policy analysis have become more fundamental and—in this writers view— more compelling as critics have applied closer scrutiny to contemporary analytical techniques.

This chapter will assess those controversies in the application of welfare economic principles in policy analysis that have shown greatest tenacity. Discussion will begin with a brief review of the development of utility theory and the concepts of efficiency as the cornerstones of contemporary policy analysis and then turn to those critiques who most directly challenge these cornerstones. The more venerable charges of distortion of public preferences and violations of the process of public discourse will be reviewed but primary attention will be given to more recent critiques who challenge both the application and the normative bases of efficiency as the primary criterion for choice in public policy. The chapter will conclude with a discussion of the implications of these critiques for the practice of policy analysis.

2. The Development of Utility Theory and Efficiency

The concept of efficiency has evolved over the past two centuries, beginning as a key element of a reformist political movement and undergoing transformation toward an ever more technical and "content-free" analytical concept. Central to the concept of efficiency is the theory of utility as developed by economists from foundations first laid by Jeremy Bentham. According to Bentham, human experience provides utility when it produces "benefit, advantage, pleasure, good, or happiness" or when it prevents "mischief, pain, evil, or unhappiness" (Bentham, [1789] 1970). Individual behavior can be understood as the pursuit of utility, based on a hedonistic calculus designed to maximize pleasure and minimize pain. The value of an act or experience was to be defined in terms of the pleasures and pains it brought to individuals; individuals were thus the ultimate arbiters of value. Drawing on these premises, Bentham called for enlightened formulation of public policy based on the principles of utility (Bentham, [1776] 1977).

For Bentham the concept of utility was rich in substantive content. The chief dimensions of utility were (1) intensity, (2) duration, (3) certainty or uncertainty, and (4) propinquity or remoteness. Also important were fecundity, meaning the likelihood that the pleasure or happiness would be followed by more of the same, and purity, meaning the likelihood that the pleasure would *not* be followed by pain (Bentham, [1776] 1977: 38–41). Bentham lists on less than 26 categories of pleasures and pains making up the "simple" roots of utility to which all specific pains and pleasures can be reduced, including (but not limited to) sense, wealth, skill, amity, good name, power, piety, benevolence, and association (Bentham, [1776] 1977: chap. 5).

Much like economists who followed him, Bentham employed money as a common metric in the measurement of utility, and he argued that the value of money itself *decreases* as the amount of money held increases—a phenomenon later dubbed "the decreasing marginal utility of money." As Bentham argued, "the quantity of happiness produced by a particle of wealth (each particle being of the same magnitude) will be less and less at every particle" (Bentham, 1843: 229).

For Bentham, the development and use of utility theory in the formulation of public policy rested on an unresolved ambiguity. On one hand, Bentham held that it would be impossible to determine the quantity of utility that an individual obtained from an experience or to compare the gains or losses of utility of any two individuals. On the other hand, unless one *could* reasonably compare the utilities of individuals, the utility calculus would provide little aid to the formulation of public policy. Bentham's solution was simply to *assume* utilities to be comparable and to justify the assumption as providing a useful tool for legislators that would be, at worst, far better than any basis for legislation that failed to take utility into account.

A central weakness in Bentham's calculus was the incomparability of individual utilities in prescribing legislation for the "greatest good." Given that the pursuit of the greatest good for the greatest number would often involve utility losses for some, could we be sure that the added value to the gainers would offset the losses to the losers? The incomparability of individual utilities would seem to preclude such assurance. Utility theorists following Bentham struggled with this problem and generally rejected Bentham's contention that utilities could be assumed comparable.

More recent utility theorists have broadened and generalized the theory of utility, effectively purging it of the substantive form specified by Bentham. Political economists Stanley Jevons (1911), Leon Walras (1926), and Carl Menger (1871), among others, altered Bentham's formulations to focus on the satisfaction to be obtained from the possession of individual goods (see Stigler, 1975: 220–241, for an overview). Among these early theorists the concept of diminishing marginal utility (holding that the increment of utility gained from possession of an added unit of a good declines as the number of units possessed increases) was deemed a general law of utility. Furthermore, most early marginal utility theorists held total utility of the individual to be derived from simple summation of the utilities gained from the goods possessed by the individual.

This formulation, however, ignored complementary and substituting goods, which, when consumed, change the utility to be gained from consumption of other goods. This problem led theorists to specify a more general individual utility function that would allow for utilities to be affected by such relationships among goods (Edgeworth, 1881). The general utility function eliminated the need to assume diminishing marginal utility for consumption of individual goods in order to assure equilibrium in economic trades; indeed, diminishing marginal utility was shown to be neither a necessary nor sufficient condition for achievement of equilibrium conditions (Stigler, 1965: 126). Still later development of utility theory, based on the concept of indifference schedules, took a further leap toward generality; the conception of individual utility itself that had underlaid the development of utility theory was abandoned as too "metaphysical" and restrictive.[1]

Utility theory has thus been marked by a progressive development away from the substantively grounded, limited theory of utility proposed by Jeremy Bentham; successively, interpersonal comparisons of utility, additive individual utility functions, the requirement of diminishing marginal utility, and even the "metaphysical" conception of utility itself have been shed in favor of increasingly general propositions.

Despite the increasing generality of the theory, the prescriptive "legislative" role of utility theory envisioned by Bentham has been preserved. That prescriptive role is embodied in the concept of economic efficiency. The normative heart of the concept of efficiency (derived straight from Bentham) holds that a social system or policy ought to be designed to maximize the satisfaction of individual wants, subject to certain limitations on the analyst's ability to specify what constitutes an "improvement" in overall want satisfaction. Thus efficiency analysis, like Bentham's calculus of pleasure and pain, is based solidly on an individualistic and utilitarian view of human activity. It is assumed at the outset that the system is made up of individuals and that each individual has an ordinally ranked set of wants or "preferences." "Society" is thus strictly an aggregation of individuals, and social welfare is no more or less than the aggregation of the welfare of the individuals that make up the society.

The chief limitation confronting the efficiency analyst is the premise that each individual holds a possibly unique schedule of preferences; without omniscient capabilities it is impossible to determine whether satisfaction of one individual's wants adds more to total well-being (or social welfare) than would satisfaction of some other individual's wants. Rather than confront the problem of the incomparability of individual utilities directly, the criterion of efficiency seeks a way around this problem.

Simply stated, an individual's well-being can occur either (a) without reduction (and perhaps with improvement) in the well-being of others or (b) with a concomitant decrease in the well-being of others. In the latter case, due to the assumed incomparability of individual utilities, it is impossible to determine whether society was a whole is made better off by the change. In the former case, when one person's gain is not offset by the losses of others, the sum of the individuals' welfare can unambiguously be said to have increased. This represents a clear-cut increase in the efficiency with which wants are satisfied.

According to this strict criterion of efficiency, dubbed the Pareto optimality criterion, if at any time any individual can be made better off without reducing the well-being of others, the system is not operating strictly efficiently. There exists no uniquely efficient allocation of resources; beginning from any suboptimal distribution of wealth, movement toward efficiency can be achieved by distributing the added increment of well-being in countless ways among the members of society. Thus many Pareto superior solutions exist, differing according to the distributions of goods achieved.

Unbending application of the strict Pareto optimality criterion would impose severe restrictions on government action: No policy, no matter how beneficial it might be to the community as a whole, could be taken that diminished the well-being of even one individual. In the extreme, even an action required to maintain the viability of the community (say, maintenance of law and oder) would violate the criterion if any person, on the basis of his or her own assessment of the effect of the action on his or her utility, determined that the action would leave the person worse off than would no action at all. But clearly much of government action does just that.

The "potential Pareto principle" allows redistributions that increase net welfare such that those who gain from the redistribution *could* compensate those who lose, restoring the losers to their prior level of well-being, while the winners retain enough of their gains to be better off than they would have been without the redistribution (Hicks, 1939). In this case individuals' utilities need not be compared: as long as a common value of the good redistributed is available, such as the money value of the gains and losses to the individuals involved, it is possible to determine just how much of the improvement to the gainers must be given in compensation to the losers to assure that no one is worse off than they would have been without the redistribution. Thus the criterion specifies that a system that results in an allocation of goods from which subsequent redistribution could result in *net* increases in social well-being is not efficient. Furthermore, in the comparison of policies, the relevant criterion is: Which policy option serves to create the largest net gain in social well-being?

The potential Pareto criterion is the central normative standard in contemporary public policy analysis. Texts in policy analysis, and curricula in the major schools of public policy in the United States, widely invoke efficiency as the most prominent, and least ambiguous, of the guides for public policy analysts (Jenkins-Smith, 1990; Friedman, 1987; Stokes, 1986; Weimer and Vining, 1989).

3. Normative Critiques of Contemporary Policy Analysis

Drawing on its origins in welfare economics, policy analysis would provide objective analysis and advice; that is, for a given policy option, the results of analysis would reflect the maximized sum of objectively measured and aggregated net benefits for the individuals constituting society. Thus, in an important sense, analysis based on welfare economic principles is antipolitical; it is designed to remove social decision making "from the tumult of politics to the domain of putatively scientific, dispassionate inquiry" (Nieman, 1984). Policy analysis is to be a vehicle whereby political conflict over public policy is reduced. This element of contemporary policy analysis reflects, at least in part, the stance of the prophets of the "end of ideology," contending that the withering of ideological differences will lead to a commonality of ends, wherein only means will remain dispute (Bell, 1960; Bell and Kristol, 1965). According to Edith Stokey and Richard Zeckhauser (1978: 261),

> one objective of descriptive analysis is to narrow areas of disagreement in policy disputes. . . . Policy disagreements would lessen—and perhaps vanish—if we could predict with certainty the safety consequences of the breeder reactor, or the cost of annual upkeep of clay [tennis] courts, or whether a special shuttle bus for the elderly would be heavily used.

Analysis can thus reduce political conflict by moving the debate from argument about values—about which "men can only ultimately fight" (Friedman, 1953: 5)—to discussion of predictions about means, which can be resolved through analysis.

But critics contend that the antipolitical mode of policy analysis may serve to distort public policy by focusing on the end result of policy (maximizing net social welfare) to the exclusion of focus on the *procedure* by which policy choice is made. That procedure is held to be of intrinsic value in democratic societies, independently of the end result of policy. Policy analysts, the critics argue, typically justify process

> [e]ither in purely formal, positivist terms or in terms of a superior tendency to maximize aggregate satisfaction in the end, rather than in terms intrinsic to the

process itself in its constitutive function of defining substantive human roles, rights and relationships and structuring their evolution over time. [Tribe, 1972: 82]

Perhaps most notable, the *legitimacy* accorded decisions reached through sanctioned procedures may be largely independent of the substantive content of policy. Cognizant only of end results, analysts may fail to capture an essential element of value. In this view the value of a policy choice cannot be ascertained without considering the procedure from which it is derived.

Equally troubling to these critics, the very application of techniques of the contemporary policy analysis to values subject to discontinuous preference orders serves to *erode* those values. Kelman (1981) argues that widely held social rights or decision procedures are withheld from the run of more common questions by excluding them from the benefit-cost calculus (also see Okun, 1975, and Brown, 1990). To attempt to impute a dollar value to such "specially valued things" eliminates their special status, thus reducing their value. "Cost-benefit analysis thus may be like the thermometer that, when placed in a liquid to be measured, itself changes the liquid's temperature" (Kelman, 1981: 38). In this view, analysis not noly distorts human values but destroys them as well.

Critics are concerned that contemporary policy analysis may erode more than end values, however. An increased reliance on the essentially static and passive measures of individual preferences, as typically conducted for benefit-cost analysis, diminishes or eliminates the role of active debate and expression in a public forum as a means to develop and channel citizen preferences (see, e.g., Cummings et al., 1986; Brookshire and Coursey, 1987). Critics argue that application of the efficiency criterion is predicated on the existence of a universe of individual preference functions that may be tapped in order to "discover" optimum policies. The role of the analyst, using shadow prices to inform willingness-to-pay analysis, is to determine the value of particular options based on the given distribution of tastes. This vision of democracy, with its emphasis on accurate *reflection* of individual tastes in public policies, radically departs from the conception of the *process* of democracy—and participation in particular—as important to the *formation* of tastes, the legitimization of public choice, and the full development of the political individual (Pateman, 1970; Benello and Roussopoulus, 1971). At bottom, the emphasis on process in democracy is based on the contention that the deliberative process is *more* than a simple summation of tastes. It is a process by which individuals *develop* policy preferences through exposure to the preferences of others and reasoned discourse, or through the competition for votes and necessity for compromise. Preferences are formed, as well as expressed, as they are identified through political processes.

The policy analytic techniques employed to measure citizen preferences depart from the process views of democracy in a number of ways. Benefit-cost analysis, for example, commonly employs market prices, or estimated shadow prices, to calculate the value of benefits produced or resources used in public policy. Taking a more direct approach, many major cities now incorporate annual or biennial surveys of citizen opinions on tax and expenditure issues as a routine part of policy development (Hess, 1980; Stipak, 1980). Thus indirect measure through price or price estimates, or direct solicitation of preferences through surveys, supplements or replaces more traditional processes of politics.

How have proponents and practitioners responded to this critique? Quite broadly, they have argued that the critics misconstrue the role to be played by the analyst in the policy process. According to Allan Williams (1977: 519–545), rather than *precluding* the processes of politics, the use of analytic techniques can usefully serve as but one "loop" in the iterative process of arriving at decision. Thus policy goals are specified and provided to analysts, who then determine what policy options best achieve these goals. Options in hand, the analysts submit their results to policy-makers who again assess goals in light of necessary means. Thus analysis plays a constructive and informative role in the policy process.

Furthermore, empirical research on the applications of policy analysis indicates that analysis has become well integrated into the policy process, with analysis employed by many sides in the political debate (Jenkins-Smith and Weimer, 1985; Jenkins-Smith, 1990). As policy issues arise, individuals, interest groups, or public agencies tend to mobilize analytical resources to define the problem, define the causes, and specify probable policy solutions. Others, whose interests may be harmed by the proposed solutions, mobilize additional analytical resources to redefine the problem, identify other causes, or propose "better" policy solutions. In the process analysis becomes employed on two (or more) sides to the debate. Thus analysis is often integrated into the policy process, rather than supplanting it as the critics charge.

4. Public Versus Private Values

One controversy centers on the use of prices, either actual or inferred, as indices of citizen preferences for public policies. Market prices result from a myriad of private, individual choices regarding consumption and production of the good in question. In using those prices, critics contend, the analyst wrongly presumes that the citizen values goods exchanged in purely *private* transactions identically with the value of those things in *public* use. Thus, Kelman (1981: 38) contends, policy analysts "insidiously" assume that "there should be no difference between private behavior and the behavior we display in public life." Social values that for some reason are not expressed in private behavior are excluded from the calculus of public decision, and therefore the valuations reached through benefit-cost analysis are flawed.[2] More importantly, the use of private preference and behavior reflected in price as a guide for public decision would seem to lock public decision into the pattern set by private behavior; rather than exploring what values *ought* to be served, public policy would mimic existing private behavior. The formative role of politics as a shaper of public values is thus eroded.

The use of citizen surveys as a device for policy formation is similarly susceptible to attack for its exclusion of the formative qualities of process. Surveys are akin to snapshot photographs; a well-designed survey, asking the right questions, may measure the preferences of the respondents at the time of the survey and, if not methodologically flawed, adequately reflect the likely responses of the broader population. Surveys are *passive* measures, however, for which a sample of citizens' answers are solicited to policy questions about which the respondents may or may not have devoted significant thought and reflection. The important presumption underlying the use of surveys in policy formulation is that coherent preferences on policy issues actually exist, preferences that are susceptible to measurement and that are reasonably stable. Critics have argued that these presumptions are in error for a broad array of public issues, including the most important ones (Bogart, 1976; Achen, 1975; Farlie, 1978). On most complex policy issues, the nature of public opinion may be better described as a "natural force," like "currents of the air or ocean, constantly changing in their contours and directions" (Bogart, 1967: 334). Uncertainty, lack of information, the compelling novelty of the survey situation, and question construction and phrasing often make "public opinion" on policy issues unintelligible if not misleading. The point of this line of criticism is that the well-formed public opinion presumed to exist will in many cases be absent; the development of stable and intelligible public preferences occurs through the workings of the political process —the public forum for raising, defining and debating public issues. Surveys used in absence of this process, or surveys used to *replace* this process, will fail to find—or what is worse, will fabricate—what does not exist.

5. Inadequacies of Utilitarianism

What may be the most persistent controversy surrounding the application of welfare economic bases of policy analysis takes aim at the philosophical roots of policy analysis. Critics of policy analysis argue that contemporary policy analysis itself is a purveyor of a well-developed ideological perspective—that of individualistic utilitarianism (Bromley, 1990; Brown, 1991). Further, utilitarianism itself has been under extensive attack within the field of moral philosophy (Gorovitz, 1977; Smart and Williams, 1973). One serious reservation concerning utilitarianism derives from its lack of distinction among values—push-pin and poetry are accorded equal status. Within the general critique of utilitarianism, the difficulty in handling such concepts as rights and obligations, which have traditionally found bases outside the language of preference and utility, has received significant attention; can lying, unjustly punishing the innocent, or even repression of a small minority be justified on the basis that doing so increases *aggregate* well-being?

These criticisms have led Steven Kelman (1981: 34) to exclaim that "it is amazing that economists can proceed in unanimous endorsement of cost-benefit analysis as if unaware that their conceptual framework is highly controversial in the discipline from which it arose—moral philosophy." Peter Brown (1991: 6) adds that "utilitarianism leaves too much up for grabs. . . . It is compatible in principle with severe violations of human rights if total utility will be maximized by the rights violation."

Another cause for concern among critics of the utilitarian basis of policy analysis is grounded in perceived flaws in methods used for the aggregation and comparison of values. Ideal policy analysis would express the value of the costs and benefits of policy options in a common metric, preferably dollars. These valuations would be accomplished through determination of individuals' willingness to pay to obtain the benefit or willingness to accept to bear a loss. In the ideal this approach would permit the comparison of a wide range of policies over all affected values. The policy option that maximizes aggregate well-being (dollars) is selected, and those who lose would (ideally) be compensated through lump-sum transfers. Critics contend, however, that this approach ignores the *structure* of values; it ignores the possibility that certain values may have a lexicographical ordering in which some minimum level of good x must be obtained before *any* x will be traded for good y. Put differently, not amount of y can compensate for the loss of good x below some threshold. According to Laurence Tribe (1972: 87–88), in such circumstances the "very concept of proper distribution (of x and y) must now be defined not with respect to the single homogeneous entity called 'wealth' but with respect to the *enjoyment* of these rights as such." Where such orderings hold, Tribe argues, the principle of compensation of the losers by the winners fails; discontinuous preference orderings for rights cannot be reduced to the same "undifferentiated mass" of total welfare as continuous preference orderings for marketable goods and services.

Although recent utilitarian theorists have sought to find a natural basis in enlightened self-interest for rights and obligations (e.g., derived from within Rawls' "veil of ignorance"), utilitarianism remains a contentious basis for prescriptive political theory (Harsanyi, 1985; Rawls, 1971; Barry, 1973; Bluhm, 1983). Richard Zerbe (1988) makes a very cogent argument that use of a conceptual device like the veil of ignorance *can* permit utilitarianism to handle concepts like rights and justice. Though many rights cannot be derived from within the language of utilitarianism, the application of efficiency criteria *can* be made consistent with a specification of those rights. For example, once property rights are defined, benefit-cost analysis could impute a value of zero to stolen goods. Critics (e.g., Bromley 1990; Brown, 1991), however, maintain that the utilitarian bases of efficiency analysis are incorrigible and, when employed as the normative core of policy analysis, will seriously distort analysis, mislead policy-makers, and ultimately diminish the use of policy analysis.

In a recent and illustrative debate, for instance, a critic of the techniques of policy analysis charged that the underlying philosophy of benefit-cost analysis—individualistic utilitarianism—would permit what are considered to be morally reprehensible acts in the interest of maximizing utility (Kelman, 1981). A defender of those techniques responded

> [the critic] ... hints that "economists" are so morally numb as to believe that a routine cost-benefit analysis could justify killing widows and orphans, or abridging freedom of speech, or outlawing simple evidences of piety or friendship. But there is nothing in the theory or practice of cost-benefit analysis to justify that judgment. Treatises on the subject make clear that certain ethical or political principles may irreversibly dominate the advantages and disadvantages capturable by cost-benefit analysis. [Solow, 1981: 41]

In other words, the economists and policy analysts, like other people, take recourse to "other ethical or political principles" that may overwhelm the results of benefit-cost analysis.

6. Hard Versus Soft Values

One of the most common criticisms of contemporary policy analysis is that, in the zeal to quantify, analysts tend to underemphasize those costs and benefits that are intangible or that are external to market valuation (Tribe, 1971, 1972; Kelman, 1981: 33–40; Paris and Reynolds, 1983: 118–123). Though it may eventually prove technically feasible, valuation of nonmarketed goods, such as the value of a pleasant view or of the right to life (Zeckhauser, 1975), has proved difficult, and consensus regarding appropriate techniques elusive. Critics of analysis contend that these "soft" values tend to be ignored, whereas easily measured values are emphasized; when attempts at valuation *are* made, that valuation may be more akin to "subjective guesses" than objective science (Paris and Reynolds, 1983: 120).

7. The Problem of "Standing" in Policy Analysis

Taking a somewhat different tack, one particularly compelling critique of benefit-cost analysis points out that, for analysis to be applied to a specific policy, the analyst must decide *which preferences count*, that is, which preferences have "standing" in benefit-cost analysis (MacRae and Whittington, 1986 and 1988; Brown, 1986). In the abstract, benefit-cost analysis should count *all* benefits and costs associated with the policy under scrutiny, regardless of who bears those benefits and costs. In point of fact, however, analysts routinely reject many preferences as illegitimate; the lost value to criminals of illegal activity is usually not counted as a cost in analyses of criminal justice policies[3] nor are the benefits or costs of immigration policies for illegal aliens. Debates over how to count benefits and costs for future generations, fetuses, nonhumans (e.g., endangered species), inanimate objects (e.g., rivers), and others are indicative of the breadth of the standing problem (Weimer and Vining, 1989: 78–79).

For contemporary policy analysis, the standing issue presents a particularly thorny problem: How are analysts to decide which preferences to include or exclude? Given that *some* preferences are socially (and politically) unacceptable, the analyst must make such a decision, and making that decision forces the analyst outside of the (relatively) safe domain of efficiency analysis. *Some* criteria of justice or equity must be invoked, at least implicitly. The great danger here is that the analyst's criteria of justice will masquerade behind a facade of objectivity and thus be opaque to decision makers, the public, and even the policy analyst.

8. Efficiency and Institutional Transactions

One of the most important recent contributions to the debate over application of welfare economic principles to policy analysis is made by Daniel Bromley (1989a). Bromley argues that a critical class of economic and political decisions are made regarding the choice sets of individuals and groups and that those choice sets are specified and modified through "institutional transactions" such as the specification of rights and obligations. Two of Bromley's points are of particular relevance here: that the specification of efficiency is often predicated on existing institutional designs, which are themselves based on prior institutional transactions or accident; and that the traditional welfare economic dichotomy of policy change resulting in either efficiency gains or redistribution of wealth is too restrictive. These arguments, according to Bromley, undermine the conventional uses of welfare economic concepts in policy analysis.

For Bromley, public policy is best understood as a matter of defining the choice sets of individuals (or classes of individuals). To specify a new right (such as the right *not* to breath cigarette smoke-filled air on passenger airplanes) is to redefine the choice sets of individuals. What was once a nonright for the non-smoker, and a privilege for the smoker, becomes a right (to clean air) for the former and an obligation (not to smoke in certain areas) for the latter. More broadly, choices are made within a complex of institutions (defined as conventions and rules or entitlements) that establish what is a right, obligation, privilege, or non-right. Institutional transactions take place when these institutions are altered.

Applied to the concept of efficiency, Bromley makes a simple point: What is "efficient" is dependent on the existing set of institutions. First, Bromley argues (following Kahneman and Tversky, 1983) that individuals and decision makers tend to treat expected losses and gains differently. With respect to the domain of *gains*, risk aversion predominates: Individuals are prone to take the "sure thing" even if the expected value is less than some riskier choice. Regarding the domain of *losses*, however, risk acceptance is prevalent: The chooser tends to gamble on that option that *might* result in least loss, even if the expected losses of the option are greater than those for some other, less risky option. That means that decision makers will generally accept riskier strategies, and perhaps incur greater costs, to avoid a probabilistic loss than they will to obtain a probabilistic benefit.

Bromley points out that, for many policy issues, what *counts* as a gain or loss is dependent on existing institutions. For example, reductions in existing environmental or safety standards are generally considered losses to those currently "entitled" to them, whereas increases in such standards would be considered a gain. Given that gains and losses tend to be valued differently, efficiency analysis of a change in standards may be dependent on the nature of the existing set of standards, entitlements, rights, and obligations. Thus the current structure of institutions is critical for specification of costs and benefits. Finally, Bromley points out that existing institutions themselves result from prior "institutional transactions" or even historical accident. Why should such institutions be considered sacro-sanct? And, if they are not sacrosanct, the analyst would be remiss not to consider the efficiency implications of a policy from the standpoint of different institutional arrangements. Thus Bromley's charge is that efficiency analysis, as conventionally employed, is inherently "conserva-tive" in that it imputes a special (and unjustifiable) status to the existing constellation of institutions.

Bromley (1989b) carries his point further by arguing that the conven-tional dichotomy between policies that promote efficiency gains (which enlarge the pie) and transfers of wealth (which redivide the pie) is underspecified. Given this dichotomy, institutional transactions can be either efficient or merely redistributive. Bromley argues that this conven-tional view ignores the possibility that a reallocative policy may be socially efficient. What might appear to be "merely redistributive," as when mine employees demand greater expenditures for mine safety, may be stimu-lated by a shift in social preferences toward greater mine safety. If so, the reallocation from mine owners to mine workers, though redistributive, might be socially efficient. More generally, demands for policy change can result from changes in collective attitudes about the weights and valuations of elements of a nation's full consumption set. Note that changes in these weights and valuations may be incremental (e.g., as a society gradually becomes more concerned about environmental quality) or abrupt (as when the franchise is enlarged, adding new citizens who carry different weights and valuations). In either case, the change results in demands for institu-tional changes that might add to net social utility and should not be branded as "rent seeking." Bromley dubs such changes "reallocations of economic opportunity." Such policies should be kept conceptually distinct from reallocative policies that are not driven by changes in collective attitudes or relative prices, policies that Bromley calls "reallocations of economic advantage."

One import of Bromley's reformulation of the efficiency and redistribu-tive effects of policy change is that it requires the policy analyst to attend to the shape and content of the social welfare and utility functions. In his view, the analyst cannot legitimately escape the need to compare welfare changes across groups, or across types of gains and losses, by reference to the strict Pareto criterion of efficiency. To do so is to ignore and denigrate a vast domain of potential social welfare gains that public officials can and do reference in the formulation of public policy. In addition, to rely on conventional efficiency analysis to dodge the issue is to accept the implicit sanctification of the existing institutional order as it defines choice sets and the distribution of income. If economists are to influence the policy process, according to Bromley, they must explicitly grapple with the claims of various groups on that process and assess the origin of the claim for a new institutional transaction; Is a claim based on a shift in the social welfare function, changes in social utility relations, or alterations in the social weighting of welfare across different groups? Or is it merely the seeking of "economic advantage" by one group over others? And, in conducting such analyses, the analyst must not fall into the trap of accepting as sacrosanct the existing institutional order.

In advocating this shift, Bromley is asking the analyst to step from under the protective umbrella of the efficiency criterion. Remember that Pareto optimality and potential Pareto optimality provide the analyst with a way around the analytically difficult problem of comparisons of individual utility. Bromley's argument is that the umbrella was a mere fiction anyway and that analysts must come to grips with the real engines of institutional change if they are to make a contribution to public policy.

This is a tall order. First, shifting the focus of policy analysis to specification of the social welfare function, or changes in social utility relations, will result in a much wider range of plausible analytical claims on behalf of a wide array of policy positions. Social welfare functions are notoriously hard to specify and may well be subject to constant change. Furthermore, to assess the efficiency of policy change from the standpoint of potential as well as existing institutional arrangements raises a practical and a philosophical problem. The number of *potential* institutional arrangements is, of course, infinite; which ones will the analyst employ in assessing the social value of change? Given that not all can be used, the choice of the subset to use will be important because (as Bromley demonstrates) the assumed institutional arrangements may well determine the analytical outcome. Is that better than the use of the existing institutional order? That leads to an underlying philosophical question: Should policy analysts accord the results of past and current political and economic processes (i.e., the existing package of institutional arrangements) as legitimate and therefore a sound base for policy comparisons? Or should the analyst invent, and compare, an array of alternative social arrangements for purposes of assessing the merits of policy change? This issue, it seems to me, is akin to the debate between the Burkean conservative, who accords great legitimacy to the existing order, and the welfare state liberal, who sees the need for extensive public intervention to achieve social ends.

9. Summary: The Dynamic of Controversies in Policy Analysis

Although far from exhaustive of the controversies focused on applications of contemporary policy analysis, the list provided here includes those that have been or (in this author's view) will be, the most vigorous. To summarize the major themes: The standard uses of efficiency criteria in policy analysis are criticized because they exclude what critics contend is the essential role in citizen preference formation performed by the policy process. Exclusion of that step confuses public and private choice, excludes the possibility of reasoned debate over what values *ought* to be inculcated (i.e., What kind of people should we become?), and in many cases inhibits the very formulation of "public opinion." In addition, analysts are forced to make decisions on the standing of preferences, requiring choice among criteria of justice—a task for which the analyst is *not* prepared through training in contemporary policy analysis. Furthermore, it is charged, the techniques of analysis distort existing preferences, reducing complex relations within and among human values to a structureless mass. "Soft" or intangible values are ignored or underemphasized when traded off against more tangible values. Finally, analysts routinely employ an inappropriate base of comparison in assessing the benefits and costs of policy change (existing institutional arrangements) and have underspecified the engines of policy change (acknowledging only efficiency and redistributive reasons). The result is that many policy initiatives that may result in net social improvement are classified by analysts as mere "rent seeking."

For some of these critics—most notably Peter Brown and Daniel Bromley—the flaws of contemporary policy analysis have resulted in the mininal influence of policy analysis in the formulation of public policy. According to Brown, analysis has not penetrated because it has been imbued with a different philosophical underpinning than the ones typically employed in personal and public choice. For Bromley, attempts to provide only dispassionate advice in the interest of maximizing net utility, ignoring the interests and influence of the various actors in the political process as they translate into social utility, relegates policy analysts to an insignificant role in the political process. Other critics—such as Kelman and Tribe— argue that we are in danger of using too much analysis and that the techniques of analysis must be transformed to overcome "the ideological structure of particular errors that . . . have flowed from the basic axioms of policy analysis and related techniques" (Tribe, 1972: 106).[4] For these critics, analysis distorts public preferences in formulation and expression, thereby threatening the effective operation of the democratic process.

How have defenders of contemporary policy analysis responded? The broadest rejoinder to the critics has been that, though there may be limitations or flaws in the techniques of analysis, tough decisions regarding the use of scarce resources must be made, and such techniques as benefit-cost analysis are useful aids to such decisions. As three federal analysts argued in defense of benefit-cost analysis in a recent debate:

> [W]e do not dispute that cost-benefit analysis is highly imperfect. We would welcome a better guide to public policy, a guide that would be efficient, morally attractive, and certain to ensure that government follow the dictates of the governed. [Butler, Calter, and Ippolito, 1981: 41–42]

But, they add, no such better guide is evident. Says another defender of benefit-cost analysis:

> [Benefit-cost analysis] is not the way to perfect truth, but the world is not a perfect place, and I regard it as the height of folly to react to the greater (though still incomplete) rigour which [benefit-cost analysis] requires of us by shrieking "1984" and putting our heads hopefully back into the sand (or the clouds). [Williams, 1977: 543]

The critics of analysis are thus viewed as hypercritical, rejecting the promising techniques of contemporary policy analysis for fear of over-blown imperfections, and as having nothing to offer in their stead.

In a nutshell, proponents, critics, and defenders seem to evoke different visions of the role analysis is to play. Following Bentham, the proponents of policy analysis have tended to be reformists. The foundations of policy analysis militate toward changes in political institutions to better map the social welfare function into public policies. At the very least, the techniques of policy analysis are seen as a significant corrective for the practice of politics as usual. For their part, the critics of contemporary policy analysis take the proponents (or perhaps, the more extreme proponents) at face value; what would the world look like, they ask, should contemporary policy analysis be fully implemented without restraint in public policy-making? Their conclusion is that such a world would be dreadful. Defenders, finally, scoff at the critics' concern, knowing full well that analysis and analytical techniques are far from singularly influential in public decisions. They point out that policy analysis competes with other institutions, theories, and methods for policy-making that—though inferior—predominate now and will probably in the future as well. The defenders need not take the critics seriously because analysis is seen by the defenders as but one all-too-insignificant piece among many in the Rube Goldberg policy machine; in the defenders' view, the critics' excesses stem from erroneously believing that economists are "morally numb" and from "having their heads in the sand (or clouds)."

Notes

1. As Vilfredo Pareto, cited in Stigler (1965: 126), wrote early in this century:

> The entire theory [now] rests on a fact of experience, that is to say, on the determination of the quantities of goods which constitute combinations that are equivalent for the

individual. The theory of economic science thus acquires the rigor of rational mechanics; it deduces its results from experience, without the intervention of any metaphysical entity.

2. Strictly speaking, this is a mistaken view of benefit-cost analysis. A perfect analysis would capture these excluded social values and would treat them analogously to externalities of market price. While conceptually straightforward, this would prove difficult to accomplish in practice, and therefore the criticism may have more weight in practice than it does in theory.

3. A noteworthy exception is Long, Mallar, and Thornton (1981).

4. Tribe suggests several reforms: (1) elimination of the attempt to provide objective analysis in favor of a more impassioned and self-consciously value-laden approach and (2) the adoption of a "subtler, more holistic and more complex style of problem solving, . . . relying at each stage on the careful articulation of a wide range of interrelated values and constraints through the development of several distinct 'perspectives' on a given problem, each couched in an idiom true to its internal structure rather than translated into some 'common denominator'" (1972: 107). Thus Tribe has in mind a radical transformation of policy analysis.

References

Achen, Christopher, "Mass Political attitudes and the Survey Response," *American Political Science Review*, 69(3) (Fall 1975), 1218–1231.

Barry, Brian, *The Liberal Theory of Justice* (Oxford: Clarendon Press, 1973).

Bell, Daniel, *The End of Ideology* (New York: Free Press, 1960).

Bell, Daniel, and Irving Kristol, *The Public Interest* 1(1), (1965), 3–5.

Benello, C. George, and Dimitrios Roussopoulos, eds., *The Case for Participatory Democracy* (New York: Grossman, 1971).

Bentham, Jemery, *Fragment on Government, in The Collected Works of Jeremy Bentham*, J. H. Burns and F. Rosen, (eds.) (London: Althone Press, 1977).

———, *Introduction to the Principles of Morals and Legislation*, J. H. Burns and H. L. A. Hart, (eds.) (London: Athlone Press, 1970).

Bentham, Jeremy, *Works of Jeremy Bentham*, vol. 3 (Edinburgh: Tait, 1843).

Bluhm, William T., "Liberalism as the Aggregation of Individual Preferences: Problems of Coherence and Rationality in Social Choice" (presented at a Conference on the Crisis of Liberal Democracy, SUNY—Geneseo, 1983).

Bluhm, William T., *Theories of the Political System* (Englewood Cliffs, N.J.: Prentice-Hall, 1973).

Bogart, Leo, "No Opinion, Don't Know, Maybe No Answer," *Public Opinion Quarterly* 31 (Fall 1967), 331–345.

Bromley, Daniel W., "The Ideology of Efficiency: Searching for a Theory of Policy Analysis," *Journal of Environmental Economics and Management* 19:1 (July 1990), 86–107.

———, *Economic Interests and Institutions: The Conceptual Foundations of Public Policy* (Oxford: Blackwell, 1989a).

Bromley, Daniel W., "Institutional Change and Economic Efficiency," *Journal of Economic Issues* 23:3 (1989b), 735–769.

Brookshire David and Don Coursey, "Measuring the Value of a Public Good: An Empirical Comparison of Elicitation Procedures," *American Economic Review* 7:4 (September 1987), 554–566.

Brown, Peter, "Ethics and Education for the Public Service in a Liberal State," *Journal of Policy Analysis and Management* 6:1 (Fall 1986), 56–68.

Brown, Peter, "The Failure of Market Failures," (Forthcoming, *Journal of Socio-Economics*).

Butler, Gerard, John Calter and Pauline Ippolito, "Defending Cost-Benefit Analysis," *Regulation* 5(2) (March/April 1981), 41–42.

Cummings, Ronald, David Brookshire, and Don Coursey, *Valuing Environmental Goods: An Assessment of the Contingent Valuation Method* (Totowa: Rowman and Allenheld, 1986).

DeLeon, Peter, *Advice and Consent* (New York: Russell Sage, 1989).

Dumont, Etienne, *Bentham's Theory of Legislation*, trans. by Charles Atkins (London: Oxford University Press, 1914).

Edgeworth, Francis, *Mathematical Psychics* (London: Kegan Paul, 1881).

Farlie, Henry, "Galloping Toward Dead Center," *The New Republic* 178(14), Issue 3300, April 8, 1978), 18–21.

Friedman, Lee, "Public Policy Economics: A Survey of Current Pedagogical Practice," *Journal of Policy Analysis and Management* 6:3 (Spring 1987), 503–520.

Friedman, Milton, *Essays in Positive Economics* (Chicago: Chicago University Press, 1953).

Gorovitz, Samuel (ed.), *Utilitarianism with Critical Essays* (Indianapolis: Bobbs-Merrill, 1977).

Harsanyi, John C., "Rule Utilitaranism, Equality, and Justice," *Social Philosophy and Policy* 2(2) (Spring 1985), 115–127.

Hayek, F., *The Constitution of Liberty* (Chicago: University of Chicago Press, 1960).

Hess, F. William, "Listening to the City: Citizen Surveys," *Urban Affairs Papers* 2 (Summer 1980), 1–9.

Hicks, J. R., "The Foundations of Welfare Economics," *The Economic Journal* 49:196 (December 1939), 696–712.

Jenkins-Smith, Hank, *Democractic Politics and Policy Analysis* (Pacific Grove, Calif.: Brooks/Cole, 1990).

Jenkins-Smith, Hank, and David Weimer, "Analysis and Retrograde Action: The Case of Strategic Petroleum Reserves," *Public Administration Review* 45:4 (July–August 1985), 485–494.

Jevons, Stanley, *Theory of Political Economy*, 4th ed. (London: Macmillan, 1911).

Kahneman, Daniel, and Amos Tversky, "Choices, Values and Frames," *American Psychologist* 39:4 (1983), 341–350.

Kelman, Steven, "Cost-Benefit Analysis: An Ethical Critique," *Regulation* 5:1 (January–February 1981), 34–42.

Long, David, Charles Mallar, and Craig Thornton, "Evaluating the Benefits and Costs of the Job Corps," *Journal of Policy Analysis and Management* 1:1 (Fall 1981), 55–76.

MacRae, Jr., Duncan, and Dale Whittington, "Assessing Preferences in Cost-Benefit Analysis: Reflections on Rural Water Supply Evaluation in Haiti," *Journal of Policy Analysis and Management* 7:2 (Winter 1988), 246–263.

MacRae, Jr., Duncan and Dale Whittington, "The Issue of Standing in Cost-Benefit Analysis," *Journal of Policy Analysis and Management* 5:4 (Summer 1986), 665–682.

Menger, Carl, *Grundsatze der Volkswirtschaftslhre* (Vienna: Braumuller, 1871).

Mill, John S., "Utilitarianism," in *Utilitarianism, Liberty, and Representative Government* (New York: E. P. Dutton, 1910).

Nieman, Max, "The Ambiguous Role of Policy Analysis and an Illustrative Look at Housing Policy" (paper presented at the annual meeting of the Western Political Science Association, Sacramento, California, 1984).

Okun, Arthur, *Equality and Efficiency: The Big Tradeoff* (Washington, D.C.: Brookings, 1975).

Oser, Jacob and William C. Blanchfield, *The Evolution of Economic Thought*, 3rd ed. (New York: Harcourt, Brace, Jovanovich, 1975).

Paris, David and James Reynolds, *The Logic of Policy Inquiry* (New York: Longman, 1983).

Pateman, Carole, *Participation and Democratic Theory* (Cambridge: Cambridge University Press, 1970).

Rawls, John, *A Theory of Justice* (Cambridge, Mass.: Harvard University Press, 1971).

Riker, William and Peter Ordeshook, *An Introduction to Positive Political Theory* (Englewood Cliffs, N.J.: Prentice-Hall, 1973).

Smart, J. J. C., and Bernard Williams (eds.), *Utilitarianism: For and Against* (Cambridge, Mass.: MA: Cambridge University Press, 1973).

Solow, Robert M., "Defending Cost-Benefit Analysis," *Regulation* 5(2)(March/April 1981), 40–41.

Stigler, George, *The Development of Utility Theory in Essays in the History of Economics*. (Chicago: University of Chicago Press, 1965).

Stipak, Brian, "Local Government's Use of Citizen Surveys," *Public Administration Review* 40 (September/October 1980), 521–525.

Stokes, Donald, "Political and Organizational Analysis of the Policy Curriculum," *Journal of Policy Analysis and Management* 6:1 (Fall 1986), 45–55.

Stokey, Edith, and Richard Zeckhauser, *A Primer for Policy Analysis* (New York: W. W. Norton, 1978).

Tribe, Laurence, "Policy Science: Analysis or Ideology?" *Philosophy and Public Affairs* 2 (Fall 1972), 67–110.

Tribe, Laurence, "Trial by Mathematics: Precision and Ritual in the Legal Process," *Harvard Law Review* 84 (1971), 1361–1365.

Walras, Leon, *Elements d'economie politique pure* (Paris: Pichon & Durand-Auzais, 1926).

Weimer, David L. and Aidan R. Vining, *Policy Analysis: Concepts and Practice* (Englewood Cliffs, N.J.: Prentice-Hall, 1989).

Williams, Allan, "Cost-Benefit Analysis: Bastard Science? And/Or Insidious

Poison in the Body Politick?" in Robert Haveman and Julius Margolis, eds., *Public Expenditure and Policy Analysis*, 2nd ed. (Chicago: Rand McNally, 1977), 519–545.

Zeckhauser, Richard, "Procedures for Valuing Lives," *Public Policy* 23(4) (Fall 1975), 419–464.

Zerbe, Jr., Richard O. "The Ethical Foundations of Benefit Cost Analysis," unpublished manuscript, University of Washington, 1988.

3 BEYOND EFFICIENCY: ECONOMICS AND DISTRIBUTIONAL ANALYSIS

Alphonse G. Holtmann

1. Introduction

Distributional analysis, as discussed in this chapter, refers to the distribution of well-being among the members of society. The discussion first illustrates that efficiency, as defind by most contemporary economists, is directly related to social well-being and that questions of equity and efficiency are often inextricably combined when dealing with public policy issues, requiring that the policy-maker and the analyst deal with both dimensions of these issues. This is true whether the policy under considera-'tion involves pure transfers within the economy or resource allocation to a productive project. Suggesting possible means for policy analysts to evaluate programs that influence social welfare, however, requires a better perspective on the issue of social welfare, defining terms and putting philosophical, political, and theoretical developments in historical context.

To understand the role of the public policy analyst in dealing with the distribution of well-being within a society, the chapter will briefly explore both the nature of modern welfare economics and the recent history of the interaction between government policy in market economies and the theoretical work in applied welfare economics or policy analysis. Welfare economics is the normative branch of the discipline that deals with reaching judgments on what ought to be, whereas positive economics is that branch of the discipline that deals with explaining how the economy functions. Deciding whether more funds should be spent on a Head Start program is within the domain of welfare economics. Explaining why oil prices went up during the last several decades is an exercise in positive economics.

Individual well-being is the foundation of modern welfare theory, which is not an unreasonable foundation for a theory of welfare in a society that relies on markets to distribute most goods and services. The principal notion of welfare theory is that individuals can order choices available to them in a fashion that will allow them to gain the greatest satisfaction from the choices available, usually given some constraints on the choices. If a fully informed individual, given a choice between remaining at home or working at the prevailing wage, decides to remain at home, one would conclude that the individual's welfare or utility would not be increased by working. The chapter will discuss not only the role of individual satisfaction or choice as the foundation of welfare economics but some of the difficulties of measuring welfare. National income in this example will be smaller because of the individual's choice, but well-being will not have decreased according to individualistic welfare theory. Generally, however, one would expect a positive relationship between national income and social welfare.

Individual well-being is associated with social or group well-being through the Pareto principle: For a given initial distribution of endowments, society's allocation of resources is Pareto optimal if no one can be made better off without making someone else worse off. Conversely, the allocation of resources in both production and consumption is not Pareto optimal if someone's utility can be increased with no decrease in anyone else's utility. One allocation is said to be Pareto superior to another allocation if someone's satisfaction is increased by the new allocation without a decrease in anyone else's satisfaction. The ethical and technical assumptions underlying these principles are the subject matter of other chapters in this volume, but it is important to note at least two aspects of the principles that are important for public policy purposes. First, even for those who find the Pareto ethic acceptable, it is likely to be too limiting because many would find it satisfactory to help some in society at the expense of others. For instance, this author is perfectly content to tax the extremely wealthy to give to the extremely poor. Second, there are different Pareto optimal allocations for different initial distributions of endowments. Economists, unable to make interpersonal comparisons of satisfaction among individuals, are unable to compare Pareto-optimal allocations (sometimes these allocations are called efficient allocations or Pareto-efficient allocations), leading to the dilemma that economists cannot scientifically choose, at least by means of Pareto principles, among redistributions of resources that help some at the expense of others.

Apparently, theoretical welfare economics and the Pareto principles are not helpful in allowing policy analysts to determine the ideal distribution of well-being in society. But, agreeing that policy analysts cannot determine the ideal distribution of resources is not to say that they cannot be helpful to policy-makers whose decisions inevitably involve such matters. To understand the important role of Pareto efficiency in policy analysis, it helps to chronicle the development of modern welfare theory.

2. Modern Welfare Economics

As Paul Samuelson (1965) has indicated, economists since the time of Adam Smith and the Physiocrats have believed that a free competitive market leads to desirable consequences for the population. The simple logic behind this conclusion, closely related to our earlier principle that fully informed individual choice reveals welfare orderings, is that individuals trade when they can gain from the trade. Pareto (1929) and Barone (see Hayek, 1935), and later Lerner (1934), Hotelling (1938), and Bergson (1938), were able to show, under the appropriate assumptions, that a competitive market equilibrium would result in a Pareto efficient allocation of resources: Given the initial endowments, it is not possible to rearrange goods and services or production so that someone is helped without hurting someone else. The proof of this theorem is elegantly derived in Samuelson's *Foundations of Economic Analysis* (1965).

This close connection between the Pareto efficiency principle and the conpetitive market no doubt partly accounts for the domination of applied welfare economics by this criterion of welfare. But there is more to the story of theoretical developments and our current state of art in policy analysis. In the 1930s and 1940s a large literature developed—some of which has been alluded to—that not only shows the relationship between a competitive equilibrium and Pareto efficiency but rigorously proves all the theorems of modern welfare economics. The analysis provides the basis for Samuelson's chapter on welfare economics in 1947 (1965) and J. de V. Graaff's classic volume *Theoretical Welfare Economics* ten years later (1967). One theorem of this theory is that any ethical individualistic optimum can be attained through lump-sum taxes and subsidies, allowing the individuals to trade at fixed prices.

Thus after World War II when the major market economies were just reviving on a peacetime basis, welfare theory had seemingly provided a clear guide for the policy-maker. Whatever the ethical basis for favoring different individuals in society, lump-sum transfers could in principle be used to reallocate endowments and a competitive market could then achieve a Pareto-efficient allocation that would be optimal in the context of that endowment. It is difficult, however, to suggest practical tax and subsidy schemes that are lump-sum in nature, that is, taxes and subsidies that do not affect the market prices facing the consumer.

In addition, as indicated earlier, economists cannot provide the appropriate ethical standard, sometimes called a welfare function, to index transfers among individuals. In fact, as Kenneth Arrow (1963) has shown, it is impossible for any fair collective choice process to provide consistently an appropriate ordering to resolve any interpersonal difference while at the same time satisfying certain reasonable axioms. For example, majority voting is not a satisfactory vehicle for making all social choices because situations arise where there is no equilibrium. That is, in some cases where more than two options arise (helping the poor, the middle class, or the rich, for example), any selected policy can be overturned by another policy selected by the majority. Such cyclical majority problems may be fairly common, implying that one needs to know how the vote was reached before being confident that the outcome reflects the will of the majority.

That economists cannot scientifically specify a welfare function that selects among the Pareto-efficient allocations is so discouraging to many welfare analysts that they recommend that economists would be best advised to spend their efforts on positive economics (Graaff, 1967: 170). Perhaps many share that belief, but others like the notion that efficiency and equity can in principle be separated when dealing with public project evaluations. In any event, many economists became deeply involved in policy analysis.

With the state of general welfare economics basically settled by the late 1940s, economists in the early 1950s turned their attention to the assumptions that provide the basis for Pareto optimality. That is, even if one accepts the initial endowments in a static environment and assumes that the economy is perfectly competitive, it is only possible to reach a Pareto-efficient allocation of resources when all the assumptions underlying our individual welfare index are met. One crucial assumption is that the utility function (the mechanism for ordering choices) of each individual is independent of that of other individuals in the society.

An extreme case of the interdependence of individual utility functions was explored by Paul Samuelson (1954) in his work on public goods. In that classic work, Samuelson shows that certain goods provide satisfaction to all individuals in society at the same time (national defense being an example) and that these types of goods will not be efficiently provided in a competitive market. Of course, the pure public good that enters everyone's utility function when it enters anyone's utility function is an extreme case of the problem of external benefits or costs. While your consumption of medical services, educational services, or gardening services no doubt increases your satisfaction, they may also increase my satisfaction. I may be less apt to become ill when you take care of your health; I may find it less costly to transact my business because you are better educated; and I may simply enjoy observing your garden.

In all these cases of externalities and in the case of pure public goods, a competitive market will not assure a Pareto-efficient allocation of resources. Hence, government might be able to improve social welfare, in the Pareto sense of helping someone without hurting others, with appropriate taxation, subsidies, or provision of services. In addition, there are other characteristics of markets that might prevent the economy from achieving a Pareto-efficient allocation of resources. Economies of scale in production might lead to monopoly, which is generally inconsistent with Pareto optimality. Uncertainty, lack of information, and the lack of appropriate insurance markets might lead to a failure of the market to achieve a Pareto-efficient result. Though the list of factors that cause market failure (Bator, 1958), as the failure of the market to achieve a Pareto solution has come to be known, could be greatly expanded, it is noteworthy that theoretical analysts turned to these issues of efficiency after 1950, providing some of the incentive for policy analysts to also dwell on efficiency issues for several decades.

3. Public Expenditures and Human Capital

Before discussing the accomplishments and limitations of the broad spectrum of studies concerning public policy evaluation, three other events must be noted—events basically concomitant with the theoretical developments on market failure already discussed—that influenced the nature of public policy studies undertaken in the United States. Two contributions at the conceptual level influenced policy evaluation around 1960. In 1959 Richard Musgrave published his path-breaking book, *The Theory of Public Finance*, which although not unduly long (628 pages) was almost encyclopedic in its coverage of modern public finance, including the theory of public expenditures. In that volume Musgrave divided the public household, as he called it, into the allocation branch, the distribution branch, and the stabilization branch, stressing the proposition mentioned earlier that, at least conceptually, one cound separate the issues of equity and efficiency—the major concerns of the distribution and allocation branches, respectively. While clearly indicating that there was no simple normative rule for evaluating public policy, Musgrave suggested that, as an analytical tool, the allocative operations of government policy could be separated from the distributional operations. This separation of equity and efficiency was not new, being implicit in the basic theorem of welfare economics that lump-sum transfers of income could be used to attain distributional equity, but Musgrave's book formalized the approach for policy analysts during this period.

It was natural that the early work in project evaluation was aimed at services already in the government sector; river development, public health programs, and education were early candidates for public policy analysis. Most of these early analyses concentrated on the efficiency aspects of the evaluation of a project of investment and not the equity aspects. In a detailed analysis of U.S. river projects, John Krutilla and Otto Eckstein state, "We take for granted that political, judicial, and other social processes in democracy tend to adjudicate disputes involving the distribution of income" (1958: 49). These scholars explicitly adopted the procedure later suggested by Musgrave.

Of course, some of the early project evaluations considered distributional questions, but these studies clearly attempted to determine the impact of the distribution of costs or benefits on efficiency rather to analyze the equity dimensions of the distribution of costs and benefits per se. For example, Burton Weisbrod (1962), in "Education and Investment in Human Capital," discusses the possible distribution of benefits from education among different groups through time and by location, showing that all beneficiaries are not likely to be able to express appropriately their demand for education. Although the equity considerations are recognized, his article emphasizes that external effects can cause efficiency problems, resulting in over- or underinvestment in education. As this example demonstrates, there is a distinction between looking at the distribution of costs and benefits because they influence an efficient allocation of resources and looking at the costs and benefits because they influence the equity of the allocation of resources. In any case, it is reasonable to say that most of the early focus in project evaluation was on efficiency.

Note that the preceding discussion concerns investments in education, thus relating to the second event that influenced the nature of project evaluation for the last several decades. In 1961 T. W. Schultz of the University of Chicago extolled the virtues of particular expenditures on people that could be considered as investments: Expenditures made today result in a stream of future benefits for the individual and perhaps society. This notion of human capital, though not completely new, captured the imagination of a large number of economists who quickly set out to measure the returns to expenditures on health, education, migration, information, and training in the economy. In 1970 the annotated bibliography *Cost-Benefit Analysis and the Economics of Investment in Human Resources* listed 389 papers that had been written on some aspect of policy analysis in this area (Wood and Campbell, 1970).

This interest in investments in people was of major importance to policy analysts for two reasons. First, these types of investments in people might be rather important to the economic growth process. After all, the United States, the richest country in the world, makes large investments in its people and thus provides a model for other countries. Second, expenditures on health, education, and other forms of human capital are thought not only to influence growth in developing economies but also to have particular consequences for the achievement of Pareto efficiency in any market economy. Thus the question naturally arises as to whether Pareto efficiency requires that developed economies like that of the United States devote more resources to these investments than is generated through market forces. It is common, even today, to hear individuals speak of underinvestment in human resources. That is, it might be possible to make everyone better off by increasing these types of expenditures. Finally, there is the view that these investments in people could reduce poverty.

Many of these human services are, of course, already provided by government, and few people question the government role in supporting them. So the issue arises as to the amount of service provided by government and the level of government—federal versus state and local government—that should support these services. Should, for example, Head Start be initiated, and how should it be financed? Today's policy suggestions concerning child day care and aid to dependent children have much of the same rationale as these earlier projects. Again, although some analysts address the issue of the distributional consequences of these investments, the emphasis of most studies is on the efficiency issue.

4. The Great Society

Many of the Great Society programs brought to fruition during the Johnson administration (though some had been conceived in the Kennedy presidency) reflected a fundamental change in the nature of the federal government's social programs. Although these administrations followed those since the New Deal in expanding and modifying the money transfer programs, particularly those associated with Social Security, many new in-kind transfer programs were initiated during this period—a time, as we indicated earlier, of great activity in project evaluation and analysis. Many of these programs, of course, continued in the presidencies of Nixon, Ford, Carter, and Reagan, but the surge in the growth of in-kind transfer programs took place in the Johnson administration, when in-kind transfers grew in nominal dollars by 84.6 percent, a growth rate that declined to 4.8 percent by the first term of the Reagan administration (Browning, 1987). In-kind transfer programs, such as Head Start, Upward Bound, Manpower Development and Training, Area Redevelopment, and neighborhood health centers, initiated during the Johnson era were related to investments in the poor, not purely income transfers to the poor, though the latter were also expanded in the War on Poverty. Many of these programs had great appeal to policy analysts, particularly economists, because the programs emphasized investments in people as had been highlighted by Schultz and given much theoretical and empirical content by such people as Gary Becker (1964), Jacob Mincer (1962), Burton Weisbrod (1962), George Stigler (1962), and numerous others and because many of these investments might be justified on allocative efficiency grounds. Without stretching the analytical framework, one can imagine that investments in education, health, and training of the poor might represent a Pareto improvement in resource allocation, particularly if any adverse changes in the income distribution might be addressed through other government tax and subsidy programs. Thus, to a large extent, it was easy to analyze these programs purely in terms of efficiency: Could some be made better off without hurting others? Though some analysts mention the possibility of distributional problems arising and though some commentators stress the actual redistribution of income that takes place through these programs because beneficiaries of the programs are not identical to those who pay the taxes to support them, most studies stress efficiency and concerns with equity arise somewhat later.

In retrospect, it is perhaps not difficult to see why policy analysts, at least in the United States, were largely concerned with the efficiency of in-kind programs in their evaluations. First, the transfer programs under Social Security emerged when modern welfare economics was rejecting the idea that interpersonal utility evaluations were possible, making a scientific evaluation of these transfer programs appear vacuous. In addition, the Social Security programs seemed to reflect a social consensus that was intact from the Roosevelt administration until most recently. Second, the in-kind programs stressed during the War on Poverty had the charm of representing the newly rediscovered notion of investing in people, and as investments, the rates of return to these programs could actually be calculated and compared to the returns on other investments in the economy, including other government investments in highways, flood control, and the like—the redistributional consequences of all government investments being left to other government devices or, perhaps, considered as desirable fringe benefits of the programs. In any case, contributions to national product were most often the primary criterion of early project evaluations, though certainly nonmeasurable cost and benefits were also stressed—the possible role of education in promoting democracy, for example. Finally, expenditures on people, as Schultz had stressed, were like other government investments, promoting growth in the economy over time and allowing everyone to be better off in the future.

Although the preceding synopsis has concentrated on the United States experience, other market economies like those of Great Britain and France seemed just as concerned with efficiency in their formal project evaluations and, at the same time, were initiating programs that involved extensive government determination of resource allocation and income distribution through government involvement in activities ranging from the provision of medical care to generating electric power (Nelson, 1964).

5. Linking Equity and Efficiency in Policy Analysis

As has been shown, the particular emphasis given to the Pareto efficiency concept by the project analyst results from complex interactions between the apparent needs of public decision makers and the analytical tools available during a particular period. Nevertheless, it has been recognized for some time that an appropriate welfare function to aggregate individual utilities would allow the social planner to select among Pareto-efficient allocations, thus permitting the evaluation of projects on the basis of their contribution to social welfare (Samuelson, 1965).

The problem is, and always has been, that scholars cannot agree on the appropriate welfare function because such a welfare function implies interpersonal utility comparisons. Though agreement on the appropriate social welfare function for society is unlikely, this notion of a social welfare function can be very useful in evaluating public projects because it permits the combining of the equity dimensions of a project with those of efficiency in a manner that allows thoughtful consideration of the issues. Also, it is perhaps worth noting at this point that Arrow's possibility theorem does not rule out the existence of a social welfare function but only indicates that fair social decision rules cannot consistently produce such a ranking device.

A social welfare function allows us to translate gains and losses of satisfaction of different individuals into a measure of social well-being, allowing us implicitly to make interpersonal utility comparisons. To consider the first of two extremes, we might have a Benthamite welfare function of the form $W = \Sigma U^i$, which implies that social welfare is increased when anyone's satisfaction is enhanced and where W is social welfare, U^i is an individual's utility function, and i goes from 1 to n members of the population, or a Rawlsian welfare function of the form $W = \min(U^i, \ldots, U^n)$, which implies that social welfare is improved only when satisfaction of the person who is worst off is improved. Or, even more generally, consider a social welfare function of the isoelastic form $W = [1/(1 - \rho)]\Sigma[(U_i)^{1-\rho}]$, which represents the Benthamite form for $\rho = 0$ and approaches the Rawlsian form as $\rho \to \infty$ (Ballard, 1988: 1028). In the case of the isoelastic welfare function, $\partial W/\partial U_i = (U_i)^{-\rho}$, implying that larger values of ρ give greater weight to individuals with lower utility levels.

If we were to visualize these welfare functions in terms of social indifference between the utility of two individuals, the Benthamite case would generate social indifference curves that are straight lines with a slope of -1, implying that society is indifferent as to the particular individual who gains from a program. Alternatively, Rawlsian social indifference functions form right angles, implying that helping anyone but the least well off person leaves society on the same indifference function. These examples, of course, form the polar cases of more general isoelastic functions with less extreme values of ρ that allow interpersonal comparisons of individuals' satisfaction and some degree of substitutability of satisfaction among the individuals.

This approach of integrating efficiency analysis and distributional analysis has been recognized for some time and is becoming increasingly important in evaluating projects that stem from concerns for either allocative efficiency or distributional justice. Burton Weisbrod (1970) was one of the earliest proponents of using a social welfare function approach as a means of making practical policy decisions. In his work Weisbrod suggests a social welfare function of the form $W = ay_1 + by_2 + \ldots + my_n$, where W is social welfare, y is the amount of individual income, and the coefficients reflect the marginal increase in welfare associated with a change in an individual's income. Thus in the two-person case the marginal rate of substitution of income between the two people would be $dy_1/dy_2 = -b/a$, allowing us to evaluate transfers of income among individuals.

The idea behind Weisbrod's analysis, however, is not simply to proclaim weights for interpersonal comparisons of income but rather to try to determine these weights from government rankings of projects that had been determined through benefit-cost analysis. As he indicates, the virtue of this procedure is in its confronting the weights used by the decision makers with those held implicitly by others in the society and in its ability to forecast the government's choices among programs. Although Weisbrod illustrated his approach using actual data from federal river projects, the approach has not been empirically applied, to this writer's knowledge.

Perhaps the limitation of this approach is that it forms a social welfare function that comes out of the political process, rather than use a social welfare function to help form the decision maker's views. Of course, to the extent that there is an iterative process, this might not be a powerful objection. In any case, this effort was one of the earliest to incorporate distribution theory into project evaluation in a practical way, though in a still earlier paper Stephen Marglin (1962) had fully outlined the technical procedures for introducing distributional criteria into project evaluation.

As Marglin shows, the utilities of those included in the welfare function can be differentiated by almost any characteristic: race, region, sex, income group, level of disability, and the like. This type of disaggregation according to group membership is often of great interest to policy-makers. As shall be seen, a number of positive distributional studies concern themselves with the relationship of benefits accruing to whites versus blacks, young versus old, and so on, suggesting that the distribution of costs and benefits to certain groups of individuals is crucial for meaningful public policy. For any particular project, a given division of the population may appear sensible, although disaggregation by different population characteristics makes comparisons of different programs more difficult.

Using a social welfare function in a recent analysis of U.S. metropolitan school fiscal reform, Robert Inman (1978) analyzed six proposed fiscal reform programs in New York State for three different social welfare specifications—utilitary (pro–middle class), Rawlsian (pro-poor), and equal school spending—to evaluate the programs. Among other things, he finds that there is no dominant reform proposal and concludes that the legislative process may collapse into a pro-poor versus pro–middle class debate. Inman suggests that a possible solution to the debate may be compromise plans that satisfy legislators favoring the poor and legislators favoring the middle class. This analysis, then, provides policy-makers with information concerning the implications of their choices for distributional equity, which allows them to make decisions that can be defended to their constituencies.

Social welfare functions have also been used in recent studies of the efficiency costs of redistribution policies. Whereas much of the earlier discussion focused on introducing distributional considerations into analyses that are focused on efficiency, the efficiency costs of pure transfer programs have become an increasing concern to the social policy analyst. Programs that attempt to transfer resources from the more affluent to the poorest often must take more than a dollar from the affluent to transfer a dollar to the poor. In an early analysis Arthur Okun (1975) refers to this problem as the leaking bucket, but more recent analysts, refer to it as the marginal efficiency cost of redistribution (Browning, 1987).

In a 1988 study Charles Ballard uses a computable general equilibrium model to calculate the marginal efficiency cost of redistributing income through two programs: pure cash transfer programs and wage subsidy programs. Assuming that taxes finance the redistribution programs, he finds that a pure cash transfer program implies that the more affluent are made worse off by between $1.50 and $2.30 for every dollar transferred to the poor and that a wage subsidy program tends to allow a dollar for dollar transfer from the high-income group to the low-income group. Though, as he indicates, the costs of a cash transfer are high, they are not as high as earlier estimates of these costs made by Edgar Browning (1987). Nevertheless, how is one to evaluate the cost of the transfer? This is the very question that Weisbrod raises when he suggests finding a social welfare function to determine the marginal rate of substitution of income among individuals.

Indeed, Ballard uses a social welfare function of the isoelasticity form mentioned earlier to determine critical values of ρ for which such transfers would be acceptable, finding that one does not have to be anywhere near the Rawlsian position to accept the costs of these seemingly expensive cash transfer programs.

Although a number of other studies that employ a social welfare function as a means of making interpersonal comparisons among groups in society can be cited, these few examples are sufficient to make clear that a social welfare function is a useful tool for applied policy analysis. And though it is not likely that any particular social welfare function will gain wide acceptance, alternative specifications of the welfare function provide the policy-maker with important information in making decisions that will actually result in gains to some and costs to others.

6. Fairness

Though the preceding social welfare approach deals with questions of equity in a formal and explicit manner through interpersonal utility comparisons, it is inconsistent with, or at least not in the tradition of, the individualistic approach that is the foundation of the Pareto principles and much of the modern welfare theory discussed earlier. Recent work on fairness (Baumol, 1986; Varian, 1990), however, raises the possibility that analysts can combine Pareto notions of efficiency with notions of fairness to make judgments about efficiency and equity that result in the individual being better off and judging the result as fair. As expected, there will be situations in which an allocation results in a Pareto improvement but is not judged to be fair.

Like the Pareto approach to efficiency, which starts with the "weak" value judgment that a reallocation that helps some and does no harm to others is a Pareto-superior allocation, the theory of fairness or equity starts with the value judgment that an allocation is fair if no agent prefers another's allocation to his of her own (Varian, 1990). At the outset, it should be noted that it is not the utility or satisfaction from another's allocation that one must not envy, but the allocation itself, so there are no interpersonal utility comparisons involved.

Now to see how this framework functions, consider attempting to distribute a fixed bundle of goods among n individuals. Theorists in this area like to use cakes to represent the bundle, which is a matter of taste, of course. According to the preceding definition, n equal shares of the cake will be fair because no one envies anyone else's share. But, of course, this division of the cake need not be Pareto efficient. Will trade result in a Pareto-efficient allocation?

To see the problem here, consider three individuals who have shared two cakes, one with nut topping and one with raisin topping, and assume that the shares are such that each person received one third of each cake. The allocation is fair because no one would select another's allocation. Now suppose two of the individuals like nuts and one likes raisins, and suppose the raisin lover trades his nut-topped piece to one of the nut lovers for a raisin-topped piece. The allocation will be Pareto optimal, but it will no longer be fair. The one nut lover will envy the new share of the other nut lover.

Suppose, however, that the raisin lover cuts his nut-topped piece in half and trades one-half to each nut lover for each nut-lover's raisin topped piece. Now note that the resulting allocation is Pareto optimal and fair according to our definition. In fact, generalizing from this example, it can be shown that a competitive equilibrium from an equal division must be a fair allocation. And, of course, we know that a competitive equilibrium is a Pareto-optimal equilibrium.

This simple cake example (Baumol, 1986) highlights the problem that economists sometimes encounter when making policy recommendations. That is, it is clearly possible to make a recommendation that results in a Pareto improvement that is deemed unfair by at least one appealing measure of fairness. Thus society may be unwilling to make Pareto-superior moves that are deemed unfair by some members of society.

The idea of fairness, as defined in this relatively recent literature and exemplified by the work of Hal Varian (1990) and William Baumol (1986), seems to show great promise for being helpful to public policy analysts in attempting to show the relationships between efficiency and equity in any particular recommendation. Baumol (1986: 104–107), for example, shows that fairness (lack of envy) could require overcompensation for air pollution victims, resulting in a welfare loss to society when damages are equally spread among the population and people reduce their pollution protection because of the compensation. His purpose is to show that policy analysts will have to find means of making trade-offs between equity and efficiency in many public policy decisions because it will be impossible to achieve maximum efficiency and fairness simultaneously. He also shows that the concept is useful in analyzing public utility pricing. In any case, it appears that it might be possible to integrate concepts of fairness (lack of envy) with Pareto efficiency in a manner that will help policy analysts make better recommendations to policy-makers.

7. Positive Economics

Policy-makers are likely to be interested in whether a particular policy will actually do what it is intended to do, who will gain and who will lose from it, and its implications for growth. Consequently, positive economics can play an important role in distributional analysis by giving policy-makers the information they need to make their own distributional assessments.

Thus, even if one eschews the tools of welfare economics, one can still be helpful to the decision-maker. For example, in recommending criteria for choosing alternative means for redistributing income, Burton Weisbrod (1970) mentions six criteria that might be considered when evaluating a redistributive program: administrative cost, target efficiency, allocative efficiency, consumer versus taxpayer sovereignty, flexibility over time, and nondemeaning benefits. (Because stigma may be attached to receiving a particular government benefit, delivery systems that identify recipients are sometimes thought to be demeaning; i.e., people might refuse to use food stamps because redeeming the stamps identifies the user as poor.) Such a set of criteria might be appropriate for any program undertaken with government support. Putting aside the question of the particular criteria to be used, the general idea is that the analyst can point to various aspects of a program that are of interest to the policy-maker and then allow the political process to determine the final outcome. Further, Weisbrod suggests (1978) that information gleaned from questionnaires on the attitudes of groups affected by a government program would help policy-makers in reaching decisions.

Much of the recent work in applied welfare economics falls into this positive genre. For example, James P. Smith and Finis Welch (1989) recently reported a comprehensive study of the relationship between black and white males' incomes over the last 40 years, concluding that substantial progress has been made in narrowing the income gap between these groups. Obviously, there are dimensions of well-being other than income, and different individuals will determine progress in closing the income gap as too fast or too slow, but it is important in evaluating our racial equality programs to know what is happening. In a similar vein, this author's work finds that reducing the major diseases in the United States would result in gains to both white and black males but would not change their relative economic positions, as measured by the present value of future income (Holtmann, 1973a). Unlike the Smith-Welch analysis, which provides positive information on the results of programs aimed at reducing inequality, my results offer information on the impact of inequality from programs meant to accomplish other ends.

Of course, this type of descriptive information is helpful in evaluating all types of programs and is becoming increasingly important in evaluating social programs. As an example of this trend, a recent book by Sheldon Danziger and Kent Portney (1988) reports 12 essays that deal with what gets distributed to whom and from whom. These essays cover topics ranging from the distributional consequence of state tax reform to an analysis of child support. Thus this volume shows that the long history of generally positive analysis of government programs can be applied to both distributional and efficiency questions. Such studies are certain to provide quantitative measures where only guesses were available before, and they are likely to provide new methods for measuring difficult-to-measure costs and benefits from programs. There is therefore a continuing need for this type of analysis.

8. Organizational Form: Efficiency and Fairness

Until relatively recently, evaluations of projects to implement either money transfers or in-kind services did not consider the type of organization that would deliver the service or make the transfer. If, for example, more health care or education is deemed necessary on efficiency grounds, the type of organization that might deliver the service is completely outside the realm of the analysis. Spurred by the analysis of Weisbrod (1975) and Hansmann (1980), the question of organizational efficiency has been raised in several recent studies, particularly those dealing with not-for-profit organizations. Thus the project analyst has one more dimension of the project to deal with: to recommend the appropriate organizational motif to best accomplish the efficiency or equity goals of a particular program.

The recent literature voices two major concerns about the appropriate organization for service delivery: Do not-for-profit organizations emerge in a market economy because of some sort of market failure? And, how does one choose among government, for-profit, and not-for-profit organizations in industries where all three exist? Again, efficiency is the main concern in most studies of not-for-profit firms, with earlier studies suggesting that these institutions are inefficient and more recent studies suggesting that they enhance efficiency (Holtmann, 1988). But little has been done to relate questions of equity, distribution of services, and fairness to the analysis of not-for-profit organizations.

This area appears to be fruitful for future research. For example, are different groups of people served by government entities, for-profit firms, and not-for-profit organizations when they exist in the same industry? The nursing home and child care industries are examples where all three types of organizations exist. Are trade-offs between efficiency and equity made differently in different organizational settings? We know, for example, that there are more often waiting lists in not-for-profit nursing homes than in for-profit homes. Also, donations are a major source of revenue for many not-for-profit organizations, but not for government or for-profit organizations. Do these differences relate to perceived differences in efficiency among organizations or perceived differences in the way organizations handle issues of equity?

It seems, then, that many program evaluations should include recommendations concerning the appropricate delivery system to accomplish the goals of improving efficiency and redistributing income (Nelson, 1977).

9. Beyond Static Efficiency and Equity

To summarize, it is clear that project evaluation and policy analysis have emerged from a classic beginning based on modern welfare economics and Pareto efficiency to become a modern discipline of policy analysis (see Friedman, 1984). This discipline continues to rely on a strong theoretical foundation associated with more refined concepts of welfare functions and fairness, allowing the analyst to better interpret empirical estimates of the consequences of social programs for both efficiency and equity. In addition, the large number of data sets that contain information concerning various social programs and the increasing power of computers allow better empirical understanding of these social programs. Thus policy analysis has not stagnated at the level of efficiency analysis but has moved on from there at an encouraging rate.

Unresolved issues remain, however. Most of our present policy analysis deals with efficiency and equity in a purely static environment. Dynamic questions are more difficult to handle, but they go to the heart of the matter for some programs (Stiglitz, 1979). Of course, in the classic purely competitive economy, prices would exist that allow consumers and producers to make the appropriate intertemporal decisions. But the dynamics of both public and private decisions mean that those decisions will affect generations who cannot be directly involved in them, as we have not yet found a satisfactory means of evaluating, in terms of either efficiency of equity, these distributions over time.

Nevertheless, many studies, such as those concerning the influence of pollution on the environment or those conerning the impact of social security programs on savings (Feldstein, 1976) and retirement decisions (Burtless and Moffitt, 1984), have already started policy analysts down the road to further incorporating growth into analyses. For, in many cases, the policy analyst might have to consider not only trade-offs between equity and efficiency in a static sense but also the potential impact on growth and intergenerational equity of any social program.

Intergenerational equity can be considered within the context of a social welfare function, as interpersonal equity was considered in section 5, where the satisfaction of future generations is an argument of the function. Alternatively, studies of completed projects can be used to suggest the possible impact of current projects on future generations. For example, Burton Weisbrod (1971) calculated the rate of return from the successful development of the polio vaccine, and Holtmann (1973a) calculated the gain from developing the vaccine at a faster rate, providing some guidance for evaluation of current research and development projects that will benefit future generations. Hence, as the analysis of distributional questions expands to include future generations, current analytical concepts and past experience can supplement new methods of analysis.

10. Conclusions

As policy analysts become more involved with issues of equity or fairness, their role as scientific evaluators versus advocates will become increasingly important. Though lack of appropriate data and lack of agreement on the appropriate empirical measures of particular costs and benefits (for example, the lack of agreement on the appropriate discount rate to be used in project evaluations) presently leave ample room for disagreement on the merits of any particular public program, evaluations based on efficiency criteria offer the decision makers seemingly objective evidence. After all, if all the costs and benefits of a program can be measured accurately, the project in question either offers a potential Pareto-superior allocation for society or it doesn't. Of course, a potential improvement in welfare is not a sufficient condition for adopting a program unless all those injured by the program are in fact compensated for their losses. But, as we indicated, this need not be an issue for the analyst who logically separates the efficiency issues from those of equity.

If the incorporation of distributional analysis into project evaluation leads to highly subjective recommendations, varying greatly from one analyst to another, many will abandon the field as some early theorists abandoned welfare economics. In addition, policy-makers will be less inclined to rely on one evaluation that can be considered objective, increasing the cost of project evaluation. However, recent developments in the theory of equity are rooted in traditional welfare theory, suggesting that analysts will be cautious as they incorporate distributional analysis into public policy analysis. Hence, though advances in this area may be slower than we would like, the integrity of the growing field of public policy analysis will be enhanced.

References

Arrow, Kenneth, *Social Choice and Individual Values* (New York: Wiley, 1963).

Atkinson, Anthony, and Joseph Stiglitz, *Lectures on Public Economics* (New York: McGraw-Hill, 1980).

Ballard, Charles, "The Marginal Efficiency Cost of Redistribution, *American Economic Review* 78:5 (1988), 1011–1033.

Bator, Francis, "Anatomy of Market Failure," *Quarterly Journal of Economics* 72:3 (August 1958), 351–379.

Baumol, William, *Superfairness: Applications and Theory* (Cambridge, Mass.: MIT Press, 1986).

Becker, Gary, *Human Capital* (National Bureau of Economic Research, 1964).

Bergson, Abram, "A Reformulation of Certain Aspects of Welfare Economics," *Quarterly Journal of Economics* 52:2 (1938), 310–334.

Browning, Edgar, "On the Marginal Welfare Cost of Taxation," *American Economic Review* 77:1 (March 1987), 11–23.

Browning, Edgar, and William Johnson, "The Trade-off between Equality and Efficiency," *Journal of Political Economy* 92:2 (1984), 175–203.

Burtless, Gary, and Robert Moffitt, "The Effect of Social Security Benefits on the Labor Supply of the Aged," In Henry Aaron and Gary Burtless, eds., *Retirement and Economic Behavior* (Washington, D.C.: Brookings Institution, 1984), pp. 135–171.

Danziger, Sheldon, and Kent Portney, *The Distributional Impacts of Public Policies* (New York: St. Martins Press, 1988).

Feldstein, Martin, "Social Security and Savings: The Extended Life Cycle Theory," *American Economic Review* 66:1 (1976), 77–86.

Friedman, Lee, *Microeconomic Policy Analysis* (New York: McGraw-Hill, 1984).

Graaff, J. de V., *Theoretical Welfare Economics* (New York: Cambridge University Press, 1967).

Hansmann, Henry, "The Role of Non-Profit Enterprise," *Yale Law Journal* 89:5 (1980), 835–901.

Hayek, Fredrick, ed., *Collectivist Economic Planning* (London: Routledge, 1935), 245–290.

Holtmann, Alphonse, "Theories of Non-Profit Institutions," *Journal of Economic Surveys* 2:1 (1988), 29–45.

———, "The Size and Distribution of Benefits from U.S. Medical Research: The Case of Eliminating Cancer and Heart Disease," *Public Finance* 28:3–4 (1973a), 353–361.

———, "On the Optimal Timing of Research Expenditures," *Inquiry* 10 (March 1973), 47–49.

Hotelling, Harold "The General Welfare in Relation to Problems of Taxation and of Railway and Utility Rates," *Econometrica* 6:2 (1938), 242–269.

Inman, Robert, "Optimal Fiscal Reform of Metropolitan Schools," *American Economic Review* 68:1 (March 1978), 107–122.

Krutilla, John, and Otto Eckstein, *Multiple Purpose River Development* (Baltimore: Johns Hopkins Press, 1958).

Lerner, Abba, "Economic Theory and Socialist Economy," *Review of Economic Studies* 2:1 (1934), 51–61.

Marglin, Stephen, "Economic Factors Affecting System Design," in Arthur Maass et al., ed., *Design of Water-Resource Systems* (Cambridge, Mass.: Harvard University Press, 1962), pp. 129–225.

Mincer, Jacob, "On-The-Job Training: Costs, Returns, and Some Implications," *The Journal of Political Economy* 70:5 Part 2 (October 1962), 50–79.

Musgrave, Richard, *The Theory of Public Finance* (New York: McGraw-Hill, 1959).

Nelson, James, ed., *Marginal Cost Pricing in Practice* (Englewood Cliffs, N.J.: Prentice-Hall, 1964).

Nelson, Richard, *The Moon and the Ghetto* (New York: Norton, 1977).

Okun, Arthur, *Equality and Efficiency: The Big Tradeoff* (Washington, D.C.: Brookings Institution, 1975).

Pareto, Vilfredo, *Manuel d'Economie Politique* (Paris: Marcel Giard, 1929).

Samuelson, Paul, *Foundations of Economic Analysis* (New York: Atheneum, 1965).

Samuelson, Paul, "The Pure Theory of Public Expenditures," *Review of Economics and Statistics* 36:4 (1954), 387–389.

Schultz, Theodore, "Investment in Human Capital," *American Economic Review* 51:1 (March 1961), 1–17.

Smith, James, and Finis Welch, "Black Economic Progress after Myrdal, *Journal of Economic Literature* 27:2 (June 1989), 519–564.

Stigler, George, "Information in the Labor Market," *The Journal of Political Economy* 70:5 Part 2 (1962), 94–105.

Stiglitz, Joseph, "A Neoclassical Analysis of Natural Resources," in Kerry Smith, ed., *Scarcity and Growth Reconsidered* (Baltimore: Johns Hopkins Press, 1979), pp. 36–66.

Varian, Hal, *Intermediate Microeconomics* (New York: Norton, 1990).

Weisbrod, Burton, "Income Redistribution Effects and Benefit-Cost Analysis," in Samuel Chase, ed., *Problems in Public Expenditure Analysis* (Washington, D.C.: Brookings Institution, 1968), pp. 177–208.

Weisbrod, Burton, "Distributional Effects of Collective Goods," *Policy Analysis* 5:1 (1978), 67–95.

———, "Toward A Theory of the Voluntary Non-Profit Sector in a Three Sector Economy," in Edmund Phelps, ed., *Altruism, Morality and Economic Theory* (New York: Russell Sage, 1975), 171–195.

———, "Costs and Benefits of Medical Research: A Case Study of Poliomyelitis," *Journal of Political Economy* 79:3 (May–June 1971), 527–544.

———, "Collective Action and the Distribution of Income: A Conceptual Approach, "in Robert Haveman and Julius Margolis, eds., *Public Expenditures and Policy Analysis* (Chicago: Markham 1970), pp. 117–141.

———, "Education and Investment in Human Capital," *Journal of Political Economy* 70:5 Part 2 (October 1962), 106–123.

Wood, Donald, and Harry Campbell, *Cost-Benefit Analysis and the Economics of Investment in Human Resources* (Kingston, Ontario: Industrial Relations Centre, Queen's University, 1970).

4 BEYOND SELF-INTEREST

Amitai Etzioni

1. Introduction

When asked why he contributed to a beggar, and was this not due to Christ's commandment, Thomas Hobbes responded that he did so "with the sole intent of relieving his own misery at the sight of the beggar" (Losco, 1986: 323). This statement captures a belief held for centuries by many social philosophers and social scientists, by the public-at-large, and championed by the neoclassical school of thought: that human behavior can be explained by self-interest. Altruistic acts, to the extent that they are recognized at all, are depicted merely as another means of pursuing one's own interest.

Socio-economists strive to correct this way of thinking with a deontological ethic based on a force beyond self-interest—that of moral and social causes. This ethic presents arguments and evidence that people are not driven solely by self-interest but are also significantly directed by their moral considerations. These moral factors represent a source of action and valuation distinctly different from, and often conflicting with, self-interest. Acknowledging this distinction, this chapter shall endeavor to show, allows for more productive conceptualization, is more predictive, and is ethically sounder than self-interest-only approaches. The first section is based on substantive arguments. The following two sections present evidence of moral behavior in support of these arguments, both in individual and public choices. The final section illustrates the policy implications of including these moral factors in one's analyses.

2. As Reflected in Utility Theory

The self-interested, "Hobbesian" view is currently represented in the neoclassical school of thought. Neoclassicists hold that individuals seek to "maximize" one utility: their self-interest, also defined as pleasure, happiness, and consumption. This concept of utility, as developed late in the eighteenth century largely by Jeremy Bentham and widely used by neo-classicists, holds that "[all] actions are directed toward the gain of pleasure or the avoidance of pain" (Dyke, 1981: 31). Moreover, many utilitarians grant moral approval to pleasure: pleasure is "good"; pain is "evil."

An analysis of this school, specifically its theory of economic utility, uncovers sound conceptual reasons for distinguishing moral causes from those of self-interest. Clearly, self-interest, or pleasure, accounts for a good deal of human behavior, and to this extent the concept of utility is logical, proper, and productive. To assume, however, that all (or virtually all) behavior is explainable in the narrow terms of self-interest is too simplistic. Many actions are either pleasurable or moral but often not both. Many times, pursuing one's pleasure is in conflict with carrying out one's moral duties (an area to be addressed in more detail later). Furthermore, ascribing a moral goodness to pursuing one's pleasure represents a gross value judgment which once removed, allows for the recognition of other sources of value.

When one contemplates the substance of the term "moral behavior," the kinds of acts the term encompasses, one finds that living up to one's moral obligations, discharging one's duties, and doing "what's right" evokes a feeling distinctly different from that of indulging one of the senses, satisfying a personal need, or doing something "fun." Indeed, many moral acts are explicitly based on the denial of pleasure in the name of the principle evoked. Doing penance, abstention from premarital sex, and Ramadan fasting are not what most people consider sources of pleasure. True, acting in line with one's moral precepts produces a kind of satisfaction, a sense of moral worth, but it is more the kind one gets when a hard day's work is done than the pleasure of getting off work early with full pay.

Moreover, although pleasure and living up to one's moral commitments are not always or necessarily in conflict, very often they do conflict in terms of their call on resources (the time, energy, and assets dedicated to one behavior are often required by the other as well, a major factor, for example, in the life of parents who work outside of the home). Quite frequently pleasure-seeking acts and moral commitments are also incompatible in terms of the behavior expected and rewarded (e.g., when managers are under great pressure to increase profits but also not to violate the rules of the game; using kickbacks or bribes to get more business are cases in point).

In an attempt to counter challenges that the prevailing concept of utility is amoral, asocial, and counter to basic, observable behavior, neoclassicists point to a concept of utility that is different but goes under the same name: one that contains service to others and a commitment to moral values. A simple conceptual device is used: The consumption or pleasure by others is made into the actor's pleasure, hence the "interdependent" utility. Essentially, this concept attemtps to explain pleasure, self-interest, and the opposite kind of behavior—caring for others and for the community—in the same self-interested terms. To convert altruism into self-interest is, however, to misunderstand altruism. By assuming self-interest to be the foundation for all behavior, including self-denial and altruism, the interdependent concept fails to account for motives, such as the actor's belief that the altruistic act was the right thing to do, regardless of whether it brought him or her pleasure. Also as a result, the concept of interdependent utility ceases to differentiate between people's preferences; moral preferences are lost among a myriad of others, the preference for honesty being on par with a taste for peanut butter (McPherson, 1984: 243).

Furthermore, expanding the concept of utility to explain, in this case, all motives for human activity violates a rule of sound conceptualization. Once a concept is defined so that it encompasses all the incidents that are members of a given category, it ceases to enhance one's ability to explain. According to this concept, there is no behavior that does not seek to maximize an actor's self-interest. As a result, this "theory" fails to shed light on motivation. Affixing the labels "utility" or "self-interest" to all behavior explains nothing. Insight into what motivates behavior is lost, and the concept becomes unproductive and tautological. In short, the neoclassical approach dilutes the explanatory power of the concept to the point where it becomes quite meaningless. It thus seems, on grounds of sound conceptualization, that the quest for self-satisfactions and seeking to serve others (the public included) out of a sense of moral obligation are best kept apart.

3. What Is Moral?

If a major motivating factor is morality, how is one to distinguish between it and other factors? After several hundred years, philosophers have yet to produce a fully satisfactory definition of what is moral. Many, though, agree that statements are to be viewed as moral if they meet four criteria. First, individuals who act on the basis of moral meta-preferences sense that they "must" behave in the prescribed way. Their moral acts are experienced as *imperatives*, things they must do because they are obligated, duty bound. Most of us are familiar introspectively with this experience, doing something because it is right, as distinguishable from doing it because it is enjoyable.

The notion of an imperative is supported by the observation that people set aside certain realms as commanding a special, compelling status. Emile Durkheim (1947) points to the fact that people treat certain acts as "sacred" (which need not mean religious). Such sacred moral principles characteristically repudiate the instrumental rationality that includes cost-benefit analysis; that is, people feel obligated to save a life or donate blood without calculating the potential payoffs (Goodin, 1980).

The need for additional criteria to characterize moral acts arises out of the fact that there can also be nonmoral imperatives, for example, obsessions with a forlorn love or even with an object, such as an illegal drug or a fetish. The addition of two other criteria helps here to separate moral imperatives from others (Childress, 1977).

Second, individuals who act morally are *able to generalize* their behavior—they are able to justify an act to others and to themselves by pointing to general rules. Statements such as "because I want it" or "I need it badly" do not meet this criterion because no generalization is entailed. "Do unto others as you wish others to do unto you," on the other hand, is a prime example of a generalized rule.

Third, moral preferences must be *symmetrical* in that there must be a willingness to accord other comparable people, under comparable circumstances, the same standing or right. (Otherwise, the moral dictum is rendered arbitrary. Such an arbitrary rule would state, "This rule applies to Jane but not to Jim although there is no relevant difference between them.") Racist ideologies, although they otherwise have the appearance of a moral system in that they are compelling (to their believers) and possibly generalizable, fail to qualify as moral by this test.

Finally, moral preferences *affirm or express a commitment*, rather than involve the consumption of a good or a service. They are therefore intrinsically motivated and not subject to means-end analysis (Dyke, 1981: 11). (The fact that there are nonmoral acts that are intrinsically motivated does not invalidate this criterion. It only shows that the universe of such acts is larger than that of moral acts, and hence, as was already indicated, this criterion is necessary but not sufficient in itself.) As to the argument that moral acts themselves are not impulsive acts but reflect deliberations and judgments (especially evident when one must sort out what course to follow when one is subject to conflicting moral claims), these deliberations are not of the same kind as means-end considerations; they require judgments among moral ends.

4. In Theory of Personality

Moral commitments, especially of the absolute kind, are distinguishable from pleasurable activities because values are often "internalized." That is, individuals see values as their own and not as external conditions to which they merely adapt. Internalization has been defined as part of the socialization process in which a person learns to "conform to rules in situations that arouse impulses to transgress and that lack surveillance and sanctions" (Kohlberg, 1968: 483). Social scientists may trace the genesis of one's moral commitments to one's parents, culture, or peer or reference groups; but whatever their source, once internalized moral commitments become an integral part of the self. Thus those who feel they ought to serve their country, God, or a cause feel strongly—sometimes despite strong protestations from spouses, friends, and peers—that such actions are in line with their values and their duty. Individuals' behavior depends on whether their consideration of morality is driven by an external constraint or by their own inner values.

The strength of moral commitments is reflected in studies that show that the more individuals act under the influence of moral commitments, the more they are expected to persevere (when circumstances change). Conversely, the more individuals heed their pleasure or self-interest—for example, by calculating costs and benefits—the less likely they are to persevere. As a result, moral commitments are expected to "stretch out" the learning curve and to increase transaction costs when changes favored by economic rationality are inconsistent with moral commitments.

More specifically, the learning curve records the time lapse and the costs involved in improving performance. The level of learning costs, the shape of the curve, is determined in part by nonmoral factors (for example, the complexity of the information to be absorbed). However, assuming all these factors are equal, it is expected that learning will be slower and more costly the higher the moral objections to what is being taught.

Choices that are relatively heavily "loaded" with moral considerations are expected to be unusually difficult to reverse, to be very "lumpy" (or highly discontinuous), and to reveal a high "notch-effect" (a resistance to pass a threshold that makes behavior sticky before it is passed; the reluctance is greatly diminished or lost once passage is completed).

The concept of "transaction costs" developed to help explain "stickiness," the fact that people do not modify their behavior even when such modifications are advantageous to them, or when the expected gains of modification exceed the expected costs. It appears that the stronger the moral commitment, the higher is the return needed before these individuals will violate their implicit contracts in the face of the changed economic circumstances that favor such a violation; they will therefore absorb more of an economic loss to live up to their obligations. For example, it is considered "improper" for professors to accept an offer from another university in May to start teaching in September (because it is difficult to replace faculty so late in the academic year). This sense of propriety is said to be stronger in some universities (Ivy League?) than in others (Red Brick?). Hence, to move a professor in May from the first kind of university would take a larger salary differential than from the second kind. That is, moral behavior is "stickier" than amoral behavior.

Moral commitments may also reduce what economists call "moral hazards." Specifically, the stronger the moral underwriting of implicit contracts, the lower the transaction costs, resulting in less need to buy hedge protection (in case resources are not delivered, or workers quit, and so on) and to spend resources on legal action (such as drafting explicit contracts and litigation to enforce them).

Although this discussion has referred to specific situations, the same point has been made about whole societies. Because it is not possible to provide enough police, accountants, and inspectors to verify more than a small segment of all transactions, economies and societies require that most transactions be based on voluntary compliance. This compliance, in turn, is significantly affected by the relative level of morality within a given society (or subsociety) in a given historical period. For example, when corruption in the society is high, it acts as a major drag on economic performance. Stated differently, to the extent that moral commitments enhance the resources that can be dedicated to economic activity rather than to supervision and verification, a higher level of morality increases productivity and the GNP.

Prosocial behavior benefits when violations of moral commitments cause guilt that leads, among other consequences, to compensatory behavior. For example, in experiments, people who were first induced to tell a lie were subsequently twice as likely to volunteer to carry out a chore than those who did not lie (Freedman, 1970: 156). The relationship is often more complex: A single transgression may lead to some guilt, but only the cumulative effect of several incidents will lead to an act of remorse. The behavioral consequences include sequences or cycles in which one or more illicit acts are followed by bouts of morally approved behavior, or an increased search for, or commitment to, "rehabilitation" (or atonement) via morally approved behavior.

The concept also holds for joining welfare. Before one joins, a welfare dollar may be worth only 80 cents, but once one joins, and one is stigmatized as a "welfare client," the very next dollar may be worth 100 cents. And even if one gets off welfare and no longer receives stigmatized income, the stigma is likely to linger.

Neoclassical concepts of utility fail to explain the sources of preferences and the factors that cause them to change. Such explanations are necessary because people change their preferences as the constraints under which they "implement" them change. Hence, changes in behavior may be due to changes in constraints or in preferences, often some combination of the two. Without a conception and measurement of preference formation and dynamics, in which moral values play a pivotal role, a satisfactory theory of behavior is hard to imagine. The assumption that people's preferences are "set" or "stable," which is central to the neoclassical paradigm because it allows it to disregard changes in intentions and in those values that affect preferences, simply ignores the most elementary observations of daily experience.

Even accepting the gross oversimplification that preferences are set rather than constantly changing, morality enters into choices because of the important observation that choices are not simple, one-dimensional, one-time (or one-stage) events but are in fact multifaceted. Neoclassical psychology treats individuals as rational bundles of preferences and desires. These psychologists assume that people are unitary, that they are driven by one overriding preference (usually for "pleasure" or some other monistic "utile"). Deontological psychology, on the other hand, recognizes that people also have a moral dimension. It is increasingly realized that humans, unlike animals, are constituted by two layers of preferences, one (the metapreference) used to evaluate the other (the regular preference), and that when these two conflict, a typical struggle ensues. The simple statement, "I would *like* to go to a movie, but *ought* to visit my friend in the hospital," captures the common tension. Moral values are the most important source of these scrutinizing metapreferences.

While it is possible to study systematically the forces behind the two levels of preferences, the outcome of the struggle rarely lands on one side or the other. Rather, human behavior is frequently conflicting and not consolidated; choices are multi-faceted events. If the friend is neglected, guilt nags; if the movie is skipped today, it may appeal more strongly the next time a duty calls.

5. Evidence in Private Choices

To this point the argument has been made for recognizing a moral motivation beyond self-interest. This section presents empirical evidence, and evidence from everyday experience, of moral acts. At first one may wonder, "Why document the obvious?" After all, does anyone really doubt that a significant part of people's conduct expresses moral commitments? But the fact is that neoclassicists and many others have labored long and hard to show that practically all behavior is driven by pleasure and self-interest. Altruistic acts are accounted for as "really" being efforts to enhance one's reputation, gain social approval, and so on. This section reveals the existence of genuine (unselfish) altruistic behavior and confirms, through example, the distinct influence moral concerns have on private behavior.

A poignant example: By standard exchange theory, husbands and wives of ailing Alzheimer's patients have no reason to stay with their mates; they get nothing in return. Victims of Alzheimer's (a disease currently without as much as a dim hope for cure) slowly lose their memory, first of events and names of simple objects, until finally they cannot recognize even those members of their own family who care for them. Eventually, they require constant care and become incontinent and abusive. This means spouses of these patients labor and nurse with no promise of reciprocal care, no thanks, or even worse, with abuse in return. Nevertheless, nearly all husbands and wives of Alzheimer's patients stay with their spouses throughout their illnesses. "Exchange" theorists may try to explain this behavior by arguing that they stay rather than endure the neighbors' gossip. Yet, weighed against all of the hardships endured in caring for an Alzheimer's patient, this argument seems quite unconvincing. People seem to stay mainly because it is the "right" thing to do.

A number of major empirical studies have concluded that Americans are also giving more to charity. Members of the neoclassical school would have predicted a drop in donations after the 1986 tax reform, which included changes that made each charitable dollar more costly to the donor. Yet in 1985 total charitable donations were $80.31 billion; in 1988 they reach $104.37 billion, an increase of 13.6 percent after adjusting for inflation (Weber, 1989: 11, 14). With the advent of sharp government cutbacks in social programs in the early 1980s, polls also show that the spirit of voluntarism rose gradually throughout the decade. In 1977, 27 percent of Americans reported that they were involved in a charity or social service activity; that figure rose to 39 percent in 1987 and to 41 percent in 1989 (*Public Opinion*, 1987: 40; *Gallup*, 1989: 20). As Alan Wolfe concludes, "These latter developments in particular insure that the present period, characterized as it is by faith in the market, will not be characterized by greater private niggardliness" (Wolfe, 1989: 88).

A considerable body of experimental data also supports the existence of significant amounts of altruistic behavior. Several experiments show that many people mail back "lost" wallets to strangers, cash intact (Hornstein, Fisch, and Holmes, 1986). In another study, 64 percent of the subjects who had an opportunity to return a lost contribution to an "Institute for Research in Medicine" did so (Hornstein, Masor, and Sole, 1971: 110). The costs are forgoing the found cash, as well as paying for postage and going to the trouble of mailing the contribution. The reward? Chiefly, the inner sense of having done what is right. (For more examples of altruistic behavior, see Janis and Mann, 1977: 27; Schwartz, 19770: 283).

5.1. A Factor in Economic Behavior

Evidence shows that commitments to moral values also affect economic activities. Consider saving behavior. Neoclassical economists explain the level of saving mainly by the size of one's income (the higher one's income, the more one saves), by the desire to provide for consumption in retirement, and by the level of interest rates. However, studies show that those who enjoy high incomes, as in the United States, save comparatively less than do those in less affluent countries (International Monetary Fund, 1989).

The factors cited explain only part of the variance in the amount saved: the extent to which one believes that it is immoral to be in debt, that one ought to save for its own sake and to avoid dependence on the government or one's children, and that one ought to help one's children "start off in life."

Much research has shown that firms do not pursue one overarching goal, profit, but that they have mixed goals; they do not maximize any one utility and are internally divided rather than unified actors (Herendeen and Schechter, 1977: 1514; Bailey and Boyle, 1977: 50; Monsen, Chieu, and Cooley, 1968: 442). Among the goals that compel executives are those prescribed as morally appropriate by their peers, communities, and society as a whole. These intentions are rarely limited to maximizing profit (Donaldson and Lorsch, 1983). Neoclassical economists generally reject the work of Cyert and March (1963) because it strayed too far from the optimization paradigm. Wiliamson's work on contracting (transaction cost economics) has received some recognition because it combines optimization with bounded rationality. Yet not until the development of the principal/agent model, which allows for optimization in the face of asymmetrical information, did neoclassical economists finally accept the notion that firms could have goals other than short- or long-term (market share) profit maximization (see Moe, 1984: 739–777). However, these are but holding operations that refuse to come to terms with the existence of major independent social/moral corporate goals.

Edmund Phelps (1975: 5) notes that in the same world in which people sell unsafe products, gouge, and short-weigh, one also finds "the prevalence of altruistic behavior: A producer might advertise his product truthfully when he need not, a labor union may refrain from breaking the law when it could do so for a net gain, a benevolent butcher may abstain from short-weighing." Kenneth Arrow (1975) goes a step further to argue that since it is impossible to generate enough reinforcement agents and incentives for many elements of the implicit and explicit social contracts that sustain the market (e.g., trust in money), the whole economic system would break down if it were not for these not-self-enforcing arrangements, that is, those based on morality and government.

6. Evidence in Public Choices

The utility conception is particularly strained when it is extended to encompass "public goods" and activities on behalf of the collectivity. "Public goods" is a term introduced by Paul Samuelson to refer to those goods that can be "used by many persons at the same time without reducing the amount available for any other person" (Alchian and Allen, 1983: 99). Price mechanisms cannot work here to allocate resources rationally or to ensure "sufficient supply, efficient production, or general welfare" (Arrow, 1974). These "goods" include much of a society's culture, heritage, national defense, and environmental protection, as well as pivotal economic elements such as major segments of scientific knowledge and of the nation's infrastructure. "Activities on behalf of the collectivity" refers to acts such as voting and doing voluntary work that serve shared needs.

Government coercion and inducements are the major methods used to ensure attention to, and resources for, these public benefits. Another major method is to build on moral commitments. Civility, the individual's moral commitment to shared concerns, is the concept used to refer to the factor that leads people to contribute to the common good (for additional discussion of the concept, see Janowitz, 1983). With the concept introduced at home, cultivated in schools, fostered by the news media, enhanced by voluntary associations, and extolled from presidential and other civic leaders' "pulpits," citizens of a nation feel obliged to contribute to the well-being of the community they share.

A large number of experiments, under different conditions, most of them highly unfavorable to civility, show that people do not take free rides but pay voluntarily as much as 40 percent to 60 percent of what economists figure is due to the public till if the person were not to free ride at all. The main reason: The subjects consider it the "right" or "fair" thing to do. (For an article about these experiments, as well as a report of their own, see Marwell and Ames, 1981: 295–310.)

Another series of experiments was specifically designed to show that egoistic incentives (reputation, reciprocity) are not neccessary to create cooperation and altruism. In one experiment seven people were seated together in a room, unable to talk to one another. Each subject, with $5 in hand, was given a choice to anonymously keep the money or contribute it toward a group bonus of $10, with the understanding that if three or more subjects also contributed, everyone (including those who chose not to contribute) would get the bonus, and if three out of the group did not contribute, no one would get the bonus, including the one or two who had contributed. Hence, noncontributors received either $15 or $5, contributors, $10 or $5. The results of the experiment showed that 51 percent of the groups were "rewarded." The success rate rose to 100 percent when, in another version of the experiment, members were allowed a ten-minute discussion (used to elicit a sense of commitment) before making their choice (Dawes, Orbell, and van de Kragt, 1983).

Dawes concludes that special payments (to make people "behave") do not explain why:

> humans often appear to forgo choosing domain strategies in favor of those that have more benign collective results. People do not rip-off their neighbors whenever they know they can avoid being caught; airplane squadrons in war fly in formation even though the planes at the periphery are most likely to be shot down, and some soldiers even fall on hand grenades to save their comrades. [Dawes, 1989: 5]

7. Public Policy Implications

The position advanced here is *not* the opposite of the neoclassical position; it does not hold that people are impervious to their own self-interest. A new discipline, socio-economics, suggests that individuals are simultaneously under the influence of two major sets of factors: their pleasure and their moral duty. It is not suggested that analysis of moral factors ought to *replace* considerations of self-interest, or that the latter are inappropriate; rather, the point is that policy analysis ought to encompass both kinds of considerations. This socio-economic position is advanced as an alternative to the reductionism of neoclassicists, to the notion that people act morally only as long as it makes sense in self-interested terms. Moreover, by viewing human motivations as *co*determined (by a quest for self-interest and by moral factors), we seek to improve both the descriptive and normative bases of policy analysis.

7.1. Descriptive Implications

Voting behavior serves as an example of the socio-economic position. Neoclassicists argue that normally there is little reason for people to vote because they get nothing in exchange; they cannot reasonably expect that their vote will make a difference. They might vote therefore only when the election is close, when they feel their individual vote will make a difference.[1] There is, however, only weak evidence in support of this correlation between voter turnout and closeness of the election. And, obviously, many millions vote when the elections are not close. The explanatory and predicting factor, on the contrary, turns out to be a moral commitment: People vote because they feel it is their "civic duty" (Barry, 1978: 17). Hence, if we seek to increase voter turnout, we need not worry only or first about length of queues, or providing umbrellas, not to mention payoffs; we should also consider expanding civic education.

A recent RAND study of the external costs of smoking and drinking (costs not included in the price, such as making others sick) approaches the problem from both perspectives (Manning et al., 1989). The study concludes that from a neoclassical point of view, smokers should not be made to pay a higher price for their cigarettes, because their costs already more than pay for their harms. (A pack of cigarettes increases medical costs but reduces life expectancy by 137 minutes, lowering the amount of pension payments collected.) Even when the study considered the effects of smoking upon society (i.e., passive smokers, other than smokers and family members of smokers, and victims of fires caused by smokers), they found the taxes on cigarettes to compensate sufficiently for these deaths and illnesses. (External costs would more than double, by the way, if the authors had included those imposed on the smokers' families.)

When the study broadened its purview to encompass "other" criteria (in effect, morals), however, it openly and explicitly called attention to considerations that might lead to imposing higher taxes on cigarettes by drawing on criteria other than economic efficiency. This second approach argues that even if one accepts uncritically that one ought not interfere in private choices, there is still some room to consider it morally appropriate to act to discourage smoking. The authors point out that the young, when they "choose" to smoke—and become addicted—often are not fully informed about the consequences of their choice; hence to help them stop smoking is, in effect, to act according to their latent preference (our terminology, not theirs). Second, the fact that many smokers try to quit signals their "true" desire. Thus, even if one holds that it is wrong to interfere with people's choices once their preferences are formed, there is moral justification to act on their behalf, on needs they express, albeit not in immediate choices (e.g., not in buying cigarettes but in also "buying" stop-smoking clinics).

More generally, the neoclassical approach claims to be value-neutral by assuming that behavior reveals preferences, that the market best serves people's preferences, or "what the individuals want;" neoclassicists disregard the fact that preferences are to a large extent socially formed and hence reflect society's values, culture, and power structure. In effect, the assumption of "consumer sovereignty" reflects a value system and a social, economic, and political structure—that of mature capitalism. A more encompassing analysis must include the factors that shape or reshape preferences.

Deterring crime is another useful example. Neoclassicists analyze crime in terms of self-interested cost-benefit analysis. They argue that the probability of being arrested and convicted, the size of the penalty, and the size of the loot—or the "costs" and "benefits"—correlate with the frequency of a large variety of crimes, including murder and rape (Andreano and Siegfried, 1980; Rottenberg, 1979). The inferences are subject to considerable methodological controversies but are of no concern here. To the extent that these data demonstrate that self-interest plays a role in situations considered the domain of impulsive behavior, neoclassicists provide an important correction to the over-socialized view of crime, a view that focuses almost exclusively on the role of education, peer pressure, subculture, and other such factors. Yet to the extent that neoclassicists suggest that self-interest accounts for all or most of the variance, they vastly overstate their findings (Cook, 1980), and their conclusions tend to mislead policy-makers.

Examples of misleading statements are from Paul Rubin (1980: 13): "The decision to become a criminal is in principle no different from the decision to become a brick-layer . . . the individual considers the net costs and benefits of each alternative and makes his decision on this basis," and "tastes are constant and a change in [criminal] behavior can be explained by changes in prices [such as penalties]." They ignore the fact that despite whatever correlations are found between "prices" and level of criminality, much of the variance (in crime rates) remains unexplained, probably because moral and other social factors are at work. Such statements also overlook the fact that the "taste" for crime, like all others, is affected by normative and other social factors, for example, by the extent to which the relevant subculture disapproves of the particular kinds of crime (Grasmick and Green, 1981).

Similarly, statements such as Charles Murray's (1984: 168) that "crime occurs when the prospective benefits sufficiently outweigh the prospective costs" are not only formulated in a way that makes falsification impossible (if no crime occurs under an expected set of conditions the benefits might be said not to "sufficiently" outweigh the costs), but they also tend to mislead policy-makers into disregarding the role of education, subculture, leadership, and role models. Of special interest in this context is James Wilson's (1985) discussion of the role of various "impulse control" movements and organizations in nineteenth-century America. Wilson points out that as industrialization advanced, youngsters who once left their own homes only to work in homes under the supervision of other farmers or artisans then started to reside in boarding houses in cities without any family bonds or authority. As a result, disorderly conduct became more widespread. What followed were numerous efforts to advance control of impulse and build up inner control, self-discipline, and "character." These included Sunday schools, YMCAs, temperance movements, and various religious and secular voluntary associations. Some had other goals, but impulse control was a successful by-product; others were aimed directly at, and were effective in, instilling self-discipline.

Another example: Economists recommend various policies to encourage saving and reduce consumption, among them curtailing federal expenditures (a major source of consumption) or taxing consumption. Both policies have a cost. The first may cause a recession, which exacts huge human and economic costs; the second is regressive and imposes an unfair burden on the poor. The fact that policies have costs does not mean that they are necessarily undesirable. It does, however, point to the merit of considering other perspectives. For example, a more comprehensive policy would emphasize the accumulation of debt as socially undesirable behavior, behavior that undermines our collective well-being and threatens our future—just as debt was perceived in the 1950s. To bring about the change in saving and consumption patterns, the President, community leaders, and educators would all have a role in changing people's long-range perspectives. Such a policy would cost relatively little, would not be regressive, and rather than imposing a solution, would draw on people's values.

The policy point is that operationalizing certain programs requires work not merely on the self-interest, cost-benefit, deterrence, incentive, and police side but also on the formation of preferences side, via moral education, peer culture, community values, and the mobilization of appropriate public opinion, factors that neoclassicists take for granted. Consequently, their theories provide no analytic framework to conceptualize the ways in which preferences are formed and might be reformed.

7.2. Social and Moral Factors in the Market

Neoclassical policy analysis typically suggests that we expand market forces to allow individuals to more freely pursue their own preferences. The idea of "choice" has recently been advocated by several policy analysts as a way to "fix" public education: Parents should be free to choose which school their child will attend. Four states have introduced choice (Arkansas, Iowa, Minnesota, and Nebraska), and more than half are considering it. The policy was called the cornerstone of President Bush's 1989 Educational Summit with the governors (*Wall Street Journal*, 1989: A26).

This idea was previously tried using a voucher system. Gary Becker (1986) described that system:

> A comprehensive voucher system would require public schools to compete for students and to cover their costs with tuition revenue. Public schools could compete effectively only if they suppressed violence, instilled discipline, involved parents, offered a challenging curriculum, and controlled costs. If a public school could not attract sufficient students with tuition that covered costs, it would have to close or be sold to a private owner. [P. 19]

(For studies of the voucher system see Doyle and Finn, 1983, and Areen and Jencks, 1971).

At the same time, experience with vouchers shows the dangers of the simplistic introduction of competition into human service areas in which consumer knowledge is limited. It is far more difficult for parents to evaluate education, than, say, a can of beans. Those searching out criteria on which to base their choice of a school tend to land on measurable figures that report the results of test scores but neglect much of the other subtler, deeper, yet highly relevant aspects of education such as curriculum design and guiding philosophies of schools and teachers.

In this case, giving more information to the "consumers" is a necessary but insufficient step in implementing choice in schools. Even with all of the relevant facts in hand, consumers have a hard time evaluating large amounts of complex information. Thus, giving them scores indicating how various schools compared on numerous measures is likely to have few beneficial effects. (Consumers are already overwhelmed by the much simpler information found on cereal boxes and do not engage in proper comparative shopping.)

The moral issue still remains: When the market responds to purchasing power rather than to votes, each of which reflects one person, it never *per se* provides for the weaker members. Hence, unless externally affected, the market simply caters to the rich and neglects the poor. The essence of public education is, of course, an effort to overcome this market bias. The more market forces are relied on therefore, the greater the danger that the poor will receive less than the rich. Hence, choice should be combined with efforts to increase the resources available to public schools in poorer areas.

7.3. Social and Moral Factors and Institutional Change

Neoclassical analyses tend to focus on transactions among individuals or small units (such as households and small firm) and their aggregation in anonymous markets, that is, markets that are assumed to have no collective controls. To the extent that institutions are studied at all within this paradigm, they are generally perceived as reflecting arrangements made voluntarily and knowingly by individuals, in line with their interests and goals. Traditionally, other social sciences tended to view institutions as reflecting historical (macro-) processes, society-wide values, and power relations. We seek to encompass the influence of both individuals and that of society. We attempt to combine aggregative analysis with collective analysis by assuming that collective factors provide the context and are "priors" within which individuals act, and which in turn are affected by them.

The significance of systematically including institutional analyses arises because institutions themselves hinder or assist policy-making, and hence, even if one does not seek to modify the institutions, their effects on policy must be taken into account. For example, a multi-year economic policy formed within the United States (say, a corporate development plan) that ignored the well-established economic effects of the four-year political cycle driven by presidential elections is less likely to succeed than an economic policy that takes the cycle into account. All other things being equal, the expansive policies of election years provide a much more hospitable economic environment for a new product, or newly expanded production capacities, than do those of first-year new administrations. "Bitter medicine" is usually prescribed during this first year; hence the period tends to be economically restrictive. The cycle, in turn, reflects the Constitution and not an aggregation of individual dicisions. Similarly, one must expect little success for a policy that ignores differences among institutions—for example, shifting law enforcement functions from the FBI to local governments—because of the widespread corruption institutionalized in many local police forces. The same must be said about a policy that shifts responsibilities from the IRS or the Social Security Administration to local tax collection or welfare agencies.

Beyond accounting for the established features of existing institutions and the powerful inertia and vested interests they tend to generate, one must also recognize that institutions can be changed and policy advanced via such changes. Thus, instead of, or in addition to, using educational campaigns to encourage many millions of Americans to increase their saving, one can enhance saving by changing the tax laws, under some conditions by reducing corporate outlays of dividends (i.e., by increasing retained earnings) or, more effectively, by reducing government expenditures.

Segregating Social Security from the unified budget, and investing its surpluses into a portfolio of American and foreign corporate and government bonds, could probably do more for the American savings rate than would, say, doubling the size of funds individuals can salt away, tax deferred, in their IRAs. While a constitutional amendment to balance the budget may well create several new problems, it would modify significantly the institutional context of the struggle to reduce federal deficits.

Similarly, aside from working on individual incentive schemes, corporations often benefit when they also introduce institutional changes such as increased cooperation with labor unions (GM-UAW, in recent years), quality circles, or participatory decision making (Greenberg, 1980). (None of these are reforms sure to have the desired result; more research is needed about the conditions of success and failure.) One may argue whether individuals or institutions are more powerful; however, one conclusion is clear: Policy analysis should consider individual, aggregative, and institutional factors.

Acknowledgments

The author is indebted to Judith Lurie and Susan McDougall for research assistance. This chapter draws on the author's book, *The Moral Dimension* (1988).

Notes

1. For a more sophisticated argument that tries to reconcile voting with rational choice theory, see Uhlander (1989). It would take us too far afield here to respond to the numerous assumptions the article introduces. Even after these are made, the most the author can claim is that "some data from recent off-year elections are shown to be consistent with the model" (Uhlander, 1989: 390).

References

Alchian, Armen Albert, and William R. Allen, *Exchange and Production: Competition, Coordination, and Control*, 2nd & 3rd eds. (Belmont, Calif.: Wadsworth, 1977, 1983).

Andreano, Ralph, and John. J. Siegfried, eds., *The Economics of Crime* (New York: John Wiley, 1980).

Areen, Judith, and Christopher Jencks, "Educational Vouchers: A Proposal for Diversity and Choice," *Teachers College Record* 72:3 (1971), 327–335.

Arrow, Kenneth, *The Limits of Organization* (New York: W. W. Norton, 1974).

———, "Gifts and Exchanges," in Edmund Phelps, ed., *Altruism, Morality, and Economic Theory* (New York: Russell Sage Foundation, 1975), pp. 13–28.

Bailey, Duncan, and Stanley T. Boyle, "Sales Revenue Maximization: An Empirical Investigation," *Industrial Organization Review* 5:1 (1977), 46–55.

Barry, Brian, *Sociologists, Economists, and Democracy* (Chicago: University of Chicago Press, 1978).

Becker, Gary, *Business Week* (March 24, 1986), 19.

Childress, James F., "The Identification of Ethical Principles," *Journal of Religious Ethics* 5:1 (1977), 39–68.

Cook, Philip J., "Punishment and Crime: A Critique of Current Findings Concerning the Preventative Effects of Punishment," in Ralph Andreano and John Siegfried, eds., *The Economics of Crime*, (New York: John Wiley, 1980), pp. 127–136.

Cyert, Richard M., and James G. March, *Behavioral Theory of the Firm* (Engelwood Cliffs, N.J.: Prentice Hall, 1963).

Dawes, Robyn M. "Social Dilemmas, Economic Self-Interest, and Evolutionary Theory," to be published in *Research in Psychology: Frontiers of Mathematics* (New York: Springer-Verlag, 1989).

Dawes, Robyn M., John M. Orbell, and Alphons J. C. van de Kragt, "The Minimal Contributing Set as a Solution to Public Goods Problems," *American Political Science Review* 77:1 (1983), 112–122.

Donaldson, Gordon, and Jay W. Lorsch, *Decision Making at the Top* (New York: Basic Books, 1983).

Doyle, Dennis, and Chester E. Finn, Jr., "Educational Quality and Choice: Toward a Statewide Public School Voucher Plan (Washington, D.C.: U.S. Department of Education, National Institute of Education, November 15, 1983).

Durkheim, Emile, *The Division of Labor in Society* (Glencoe, Ill.: Free Press, 1947).

Dyke, C., *Philosophy of Economics* (Engelwood Cliffs, N.J.: Prentice-Hall, 1981).

Etzioni, Amitai, *The Moral Dimension: Toward A New Economics* (New York: Free Press, 1988).

Freedman, Johnathan L., "Transgression, Compliance, and Guilt," in J. Macaulay and L. Berkowitz *Altruism and Helping Behavior* (New York: Academic Press, 1970).

Gallup Poll (November, 1989).

Goodin, Robert E., "Making Moral Incentives Pay," *Policy Sciences* 12:2 (1980), 161–178.

Grasmick, Harold G., and Donald E. Green, "Deterrence and the Morally Committed," *Sociological Quarterly* 22:1 (1981), 1–14.

Greenberg, Paul D., and Edward M. Glaser, *Some Issues in Joint Union-Management Quality of Worklife Improvement Efforts* (Kalamazoo, Mich.: W. E. Upjohn Institute for Employment Research, 1980).

Herendeen, James B., and Mark C. Schechter, "Alternative Models of the Corporate Enterprise: Growth Maximization, An Empirical Test," *Southern Economic Journal* 43:4 (April 1977), 1505–1514.

Hornstein, Harvey A., E. Fisch, and M. Holmes, "Influence of a Model's Feelings About His Behavior and His Relevance as a Comparison to Other Observers' Helping Behavior," *Journal of Personality And Social Psychology* 10:3 (1968), 222–226.

Hornstein, Harvey A., Hugo N. Masor, and Kenneth Sole, "Effects of Sentiment and Completion of a Helping Act on Observer Helping: A Case for Socially Mediated Zeigarnik Effects," *Journal of Personality and Social Psychology* 17:1 (1971), 107–112.

International Monetary Fund, *International Financial Statistics Yearbook*, Vol. XVII, (Washington, D.C.: International Monetary Fund, 1989).

Janis, Irving, and Leon Mann, *Decision Making: A Psychological Analysis of Conflict, Choice, and Commitment* (New York: Free Press, 1977).

Janowitz, Morris, *The Reconstruction of Patriotism: Education for Civic Conscious-ness* (Chicago: University of Chicago Press, 1983).

Kohlberg, Lawrence, "Moral Development," *International Encyclopedia of the Social Sciences*, vol. 10, David L. Sills, ed. (New York: MacMillan and Free Press, 1968).

Losco, Joseph, "Understanding Altruism: A Critique and Proposal for Integrating Various Approaches," *Political Psychology* 7:2 (1986), 323–348.

McPherson, Michael S., "On Shelling, Hirschman and Sen: Revising the Conception of the Self," *Partisan Review* 51:2 (1984), 236–247.

Manning, Willard G., Emmett B. Keeler, Joseph P. Newhouse, Elizabeth Sloss, and Jeffrey Wasserman, "The Taxes of Sin: Do Smokers and Drinkers Pay Their Way?" *Journal of the American Medical Association* 261:11 (1989), 1604–1609.

Marwell, Gerald, and Ruth E. Ames, "Economists Free Ride, Does Anyone Else?" *Journal of Public Economics* 15:3 (1981), 295–310.

Moe, Terry, "The New Economics of Organization," *American Journal of Political Science* 28:4 (1984), 739–777.

Monsen, R. Joseph, John S. Chieu, and David E. Cooley, "The Effect of Separation of Ownership and Control on Performance of the Large Firm," *Quarterly Journal of Economics* 82:3 (August 1968), 435–451.

Murray, Charles A., *Losing Ground: American Social Policy 1950–1980* (New York: Basic Books, 1984).

Phelps, Edmund S., "Introduction," *Altruism, Morality, and Economic Theory* (New York: Russell Sage Foundation, 1975), pp. 1–9.

Public Opinion (November/December, 1987).

Rottenberg, Simon, ed., *The Economics of Crime and Punishment* (Washington, D.C.: American Enterprise Institute, 1979).

Rubin, Paul H., "The Economics of Crime," in Ralph Andreano and John J. Siegfried, eds., *The Economics of Crime* (New York: John Wiley, 1980), 13–25.

Schwartz, Shalom H., "Elicitation of Moral Obligation and Self-Sacrificing Behavior: An Experimental Study of Volunteering to be a Bone Marrow Donor," *Journal of Personality and Social Psychology* 15:4 (1970), 283–293.

Uhlander, Carole, "Rational Turnout: The Neglected Role of Groups," *American Journal of Political Science* 33:2 (1989), 390–422.

Wall Street Journal (October, 20, 1989).

Weber, Nathan, ed., *Giving USA* (AAFRC Trust for Philanthropy 1989), pp. 11–14.

Wilson, James, *Thinking About Crime* rev. ed. (New York: Vintage Books, 1985).

Wolfe, Alan, *Whose Keeper? Social Science and Moral Obligation* (California: University of California Press, 1989).

5 ECONOMIC THEORIES OF DECISION MAKING UNDER UNCERTAINTY: IMPLICATIONS FOR POLICY ANALYSIS

W. Kip Viscusi

1. Introduction

If decisions under uncertainty were completely straight-forward, many of the government programs now in existence would not be necessary. Regulation of many job risks and product hazards would be superfluous, as market processes would create adequate incentives for safety. Programs to provide information about risks to product purchasers and the public at large also would be unnecessary because individuals would already have sufficient information to make rational decisions. The expansive scope of the tort liability system could also be reduced because the presumption that accident victims engaged in uninformed behavior would lose force. A world in which markets provided full information about risks, and people used this information effectively, would demand much less from public policy. This chapter explores ways in which impediments to rationality arise and how their shortcomings provide an impetus for several types of policy intervention.

The actual performance of the economy, unfortunately, often falls far short of our ideal. Individuals display tendencies to overestimate some risks and to underestimate others. Market responses to risk range from inadequate to wildly alarmist. The same people who fail to buckle their seatbelts may express great alarm over the threats posed by secondhand smoke or by two grapes found in Philadelphia with traces of cyanide even though these latter threats involve less severe risks.

These difficulties have not gone unnoticed by academic researchers. A flourishing cottage industry now generates an increasing variety of anomalies and inconsistencies in choices under uncertainty. The two main messages of this literature are that people err and that in many cases the pattern of these errors is quite systematic. This chapter explores some of the most salient findings in this literature and attempts to indentify the common themes that have emerged.[1]

From the standpoint of public policy, examination of these issues is relevant for several reasons. First, assessing the pattern of errors in individual choice is important to highlight the context in which government intervention is warranted. Second, if the character of the market failure can be identified, particular kinds of policies might be implemented. For example, if the problem is one of incomplete information, the obvious remedy is to provide appropriate hazard warnings to the affected group. Finally, examining the limitations of rational behavior also indicates potential weak links in the implementation of government policies. If individual responses are not rational, even with the aid of such efforts as well-designed informational programs, more directive kinds of policy intervention should be considered.

The chapter will first analyze individual decisions to purchase insurance against losses caused by natural disasters and will then turn to overall assessment of patterns of risk perception. After considering several of the main behavioral anomalies indentified in the literature, two models of choice to address these anomalies will be presented. The chapter will conclude by indicating the potential role of public provision of information to remedy inadequacies in the knowledge individuals have about the risks they face.

2. Responses to Natural Disaster Insurance: A Second Look

An influential early study of the rationality of choices under uncertainty was that of Howard Kunreuther (1976), who examined the patterns of purchases of earthquake and flood insurance. Because these lines of insurance are heavily subsidized by the U.S. government, Kunreuther expected widespread purchase by individuals at risk, but his predictions based on standard insurance economics were not borne out. Moreover, his

Table 5–1.   Profile of Knowledge of Insurance Cost Provisions

	The Percent of Respondents Who Do Not Know Terms	
	Insured	*Uninsured*
Cost of insurance:		
Flood	17	68
Earthquake	11	76
Deductible:		
Flood	44	82
Earthquake	25	85

Source: Adapted from Kunreuther (1976: 234).

detailed analysis of the risk perceptions of potential purchasers as well as their actual purchases provided a fruitful case study for examining how individuals respond to risk and whether they take advantage of subsidized insurance.

The principal conclusion reached by Kunreuther (p. 250) was quite strong: "The expected utility model, as traditionally used by economists, provides relatively little insight into the individual choice process regarding the purchase of insurance." This section will examine some of the specific evidence developed by Kunreuther and, in particular, indicate the extent to which full rationality appears not to hold.

In assessing these results the historical context in which Kunreuther worked must be noted. At that time, economists did not question the assumption of individual rationality. Because the literature dealing with deficiencies in choice-making under uncertainty was still in its infancy, a researcher would be expected to place great weight on any flaws found in the rational choice model. Yet, in the more than a decade since Kunreuther's article appeared, a substantial literature has attacked the expected utility model as failing to capture the way in which decisions actually are made, as opposed to the way in which they should be made. Thus a retrospective examination of Kunreuther's results would permit a search for the systematic and rational aspects of the behavior that are reflected in his results as opposed to dwelling on the shortcomings of the expected utility framework.

A useful starting point is to examine the individual knowledge of the insurance terms that were offered. Table 5–1 summarizes the extent to which the insured and uninsured population groups understand the terms of insurance.

Examination of table 5–1 clearly indicates that the full-information assumption often implicit in economic analysis does not hold. The large majority of uninsured do not know the terms of insurance; even among the insured, many do not know important details such as size of the deductible. These gaps in knowledge occurred despite the fact that survey respondents were those in the household most responsible for insurance purchases.

There are also a number of positive features of the responses. Differential knowledge of the insured and uninsured follow the expected parterns. First, in every case people who purchased the insurance have a better understanding of the premiums and the deductibles than those who did not. Second, the cost of insurance is easier to remember than the deductible. As expected, almost all people who purchased flood or earthquake insurance remember its premium, even though they may not remember all of the specific provisions. Third, the fact that people do not know all of the details regarding the insurance is not necessarily a sign of irrationality. What is important is that people are being offered subsidized insurance. In effect, the government has recommended it, and if individuals take this information as a signal, they may not need to know all of the details concerning what makes the purchase attractive. The uninsured likewise are not necessarily irrational for not knowing the terms of the insurance since they may not have heard of its availability. Such a lack of knowledge may be more an indication of ineffective marketing of the insurance than of any failure of individual irrationality.

One could then raise the secondary issue of whether the consumer search process to learn about such insurance is fully rational. With the substantial stakes involved in disaster insurance, consumers have some financial incentive to acquire information about such coverage.

It should also be noted that the fact that not all people choose to purchase subsidized insurance is not necessarily irrational since individual risks differ, thus affecting the relative value of insurance. Furthermore, the prospect of government aid *after* natural disasters provides for at least some insurance without any prior purchase, and we would want to know what these expectations were before pronouncing behavior irrational.

One can obtain a more refined perspective on the expectations of the different population groups by examining the damage expected from a severe flood of earthquake (see table 5–2). Perhaps the main anomaly in this table is that 9 percent of those who purchased flood insurance, and 2 percent of those who purchased earthquake insurance, expected zero damage. Notwithstanding the careful questionnaire that was administered, it may be that some individuals did not properly understand the survey,

Table 5–2. Individual Expectations of the Damage From Severe Floods or Earthquake

	Flood			Earthquake		
Damage Claims ($)	% Insured	% Uninsured	% Insured/ Uninsured	% Insured	% Uninsured	% Insured/ Uninsured
0	9	29	.31	2	12	.17
≤10,000	22	26	.85	13	19	.68
10,001–30,000	37	24	1.54	32	27	1.19
>30,000	24	12	2.00	47	34	1.38
Don't know	8	9	.89	6	8	.75

Note: In addition to drawing on data in Kunreuther (1976: 234), this table includes statistics on the "Insured/Uninsured" calculated by the author.

perhaps confusing the probability of severe damage with the absolute level of the damage. Another possibility that was borne out in the interviews by Kunreuther and co-workers (1976) is that even when there was no assessed risk, consumers valued the peace of mind that insurance provided.

More specifically, Kunreuther and his colleagues examined whether insurance would be attractive from an expected value standpoint by examining the contingency price ratio, which gives the relative odds that the adverse event will occur. Many consumers who purchased insurance even though they understood that it had a low perceived expected payoff did so because they indicated that having insurance provided reassurance. This beneficial effect is similar to influences such as anxiety and regret that have played an important role in the subsequent literature. In particular, insurance is a multiattribute commodity that provides a diverse set of consumer benefits not readily captured by the standard expected utility model.

A principal inference from table 5–2 is that the overall relationship between insurance purchases and damage percentions is quite plausible. In terms of distribution of the expected claims for both flood insurance and earthquake insurance, the groups with the highest expected damage claims are generally more likely to purchase insurance. The best statistics for assessing the rationality of these patterns are the rations of the insured to the uninsured purchasers for any particular damage claim group shown in the third and sixth columns of table 5–2. The fraction of each damage claim category purchasing insurance steadily rises as one moves to the higher claims groups.

Kunreuther also explores detailed measures of the rationality of insurance purchases, using information on individual decisions and risk perceptions. Once again, some of the patterns are plausible. For example, the assessed probability of a severe flood or earthquake is higher for those who purchase insurance than for those who do not.

Nevertheless, the results do not accord with fully rational insurance purchases, as Kunreuther demonstrates quite convincingly. The two key variables driving insurance purchases are the perceived seriousness of the disaster (often coupled with past experience) and discussions with friends and neighbors. These variables are consistent with a fully articulated Bayesian model of insurance decisions and with the literature on the psychology of risk perceptions. However, the standard expected utility model in the insurance literature placed little emphasis on these concerns.

3. Aspects of Risk Perceptions

The inadequacies in individual risk perceptions are now well established in the literature. In particular, individuals may not accurately assess the probabilities of the adverse events that may affect them. One identified variation concerns size of the risk. Once a risk is known, people tend to overestimate low probability events and underestimate larger risks. These regularities have been documented in detail by Fischhoff and colleagues (1981). Among the small risks that are overestimated are those of dying from botulism, tornadoes, floods, pregnancy, and smallpox vaccinations. The substantially hazardous yet under-estimated risks of dying include from diabetes, stomach cancer, stroke, heart disease, and homicides.

Combs and Slovic (1974) attribute this effect to an availability bias. The greater media coverage of some events assists consumers in recalling them. The media coverage effect is also consistent with a Bayesian learning model since it represents a potentially valuable source of information.[2] Unfortunately, this coverage may provide inaccurate information regarding the relative magnitude of risks.

A systematic bias in risk perception assumes, of course, that individuals are aware that the risk is present at all. Hidden risks, such as the hazards from unknown carcinogens, may be neglected altogether if individuals have no awareness that a risk is present. Once they have some awareness of the risk, however, they tend to overestimate the extent of the hazard for very small risks. The implications of this result are reflected both in the actions that individuals take as well as policies that government implements. Low-probability events, such as being killed by a terrorist attack while vacationing in Europe or dying from eating Chilean fruit, often evoke large responses. In contrast, individuals have been reluctant to wear seatbelts voluntarily but have been compelled to comply by mandatory seatbelt requirements in many states, which have not resulted in full compliance. Similarly, large controllable probabilities such as the risks posed by our diet often merit little attention, whereas we focus instead on minuscule hazards such as those that have been targeted by the media.

The pattern of bias in risk perception is not altogether inconsistent with rational behavior. Consider a simple Bayesian learning model in which we initially begin with the same risk perception for all classes of risk. As we acquire additional information about each risk, our perceptions will move closer toward the truth. Yet, because we have less than complete information, in our move toward the true probabilities we will continue to overestimate the very small risks and underestimate the very large risks. Although there are other possible explanations for the size-related bias in risk perception, this possibility is also quite plausible and is consistent with rational behavior on the part of imperfectly informed individuals. At this juncture, we do not know whether the central difficulty is that there are flaws in individual decision making or whether people simply do not have full information about the risks they face.

A second aspect of these risk perception patterns is that individuals appear to overestimate low-probability events and accurately perceive events of zero risk as truly posing no hazard whatsoever. As a result, there is a jump in individuals' risk perceptions when they move from no-risk situations to ones posing very small risks. This pattern has been documented in a variety of studies of risk perception and is reflected in the emphasis of government policies, such as the Delaney clause prohibiting the use of carcinogenic food additives even at very small risk levels.

Similarly, most government agencies attempt to eliminate all risks that are judged to be "significant." As our ability to detect risks has improved, however, the threshold for significance has steadily declined. We consequently run the risk that the stringency in the regulatory policies will be dictated by our measurement technologies rather than by the overall merits of these efforts.

Widespread media attention, often exceeding the relative importance of risks, contributes to a bias in public policy.[3] The damage inflicted by tornadoes, floods, and earthquakes is highly touted by the media. Easterners express fear of ever having to move to San Francisco and face the perils of earthquakes, but they are far less reluctant to live in cities with higher homicide rates and greater risks of death from air pollution than posed by earthquake hazards.

An excessive emphasis on dramatic and highly publicized risks does not necessarily imply that individuals are irrational. One can envision a process whereby one forms risk perceptions by utilizing available information to update one's probabilistic judgments. The extensive coverage provided to natural disasters does not indicate the levels of risk involved, only selective body counts. If the media primarily provide evidence of highly prominent adverse outcomes, we would expect individuals processing this information to form correspondingly high risk assessments. In effect, the media are giving people the numerator of the risk but not the denominator. If information about the numerator is repeated sufficiently often, particularly if it is provided to a degree far in excess of its overall relative value, flawed risk perceptions are likely to result.

A variety of other systematic biases have been observed in the perception of risks by individuals. People tend to underestimate risks that are within their control. For example, most of us believe we are above-average drivers, and few of us regard ourselves as being average or below average.[4] Similarly, most parents believe they are above average in the safety precautions they take for their children.[5]

The character of the risk is also of consequence. Risks such as cancer or the chance of being killed by an explosion evoke substantial fear and dread. As a consequence, they tend to be relatively overestimated once they are called to people's attention.

The statistics in table 5–3 illustrate several of these aspects of individual risk perceptions as they affect economic decisions. Consumers participating in the study were told that the starting risks posed by different pairs of products were each 15/10,000. They were then asked to value incremental risk reductions of 5/10,000 for each of the two risks. Table 5–3 provides their valuation of each successive incremental risk reduction. The risks from household products—toilet bowl cleaner and insecticide—generally posed temporary injuries such as skin poisoning or child poisoning that respondents were told would produce nausea and stomach cramps for several days.

As people purchase successive risk reductions, their willingness to pay for risk reduction should decline. This pattern is borne out initially. At an initial risk level of 15/10,000, the willingness to pay for a risk reduction of 5/10,000 is greater than it is at 10/10,000. Once we reach a risk level of 5/10,000 and are offered the opportunity to purchase a complete elimination of the risk, however, there is a substantial jump in individual valuations. These results reflect the more general finding that people overassess low-probability events and place a premium on the elimination of risks with certainty. There is a substantial discontinuity in risk perceptions once we move from some small risk to no risk at all.

Table 5–3. Marginal Valuation of Reducing Risks by 5/10,000

Starting Risk (injuries/10,000 bottles)	Incremental Willingness to Pay (dollars/bottle)			
	Inhalation— Skin Poisoning	Inhalation— Child Poisoning	Gassing— Eyeburn	Gassing— Child Poisoning
15	1.04	1.84	.65	.99
10	.34	.54	.19	.24
5	2.41	5.71	.83	.99

Source: Viscusi, Magat, and Huber (1987: 475).

Table 5–4. Responses to Valuation Questions for Risk Increases of 1/10,000 for Each Product

Injury Pair	Percentage for Whom Product Is Too Risky to Purchase	Mean Value ($/bottle) of Positive Responses
Inhalation—skin poisoning	77.2	2.86
Inhalation—child poisoning	68.1	3.19
Eyeburns—gasing	61.5	5.52
Gassing—child poisoning	74.3	1.28

Note: This question asked subjects what price discount they would require on the new product to accept an additional risk of 1/10,000 for both injuries, starting with risks of 15 injuries per 10,000 bottles sold for both injuries. See Viscusi, Magat, and Huber (1987: 477).

Moreover, the extent of this overestimation of low-probability events may not be symmetric. From an economic standpoint, a person's willingness to pay for a sufficiently small risk reduction should have a value equivalent to his or her willingness to accept a small risk increase. For larger changes, willingness to pay amounts should be less than willingness to accept values. Individuals who gave the values for their willingness to pay for risk decreases were also asked how much of a price discount they required to be willing to accept a risk increase of 5/10,000. The universal response was that they would not purchase the product at all. As a result, the survey was reformulated, inquiring about how much of a price discount they required to accept a product that posed an extra risk of 1/10,000 of each type.

The results of this exercise are reported in table 5–4. For the overwhelming majority of consumers, the product is too risky to purchase at any price. The survey even inquired whether individuals were willing to accept a cash payment and free use of the product. As a result, these responses fully reflect all of the options economists might develop to get people to display a finite risk-dollar trade-off. Moreover, for those who were willing to state a price discount they would accept the extent of the discount given in the final column of table 5–4 greatly exceeds their willingness to pay for a risk reduction of much greater magnitude described in table 5–3.

What these findings suggest is that individual inadequacies in risk perceptions are highly complex and have profound implications for perceptions are highly complex and have profound implications for economic behavior and risk regulation policies. Most of these results represent a substantial departure from the full information world of perfect rationality. Nevertheless, many systematic patterns to these biases highlight situations in which government intervention can be most profitable. In particular, these results suggest that political pressures for intervention may be greatest when there is an upward shift in a small risk. However, it is the large, stable probabilities of an adverse event that merit the greatest public concern.

4. Behavioral Anomalies

The literature on the rationality of choice under uncertainty is replete with examples of behavior that contradicts most models of rational decision making. The frame of reference for assessing rationality is the expected utility model. Under the expected utility framework, individuals maximize a linear weighted average of the utility of different payoffs, where these weights are the probabilities associated with the outcome. This framework has strong appeal from a normative standpoint because of the plausibility of the axioms on which it is based. Some of the implications of the risk perception patterns noted in the last section are inconsistent with the maximization of expected utility. Here I consider two additional examples that illustrate fundamental deviations in behavior from the expected utility model.

Consider a situation in which you are required to play Russian roulette. For concreteness, suppose that you are unmarried and have no children and that three bullets are left in the gun. How much would you pay for the removal of one bullet? Alternatively, consider a situation in which only one bullet is in the gun. How much would you be willing to pay for the removal of this single bullet? In general, people would be willing to pay a much greater sum for removal of the final bullet than for removal of one bullet, which would not buy them complete freedom from death.

The behavior in this example, which was developed by Richard Zeckhauser, contradicts the predictions of standard expected utility theory. The purchase of a bullet when many bullets remain in the gun should be more highly valued because the expected marginal utility of money is much less when the risk of death is substantial. The opportunity cost of buying back the bullet is very low if there is a good chance that one may die. The attractiveness of purchasing the bullet that ensures survival stems from people's tendency to overestimate low-probability events. As a consequence, the inadequacies in risk perceptions discussed earlier also emerge as an influential factor that leads to prominent contradictions in the rationality of economic behavior.

Perphaps the most well known anomaly in expected utility theory is the Allais Paradox.[6] If people are confronted with two sets of lottery choices, they often give responses that are not mutually consistent. The particular example constructed by Allais can be summarized by two equations:

$$U(100) > (.10) \ U(500) + (.89) \ U(100) + (.01) \ U(0) \qquad (1)$$

and

$$(.11) \ U(100) + (.89) \ U(0) < (.10) \ U(500) + (.90) \ U(0). \qquad (2)$$

In the first case, shown in equation 1, the utility of the certain reward of $100 is preferred to a 0.1 chance of a $500 reward and a 0.89 chance of a $100 reward, since there is also a 0.01 chance that the person will receive nothing at all. Even though the expected payoff is much greater under the dominated option, the chance of losing all one's money leads individuals to prefer the certain payoff of $100.

If, however, we reduce each of these two prospects by a 0.89 chance of winning $100 so that the chance of no payoff is 0.89 for the formerly preferred case and 0.90 for the formerly dominated case, we generally find the reversal in preferences shown in equation 2. This reversal obtains even though we have simply subtracted an amount, 0.89 $U(100)$, from each side of the equation. Since subtracting any positive amount from an inequality should leave the direction of the inequality unaffected, there is a clearcut contradiction.

A wide variety of models have been developed to explain inconsistencies such as the Allais Paradox.[7] Clearly, the expected utility theory is not adequate and one must either modify our characterization of individual preferences or our assumptions regarding how probabilistic information enters individual decisions.

One possibility may be that the utility of receiving a zero payoff is not equal to zero. Moreover, how we feel about a zero payoff could depend on the other payoffs that we are missing. In a situation in which we are flipping a coin and have a chance to win a dollar, receiving no reward may matter little. However, if the reward had been $1 million, the zero outcome may be devastating. The potential role of regret has been formalized in a variety of theories.[8]

As a practical mater, it is difficult to identify any common choice situations where the Allais Paradox is encountered. The main thrust of the various anomalies that have been provided in the literature is primarily to indicate that choices under uncertainty may be flawed in some manner. They do not suggest that the particular anomalies that have been identified are prevalent or of substantial consequence. This result is not entirely reassuring since the problems that do seem to be prevalent reflect more fundamental inadequacies in the way people process and act on risk information.

5. An Example of Alternative Models of Choice: Prospect Theory

A wide variety of models have been developed to address the problems arising from choices under uncertainty. One of the most widely discussed variants of this type is prospect theory, which was developed by psychologists Daniel Kahneman and Amos Tversky (1979). Their analysis consists both of a summary of the evidence in the psychology of risk literature as well as development of an alternative model to explain this behavior. Their analysis can be described as largely descriptive in nature. The emphasis is on developing central themes in the anomalies that have emerged and then imposing suitable amendments on the nature of choice and risk perceptions to reflect these phenomena.

The range of their discussion is quite broad. For example, they review a variety of anomalies, including the Allais Paradox discussed in the last section. The generalization that Kahneman and Tversky developed as characterizing the Allais Paradox as well as similar examples pertains to the scale of the probabilities involved. In particular, bigger payoffs look better as the difference in the odds gets smaller. For example, a 0.45 chance of winning $6000 may be viewed as being clearly inferior to a 0.9 chance of winning $3000. Yet, if we shrink these probabilities by dividing them by 450 so that we have a 0.001 chance of winning $6000 as opposed to a 0.002 chance of winning $3000, our preference is generally for the chance of winning $6000. As the probabilities become smaller they tend to look more similar, and we place greater weight on the payoffs involved. Kahneman and Tversky incorporate this property within the context of their theory, noting that it is an empirical regularity, not a prediction of their analysis.

Another phenomenon that they note is what they term the "reflection effect." As economists have long claimed, people exhibit risk aversion with respect to potential gains. In contrast, however, when losses are at stake, individuals display risk seeking in the experimental contexts considered by psychologists. For example, people may prefer $3000 for sure to a 0.8 chance of winning $4000. Yet, they would rather face a 0.8 chance of losing $4000 than to incur a sure loss of $3000.

In the hypothetical lotteries presented to student subjects, Kahneman and Tversky found considerable boldness of this type with respect to risking losses. Although these results have been readily replicated in other experimental contexts, they do not seem to accord with actual behavior. The United States currently has a thriving insurance industry in which insurance firms offer coverage for a price that greatly exceeds the expected payoff. If individuals were truly risk seeking with respect to losses, they would not purchase insurance at all, much less the substantial quantities of actuarially unfair insurance that they now buy. Individual attitudes toward losses may be quite different when they are dealing with real stakes as opposed to paper losses in classroom experiments.

Moreover, even if the reflection effect does hold, it does not undermine theories of rational decision making. Claims that people are risk averse with respect to gains and risk loving with respect to losses suggest a preference pattern that is unusual but not necessarily different from what economists usually assume. Its only implication is that preferences are somewhat unconventional.

Another anomaly has more fundamental implications for the structure of utility functions. Kahneman and Tversky find that experimental subjects fail to integrate a bonus with the valuation of the lottery with which they are presented. For example, individuals tend to be unresponsive to having been told that they will initially be given $1000 before they confront a hypothetical lottery. That researchers should fail to find a lack of response to artificial endowments of wealth does not mean that base levels of wealth are unimportant. Rather, a more reasonable interpretation is that telling individuals in an experimental context that they are richer is not the same as actually making them richer. Wealth conveyance must take place before individuals transform their attitudes toward risk. Economists have produced an abundant literature indicating that there are substantial wealth effects in terms of attitudes toward risk bearing.[9] This economic evidence is more plausible than the attempts to simulate changes in wealth in classroom experiments.

In developing their theory to explain these and other experimental behavioral anomalies, Kahneman and Tversky incorporate a number of notions developed in the literature on the psychology of risk perception. In particular, they indicate that people sometimes edit the complex lotteries with which they are presented before evaluating them. Moreover, they note that people often have to resort to simplifications and methods of combining probabilities that may not accord with the pinpoint predictions of rationality.

Their assessments contain much truth regarding the manner in which people deal with complex choices under uncertainty. The main remaining task is to develop systematic frameworks for predicting how people will interpret complex lottery information. Psychologists know, for example, that the framework of the information presented is often of consequence. What they are less able to tell is how particular methods of framing will alter behavior. Ascertaining results is possible only after the fact. The major gap is in developing predictive models to assess what will happen before it has in fact been observed.

The essential elements of the Kahneman and Tversky theory are two-fold. First, individuals employ valuations for payoffs that differ from those in standard expected utility models. Figure 5–1 illustrates the shape of the valuation function. As indicated in the preceding discussion, individuals are hypothesized to be risk averse in the domain of gains, and risk loving in the domain of losses. The peculiar shape of the utility function is not the only novelty. Kahneman and Tversky also suggest that utility is a function of the changes in assets offered by the lottery, rather than the net asset position that will prevail after the lottery. Thus levels of wealth are not of consequence in their model. As indicated, this structure is not consistent with existing empirical evidence in actual choice-taking situations. At this stage, the utility function component of their analysis appears to be somewhat speculative. Moreover, the essential elements can probably be reconciled with standard expected utility models by simply letting utility functions have risk-averse and risk-loving regions.

The second component of the analysis concerns how people process probabilistic information. Kahneman and Tversky hypothesize that people attach to the payoffs decision weights that are not equal to probabilities. Essentially, probabilities are transformed into decision weights by the function $\pi(p)$. Figure 5–2 sketches the shape of the decision weight function. Kahneman and Tversky do not indicate precisely how this function behaves near zero risks, but they do suggest that risk perceptions increase sharply when one moves away from a zero probability, as a wide variety of evidence has indicated.

Moreover, their sketching of the shape of the decision weight function

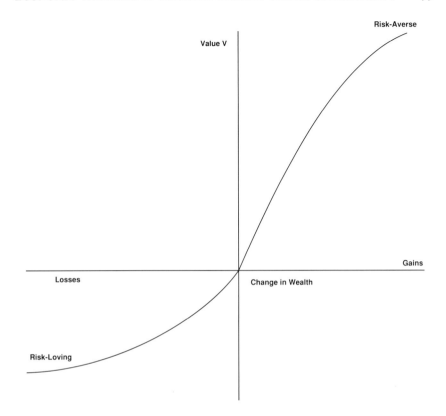

Figure 5–1.   Relationship Between Decision Weights and Stated Probabilities

implies an overestimation of low probability events and an underestimation of larger risks, a finding consistent with other psychological evidence. There is, however, no formal basis offered for the functional form they selected other than to note that it is governed by empirical regularities that have been observed elsewhere.

Although the Kahneman-Tversky prospect theory is not a generally accepted alternative to expected utility theory, it does serve to synthesize many of the experimental results. Moreover, consideration of this analysis suggests how much can potentially be lost by a move from expected utility theory. The standard expected utility model of economists has the advantage that its assumptions are quite generally appealing. As a model of behavior, it has strong predictive power. Reconciling actual patterns of choice with observed behavior tends to yield theories that by their very

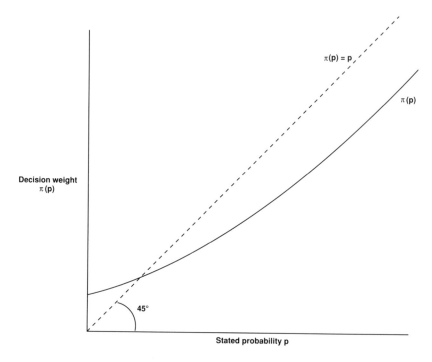

Figure 5–2. Shape of Value Function with Respect to Changes in Wealth

nature are less attractive to economists because they deviate from normatively appealing axioms. Additionally, once we begin to alter many of the
essential characteristics of expected utility theory, we lose much of the
power of having a theory. If a theory ultimately consists of a descriptive
analysis that is able to accept any behavioral pattern ex post, after having
observed it, such a theory achieves very little because it has no predictive
power.

   Most fundamentally, if the difficulty is that people are simply making
errors but would rationally choose to follow the maxims of expected utility
theory if they were appraised of the impact of their decisions, abandoning
expected utility theory may be too hasty. Expected utility may remain an
excellent reference point for anlyzing whether behavior is rational. We can
then identify departures from expected utility theory as indicating errors in
the ways in which markets function. Rather than trying to justify these
errors with an alternative theory of choice, we might instead choose to
intervene with government policies to correct the inadequacies that are
identified.

This author developed framework, termed prospective reference theory, in an attempt to retain expected utility theory while at the same time recognizing the impediments to risk perception (Viscusi, 1989). In particular, this formulation postulates that people confronted with experimental lotteries treat the information provided as partial. In particular, their perceived probability is not the same as the actual probability but is instead a weighted average of some prior probability and the information with which they are provided. For the standard classroom experiment, the assumption is that a priori people treat all lottery outcomes as being equally likely and form their posterior probability assessments as linear weighted averages of both the stated probability and the probability that would prevail if all outcomes were uniformly distributed. This approach is consistent with Bayesian learning models (following either normal or beta distributions).

This rather simple amendment to expected utility theory recognizes that people may not treat probabilistic information as being fully informative. Moreover, it incorporates the salient properties of the evidence with regard to risk perceptions, as low probabilities are overestimated, high probabilities are underestimated, and there is a jump in probabilities once we move from a zero risk situation to one in which there is a small positive risk.

Consider, for example, how one might apply the prospective reference theory approach to the Allais Paradox. For concreteness, let us consider the extreme case in which the study participant places no weight whatsoever on the stated lottery information but instead treats outcomes within a particular lottery as being equally likely. Other variants of the perceptions of stated lotteries are also possible, including a weighted average of the stated probabilities and the equal probability case. For simplicity we will confine ourselves to the extreme situation in which the stated probabilities are given zero weight, except for the certainty cases involving probabilities of 0 and 1.

In the case of equation 1, the probability of receiving a payoff of 100 remains at 1.0. However, the probability of the payoffs on the right side of the inequality in equation 1 all become 0.33 because there are three outcomes—all of which are perceived as being equally likely. In the case of equation 2, all of the lotteries involved are binary lotteries involving two possible outcomes, so that all of the associated probabilities become 0.5. Thus we are led to a reformulation of these equations given by the following expressions:

$$U(100) > (.33) \, U(500) + (.33) \, U(100) + .33 \, U(0) \qquad (3)$$

and

$$(.5)\ U(100) + (.5)\ U(0) < (.5)\ U(500) + (.5)\ U(0) \qquad (4)$$

Setting $U(0) = 0$ without loss of generality implies that these conditions become

$$U(100) > .33\ [U(500) + U(100)] \qquad (5)$$

and

$$U(100) < U(500) \qquad (6)$$

Since

$$U(500) > .33\ [U(500) + U(100)]$$

equalities 5 and 6 not only can occure with prospective reference theory, but they necessarily *must occur* for behavior to be consistent. The main manipulation of the problem is simply to treat the stated probabilities as being less than fully informative.

The advantage of this theory over models of irrational behavior is that it *predicts* almost all of the phenomena that have been identified as anomalies in the literature. Results such as the Allais Paradox and Kahneman and Tversky's general principle underlying such violations of the substitution axiom in expected utility theory are all generated as *predictions* of this model. Whereas prospect theory can be potentially reconciled with this behavior, prospective reference theory predicts ex ante that this and similar anomalies will occur. For example, it also resolves the Russian roulette paradox. As a consequence, the theory has much greater predictive power. Moreover, the situation in which people treat the lottery information as being fully informative reduces to the standard expected utility model so that the analysis need not contradict rational choice.

Consequently, it is possible to reconcile the expected utility model and the literature on the psychology of choices under uncertainty. The main deficiency in the literature is that the reference point used is that of a classical statistician rather than a Bayesian decision maker. The classroom experiments and hypothetical studies that have been conducted may not have been treated as fully informative by the participants. This behavior in and of itself can account for the anomalies that have resulted.

In short, psychologists often have used the wrong reference point to assess rationality. Rather than assuming that people are perfectly informed, a more realistic reference point for comparison would be one in which people have incomplete information but act on this information in a rational manner. Imposing this Bayesian learning structure greatly enhances the predictive power that our theories can provide.

6. Toward a Sensible Basis for Risk Policies

Perhaps the final caveat with respect to the literature on rational choice is that substantial judgment is required to assess which aberrations are important. Tversky and Kahneman (1974) frequently recount the example of assessing the contents of two urns. In particular, the task is to identify which urn has two-thirds red balls and one-third white balls as opposed to the reverse. Under one situation, we are told that the draws from an urn led to four red balls and one white ball being selected. Under a second scenario, we have drawn twelve red balls and eight white balls. Which of the two sets of draws provides stronger confidence that the urn is two-thirds red and one-third white?

Not surprisingly, experimental subjects presented with such lotteries (when recruited for the study at a local shopping mall) give incorrect answers. What is particularly note-worthy is that a swing of only one ball in terms of the draws from the urns will lead to a reversal in the assessment of the correct response. (It is left as an exercise for the reader to determine which of the answers is correct. It should be noted that the reader has much stronger probabilistic training than the typical experimental subject.)

Determining whether people can intuit applications of the laws of probability dealing with nontransparent choice situations about which they may care very little is not the best test of the rationality of individual behavior. What needs to be identified are the situations in which actual choices diverge from full rationality. Which deviations are important, and which are not? What systematic patterns of errors can be observed? What policies suggest themselves to address these difficulties? These are the truly fundamental issues that are often ignored in the literature's self-sustaining search for the new and often unimportant behavioral anomaly.

The inadequacies in choice also affect the degree to which providing risk information can potentially eliminate the market failure. The principal assumption necessary for information to be effective is that there must be a choice that the individual can make. In the case of risks traded in the market, such as job risks and consumer product hazards, there is an element of discretion that makes programs providing risk information meaningful. In contrast, in situations in which there is no discretion, particularly in the short run, risk information will be less effective. For example, the market response may be slow to incorporate information about broadly based environmental hazards ranging from air pollution exposures to toxic waste leakage into the water supply. Eventually such risks will influence long-run mobility patterns, but in most cases the individual response will not be sufficient to ensure an efficient distribution of risks because the risks are not being traded in the marketplace.

Informing individuals in these contexts may be important so that, for example, people can choose to relocate or to create safety incentives through tort liability. Residents in the Love Canal, New York, area exited quite quickly once learning of the the toxic contaminants there. Moreover, the risk information also facilitated their legal suits. Yet such information alone does not provide incentives for generators of the risks to reduce their magnitudes. There must be either a market response or action by some other social institution.

Informational policies alone are not sufficient to address environmental risks. Even in a case of risks traded in the market, provision of risk information may not always be sufficient. The major weak link in such programs is that the same kinds of impediments to sound decision making that lead to a variety or market failures in situations of risky decisions also may limit the efficacy of risk communication efforts. If we could provide full information about the risks and be assured of a rational response, market outcomes would be ideal. Human cognition, however, limits the kinds and amounts of information that public programs can effectively convey. As a result, informational efforts, correctly, do not attempt to provide comprehensive risk information; instead, they generally indicate in a succinct way the character of the risk and the pertinent precautionary behavior.

Consider, for example, the well-known case of cigarette warnings. The purpose of the warnings is to alert consumers to classes of risks posed by cigarettes, but in no instance is there any effort to convey the particular probabilities involved. Is the risk of cancer 0.01, 1, or 0.9 over a lifetime? In situations in which we convey risk information that is not specific, there should be continuing efforts to monitor the impacts of these programs on risk perceptions. Are the risk perceptions induced by the broad wording of these warnings biased in any particular direction? If so, can we select different phraseology to convey the risk more accurately?

A striking case in point is an example that took place in California. In an effort to provide consumers with pertinent risk information, California instituted a comprehensive hazard warning program under Proposition 65. That statute requires that all producers warn consumers of potential carcinogenic risks. Any product posing a lifetime cancer risk from daily consumption of at least one chance in 100,000 must be accompanied by a pertinent warning. The specific wording of the warning is as follows: 'WARNING: This product contains a chemical known to the state of California to cause cancer." Although the implementation of this act is not yet complete, experimental studies of the implications of this wording for consumers in other states indicate that the risk perceptions induced differ

Table 5–5.   Effects of Bleach Labels on Precaution-Taking (percentages)

Precaution	No Warning (n = 51)	Clorox (n = 59)	Bright (n = 42)	Test (n = 44)	Maximum Incremental Effect
1. Do not mix with toilet bowl cleaner (if toilet is badly stained)	16	23	36	40	24
2. Do not add to ammonia-based cleaners (for particularly dirty jobs)	69	68	69	84	16
3. Store in child-proof location	43	63	50	76	33

Source: Viscusi and Magat (1987: 66).

quite markedly from the trace carcinogens that are intended to be captured by this program. In particular, the average risk assessment of adult consumers seeing this warning is that the product poses a lifetime risk of 12/100, a risk assessment that dwarfs the risk threshold for labeling and greatly exceeds the risks that are believed to be associated with any of the products that will be captured by this program.[10]

This example suggests that, in evaluating programs intended to provide information about risks, we should not ignore the impediments to rationality that often led to a rationale for government intervention initially. There must be a continuing effort to monitor how the risk information is processed and to determine whether it is leading to sound decisions.

The potential efficacy of informational efforts that take the form of hazard warnings is illustrated by the results in table 5–5. This study pertained to the different precautions induced by a variety of warning labels for bleach. The table's columns provide information for four alternative labels, the first a Clorox label that has been purged of all warning information. The second label is the Clorox label currently on the market, and the third the label for Bright bleach, a brand of bleach marketed by the Kroger Company. The final label is a test label that has been redesigned based on cognitive principles for the effective design of hazard warnings.[11]

What these results indicate is that properly designed warnings can have an incremental effect. The main risk from bleach is that it will be mixed with a product such as ammonia and form chloramine gas, which is the leading source of poisoning among adults. The hazard warning would increase precautions to avoid such mixing by 16 percent to 24 percent. Similarly, the hazard warning would induce greater placement of the product in a child-proof location in 33 percent of the instances. Moreover, for families with young children vulnerable to poisoning, the efficacy is almost 100 percent.

These results suggest that warnings can influence behavior in the intended manner. Having an impact, however, does not always indicate efficacy. In the usual instance, hazard warnings are adopted in situations where precautions are usualy desirable, but that may not always be the case. Consumers, for example, may differ in the disutility they attach to wearing rubber gloves, and some individuals may therefore rationally choose not to follow this precaution when using household cleaners. Such a decision may be quite plausible based on the benefits and costs to the particular individual. What is important is that the warning alerts the consumer to the potential benefits of taking the precaution so that the individual can make an informed decision.

In many important cases, however, we do not permit such consumer sovereignty to reign. There are some precautions that we choose to make more mandatory, thus overriding individual preferences. One notable example is motorcycle helmets. Yet, many cyclists choose not to wear these helmets and several Hollywood movie stars, such as Sylvester Stallone, have visibly proclaimed that wearing helmets is not in keeping with the appropriate image that motorcyclists wish to convey. If only the motorcyclist were at risk, society might wish to condone such deliberate self-destruction. However, motorcyclists also impose substantial risks on others, notably through the accident costs imposed on automobile drivers involved in collisions with motorcyclists. In particular, if the auto driver is at fault, the cost of hitting a motorcyclist is considerably higher when cyclists do not wear helmets and thereby sustain severe injuries. Many states consequently make wearing helmets mandatory, largely in an effort to protect the well-being of nonmotorcyclists.

It may also be the case that some requirements are needed to protect the well-being of the participants themselves. Hockey helmets were long viewed with disfavor by professional hockey players who, much like the motorcyclists, believe that wearing such protective equipment would threaten their rugged image. Yet, once wearing a helmet was mandatory, complaints of this type were fewer, perhaps because players no longer risked being singled out for the apparent weakness of relying on protective equipment.

7. Conclusion

Analyses of choices under uncertainty have been a particularly active topic in the economics literature during the past decade. Perhaps the main theme of this work is that these choices are flawed in a number of ways. Individuals often do not process information well, and the decisions that result often are in substantial error.

One potential pitfall in addressing this literature is that analysts frequently attempt to summarize its implications by simply noting that people are often irrational. Such an observation is correct as far as it goes, but it does not convey the rich detail of the results found in the literature. What is most noteworthy is not that people are irrational, but rather that they have displayed systematic patterns of irrationality. Some mistakes indicate a failure to recognize properly the implications of the risk to one's well-being, whereas in other cases errors arise when people overreact to the risks they face. Thus a belief that there is an inadequacy in the way that individuals respond to risk does not necessarily mean that more governmental intervention is needed. Indeed, the situation may be that the level of risk individuals are choosing to bear is below the efficient amount. Although one would be hard-pressed to argue that government should encourage additional risk taking in these instances, at the very least government should not be engaged in efforts to further discourage such behavior by providing risk information that inflates risk perceptions that may already be too high. Rather, the objective of public policy should be to promote informed decisions and efficient bearing of risks.

The challenge for public policy is that we often need to know a great deal about the particular context before we know which action is appropriate. Thus we need to assess the extent to which people err in their risk assessments and in their subsequent behavior. Moreover, if we were going to pursue a government policy, such as a hazard warning program, we should ascertain the ways in which it will influence risk perceptions and behavior. Gaps in rationality consequently complicate the role of the policy-maker in much the same manner as they create difficulties for the individual decision maker.

Acknowledgment

The author wishes to thank Howard Kunreuther for detailed and helpful comments.

Notes

1. For alternative reviews of these issues, see Camerer and Kunreuther (1989), Fischhoff et al. (1981), Fishburn (1988), and Machina (1987). More generally, an entire journal, the *Journal of Risk and Uncertainty*, is devoted to these issues.

2. The potential for learning is particularly great when there are opportunities for search and experience. See Vining and Weimer (1988).

3. See Combs and Slovic (1974).

4. See, for example, Svenson (1981).

5. See Viscusi and Magat (1987).

6. See the discussion in Allais (1953), Camerer and Kunreuther (1989), or Viscusi (1989).

7. See, for example, the survey by Machina (1987).

8. Detailed reviews of regret theory appear in Camerer and Kunreuther (1989), Machina (1987), and Viscusi (1989).

9. See, for example, the discussion of risk taking by Arrow (1971).

10. See Viscusi (1988).

11. See, especially, chapter 2 of Viscusi and Magat (1987) for a review of these principles.

References

Allais, Maurice, "Le Comportement de L'homme Rationel Devant le Risque, Critique des Postulates et Axiomes de L'ecole Americaine," *Econometrica* 21 (1953), 503–546.

Arrow, Kenneth, *Essays in the Theory of Risk Bearing* (Chicago: Markham Publishers, 1971).

Camerer, Colin, F., and Howard Kunreuther, "Decision Processes for Low Probability Risks: Policy Implications," *Journal of Policy Analysis and Management* 8:4 (1989), 565–592.

Combs, Barbara and Paul Slovic, "Causes of Death: Biased Newspaper Coverage and Biased Judgments," *Journalism Quarterly*, 56 (1974), 837–843, 849.

Fischhhoff, Baruch, et al., *Acceptable Risk* (Cambridge: Cambridge University Press, 1981).

Fishburn, Peter C., "Expected Utility: An Anniversary and a New Era," *Journal of Risk and Uncertainty* 1:3 (1988), 267–284.

Kahneman, Daniel, and Amos Tversky, "Prospect Theory: An Analysis of Decision under Risk," *Econometrica* 47:2 (1979) 263–281.

Kunreuther, Howard, "Limited Knowledge and Insurance Protection," *Public Policy* 24:2 (1976), 227–261.

Kunreuther, Howard, et al., *Disaster Insurance Protection: Public Policy Lessons* (New York: Wiley, 1978).

Machina, Mark J., "Choice under uncertainty: Problems Solved and Unsolved," *Journal of Economic Perspectives* 1:1 (1987), 121–154.

Svenson, Ola, "Are We All Less Risky and More Skillful Than Our Fellow Drivers Are? *Acta Psychologica* 47 (1981), 143–148.

Tversky, Amos, and Kahneman, Daniel, "Judgment under Uncertainty: Heuristics and Biases," *Science* 185 (1976), 1124–1131.

Vining, Aidan, and David L. Weimer, "Information Asymmetry Favoring Sellers: A Policy Framework," *Policy Sciences* 21:4 (1988), 281–303.

Viscusi, W. Kip, "Prospective Reference Theory: Toward an Explanation of the Paradoxes," *Journal of Risk and Uncertainty* 2:3 (1989), 235–264.

———, "Predicting the Effect of Food Carncer Risk Warnings on Consumers," *Food Drug Cosmetic Law Journal* 43:2 (1988), 283–307.

Viscusi, W. Kip, and Wesley A. Magat, *Learning About Risk: Consumer and Worker Responses to Hazard Information* (Cambridge, Mass.: Harvard University Press, 1987).

Viscusi, W. Kips, Wesley A. Magat, and Joel Huber, "An Investigation of the Rationality of Consumer Valuations of Multiple Health Risks, *Rand Journal of Economics* 18:4 (1987), 465–479.

6 THE NEW INSTITUTIONAL ECONOMICS: IMPLICATIONS FOR POLICY ANALYSIS

Howard Frant

1. Introduction

Imagine a typical policy analyst—or better, an ideal policy analyst—asked to evaluate the question of whether the federal government should provide financial assistance in reconstructing deteriorated municipal water delivery systems. How might such an analyst proceed?

He might begin by trying to evaluate the extent of the problem: What the economically optimal rate of repair or replacement really was, and how much of a shortfall in capital spending that implied, if any. Next, the analyst might consider whether there were economic and philosophical justifications for a federal role, or whether the policy was one more appropriately left to states and municipalities. Then the analyst might take up the optimal design of a federal assistance program: A simple indifference curve analysis, for example, shows that a matching grant will produce a greater increase in output than a flat grant. Finally, one might examine organizational and political issues: What agency should administer the program, and what conflicts might arise between this program and other aspects of its mission? Who should receive the funds? How could such a program be made most acceptable to Congress?

When this problem was posed to the General Accounting Office (1980), their approach was quite different. The GAO looked at water systems in several cities and concluded that, while the problem was serious in some cities, it was not serious in those cities whose water systems were required to be self-financing. A clear implication of this conclusion (though not one the GAO explicitly drew) is that changing the organizational structure of public water departments is an alternative to a federal spending initiative.

Such an approach is not one that comes naturally to policy analysts. In a market-oriented approach to policy design, we tend to think of policy as various ways of altering individual incentives, with organizational and institutional considerations operating as *constraints* on policy design. Organizational issues, that is, affect implementation, and as such may need to be foreseen by the policy analyst, but only after consideration of the appropriate policy tools. We are much less accustomed to thinking of organizational structure as a policy *variable* affecting individual incentives, just like tax structure or grant structure or regulatory structure. This is surely due in part to the lack of a coherent framework for thinking about the effect of organizational structure on individual incentives. It is this lack that the "new institutional" economics tries to address.

2. The New Institutional Economics: Precursors

What exactly is the new institutional economics? Drawing the boundaries of the field is difficult because is has come from so many sources and has gone in so many directions. Indeed, the mainstream of economics today is far more "institutional" than it was a few years ago. The brief summary attempted here cannot possibly do justice to all the important contributors. The goal is simply to sketch out some main ideas and then suggest how those ideas could improve the practice of policy analysis.

One part of the new institutional economics traces back to Ronald Coase (1937), who posed the simple yet knotty question, Why do organizations exist? Economists are quick to extol the virtues of the price system as a coordinating mechanism. "Yet, having regard to the fact that if production is regulated by price movements, production could be carried on without any organisation at all, well might we ask, why is there any organisation?" (p. 388). Conversely, if there is a need for non-price organization, "why is not all production carried on by one big firm?" (p. 394).

Coase's proposal was to focus on the *transaction* as the unit of analysis: Firms will compare the costs associated with carrying out a given transaction in a market with the costs of organizing it internally. Coase suggested that the costs of market transactions included first, costs of using the price mechanism, such as discovering what prices are; second, and more importantly for the later literature, the costs of negotiating a separate contract for each transaction. Putting some transactions under the umbrella of the firm, whose workers are covered by a single comprehensive contract, is more economical. At some point, however, it becomes too costly to organize everything within one firm because of "decreasing returns to the entrepreneur function" (p. 394). The efficient size of the organization, then, is one where the marginal costs of organizational and market transactions are equal. It remained to later writers, however, to try to identify the factors that made the efficient size larger or smaller.

Another precursor of modern institutional economics is the literature on the economics of property rights. This literature points to the allocation of property rights as a key factor in determining individual incentives. Coase (1960) is again a key figure. The famous "Coase theorem," stating that the allocation of property rights does not affect efficiency in the absence of transaction costs, is widely misunderstood to this day. It is often taken to mean that property rights do not matter, while Coase's point was just the opposite. As he remarks (1988: 174): "The world of zero transaction costs has often been described as a Coasian world. Nothing could be further from the truth. It is the world of modern economic theory, one which I was hoping to persuade economists to leave." Because transaction costs *do* exist, the allocation of property rights *does* have efficiency consequences. Harold Demsetz (1967) follows Coase in emphasizing the way in which the appropriate allocation of property rights can reduce the costs of negotiating and enforcing contracts.

Armen Alchian and Demsetz (1972) made the seminal attempt to apply property rights theory to organizations. They focus on what they call "team production." Team production is group production that has inherent nonseparabilities, so that individual productivities are hard to estimate. (Their example is two men jointly lifting heavy loads into a truck.) Because monitoring true productivities is costly, it will not be efficient to monitor perfectly, and therefore each member of the team will have an incentive to "shirk" to some degree. This is a simple Prisoner's Dilemma problem—all members of the team would prefer to minimize shirking, but shirking still takes place. What to do? Alchian and Demsetz suggest that the workers could agree (obviously, this is an "as if" abstraction rather than a historical statement) to hire one worker to monitor others, giving the monitor the power to fire shirking workers. We then have the problem of who monitors the monitor. This problem can be overcome, they suggest, if the workers agree to fixed wages and give the monitor the right to residual profits, so that the monitor has no incentive to shirk. This arrangement of property rights is beneficial to all because it maximizes the size of the total pie to be divided among workers and monitor. Thus results the classical capitalist firm.

The idea that team production was the essence of the problem was, by and large, rejected by later writers. But Alchian and Demsetz did set the agenda in other respects. One key idea was the emphasis on choosing an efficient level of monitoring to reduce shirking. Another was the forceful statement of the firm as a set of contractual relations. Their views on the latter were quite radical:

> It is common to see the firm characterized by the power to settle issues by fiat, by authority, or by disciplinary action superior to that available in the conventional market. This is delusion. . . . To speak of managing, directing, or assigning workers to various tasks is a deceptive way of noting that the employer continually is involved in renegotiation of contracts on terms that must be acceptable to both parties. Telling an employee to type this letter rather than file that document is like my telling a grocer to sell me this brand of tuna rather than that brand of bread. [Alchian and Demsetz, 1972: 777]

3. Transaction-Cost Theory

At this point the literature separates into two largely parallel streams. One stream returns to Coase's focus on transaction costs and tries to operationalize it. The leading contemporary exponent of such an approach to understanding the boundary between organization and market is Oliver Williamson (1975, 1985). Williamson attempts to identify the general factors that determine transaction costs, particularly contracting costs, and relate them to specific organizational structures. He assigns a key role to Herbert Simon's (1957) idea of "bounded rationality": the idea that both information-gathering and information-processing are costly, and hence it is impossible for human beings to identify and evaluate all possible alternatives in making decisions. For Simon, organization then emerges as a way to process information. But Williamson points to a different problem: that bounded rationality makes it infeasible to respond to environmental uncertainty by writing complete contracts that cover all possible contingencies. The absence of complete contracts in turn creates scope for "opportunism"—Williamson's term for behavior that is deceitfully or dishonestly self-serving. As Williamson (1990: 12) puts it: "Given bounded rationality, *all complex contracts are unavoidably incomplete*.

Given opportunism, *contract-as-promise unsupported by credible commitments is hopelessly naive*" (emphasis in original).

How does this approach lead us back to the issue of organization versus markets? Williamson emphasizes the role of specialized commitments, leading to a "small numbers" bargaining situation. The initial transaction may be made in a competitive market. But once a contract is agreed on, and costly commitments are made, the relationship is transformed into one of bilateral bargaining. If one party must make a specialized investment that does not transfer well to other uses—in Williamson's terminology, if "asset specificity" is high—that party is vulnerable to opportunism, since the other party can threaten to break off the relationship and so render the investment worthless. The other party may thus be able to extort a higher payment.

The alternative is to substitute some sort of governance mechanism so that continual contract renegotiation is not required. For example, we might move the transaction out of the market and into the organization. But this entails costs as well. Williamson (1985) contrasts the "high-powered" incentives that usually exist in markets—the ability to appropriate the gains from a transaction for one's personal use—with the relatively "low-powered" incentives in organizations. High-powered incentives have the advantage of encouraging efficiency but the disadvantage of encouraging opportunism. The choice between organization and market involves a weighting of these two factors.

Consider the labor market, for example. An employee may acquire specialized job knowledge that would be expensive to replace; this gives the employee more bargaining power than a new hire would have. Williamson, Wachter, and Harris (1975) discuss how many features of so-called "internal labor markets" are effective in reducing the incentive of employees with job-specific knowledge to extort a higher ex-post payment from employers. A specific empirical prediction is implied: Many jobs are not characterized by acquisition of highly specialized knowledge and thus should have less elaborate governance mechanisms.

Note that although this view follows the Alchian and Demsetz view of the organization as a set of contracts, it disagrees sharply with the claim that organizations are characterized by continual renegotiation of contracts. People may have entered an organizational relation precisely to avoid this. In particular, transactions requiring long-term advance commitments may be more viable in organizational contexts. If contracts are the essence of the firm, then some of the contracts are long-term ones; thus there *is* a difference between my employee and my grocer.

An obvious application of these ideas is to the question of vertical integration. The decision whether to integrate vertically or not is, after all, simply the organization-or-market decision. The issue of vertical integration has never reposed very comfortably in the "old neoclassical" framework, under which there is no theory of the organization-or-market decision. In a competitive market, the opportunity cost of an input ought to be the same whether or not it is produced in a plant owned by the firm. On the other hand, a firm with market power might use vertical integration in a strategic way; this leads one to view all cases of vertical integration with suspicion as being potentially anticompetitive. Williamson's approach, in contrast, explains why, in some cases, a firm might want to be vertically integrated independent of any aspirations to market power.

4. Agency Theory

The second stream in institutional economics is agency theory. An important antecedent of this work is the literature on the economics of insurance, especially that dealing with "moral hazard." The moral hazard problem arises because an insurer cannot perfectly observe the behavior of insurees. Since insurees do not bear the costs of their own risky behavior, they will engage in more of it than if uninsured, and more than would be efficient if their behavior could be monitored. The optimal contract under these conditions will in general sacrifice perfect efficiency in risk-spreading, making insurees bear some of the risk in order to improve incentives (Spence and Zeckhauser, 1971). Thus insurance policies commonly include such features as deductibles and co-payments.

This idea was quickly formulated more generally as the problem of an "agent" (analogous to the insuree) who has information not accessible to the "principal" with whom she is transacting in an environment with exogenous uncertainty. The information asymmetry is typically portrayed as relating to "effort." Obviously this is easy to relate to the Alchian and Demsetz emphasis on shirking, but in a more general sense effort in these models is simply something that has a negative effect on the utility of the agent but a positive effect on the total product of the transaction. (As will be noted later, the significance of the term "effort" is often misunderstood.) The key problem is the difficulty in monitoring the agent's effort— perhaps because of exogenous uncertainty, perhaps because of the sort of nonseparabilities in production that concern Alchian and Demsetz, perhaps because of informational barriers. A series of theorems were developed about the forms of optimal contracts between principal and agent, under various conditions of uncertainty and risk aversion (see Ross, 1973; Harris and Raviv, 1978; Holmstrom, 1979; and Shavell, 1979).

Michael Jensen and William Meckling (1976) were apparently the first to use the term "agency" in a specifically organizational context. Their account starts with the classical capitalist firm owned by a single entrepreneur. Jensen and Meckling, however, focus on what happens as the entrepreneur begins to sell off shares of the firm to outsiders (to raise capital, diversify, and so on). At this point governance problems arise, for the entrepreneur-manager now shares the cost of his actions with others (much as in the insurance case) and thus has increased incentive to shirk—by granting himself too many perquisites, for example. Jensen and Meckling point out that if investors are rational, entrepreneur-managers will bear these costs when they sell shares, and therefore it is in their interest to put in place mechanisms to keep shirking to a minimum. They use the term "agency costs" for the combination of the costs of the mechanisms and the unavoidable efficiency losses that arise because it is too costly to control all actions.

Jensen and Meckling hark back to Alchian and Demsetz in their view of organizations as contractual relations; for them organizations are "simply *legal fictions which serve as a nexus for a set of contracting relationships among individuals*" (p. 310; emphasis in original). Eugene Fama (1980) goes further, arguing that ownership of the firm is largely a meaningless concept. He too views the firm as a nexus of contracts between individuals, but he insists on the absence of a privileged position for either management or the shareholders. The latter he views as merely individuals who specialize in risk bearing. This idea—we could call it "ownership illusion"—was extended by Fama and Jensen (1983a, b). If shareholders are just residual risk bearers, they ask, why should they also be those with ultimate control over the decisions of the organization? Alchian and Demsetz would have ascribed this to the need to motivate monitors; Fama and Jensen instead point to the agency problems that could arise in defining what the residual would be if other parties had control. But, they add, in complex orgainzations there is a need to specialize the management and risk-bearing functions, and this requires the development of organizational structures (such as boards of directors) to oversee the decisions of managers. They also discuss why the possibility of agency problems means that certain organizational forms have advantages in certain situations—for example, that nonprofit status (meaning the absence of a residual claimant) enables one to solicit donations by reassuring donors that their gifts will not simply be diverted to the residual claimant. They make a selectional argument: The organizational forms that survive will be those that have the lowest costs, including agency costs.

The parallels between the agency approach and the transaction cost approach should be apparent. The agency problem is just the problem of opportunism: Those whose behavior cannot be monitored with precision have an incentive to behave ex post in ways that they would have agreed to exclude ex ante if such an agreement were possible. If people are rational, the primary impact of opportunistic behavior will be on efficiency rather than equity; that is, some potentially beneficial transactions will not take place because of the threat of opportunism. The focus is then on determining what sort of institutional structures—organizational, legal, perhaps even cultural—can be developed to reduce this threat.

The differences between the two streams are less significant than are the similarities. But the transaction-cost theorists tend to differ from the agency theorists, at least those already cited, with respect to the issue of long-term versus spot contracting. As we have seen, the transaction-cost theorists place more weight on the long-term nature of many relationships and on the scope for opportunism that is created by the need to make long-term commitments.

5. Institutional Economics in the Public Sector

As should be apparent from the discussion so far, the new institutional economics has been almost exclusively concerned with the private sector firm. As Terry Moe (1984) has pointed out, there are dangers in a too-facile adaptation of this framework to the public sector. To take only one example, there is an implicit or explicit assumption in much of the literature that economic Darwinism will lead to selection of the organizational form that is relatively, if not absolutely, efficient. It is by no means obvious that any similar mechanism operates in the public sector. But efficiency arguments are not the essence of a new institutional approach (statements to the contrary by some of its leading practitioners notwithstanding). A new institutional approach is one that opens up the black box of the organization by analyzing the incentives facing rational individuals. There is nothing intrinsic in such an approach that requires us to maintain that outcomes will necessarily be efficient.[1]

Of course, the application of models of rational choice to the public sector is an idea now in use in a number of existing literatures. One is political scientists' mathematical approach to "positive political theory." This literature, well summarized by Peter Ordeshook (1986), uses game theory, social choice theory, and other fruits of mathematical economics to investigate the effects of different institutional forms on outcomes. In general, however, this literature has focused much more on voting and legislatures than on bureaucracies. (A fascinating exception is Gary Miller and Terry Moe's [1986] application of some social-choice theorems to decision making in organizations.)

Another related literature, going back to James Buchanan and Gordon Tullock (1962), now goes under the name of "public choice." Though this literature had no discernible impact on the institutional-economics literature, it has many parallel features. Buchanan and Tullock's problem of designing a constitution that commands unanimous consent is analogous to the problem of designing an efficient contract or organization, and their idea that finding the optimal structure involves weighing the costs of organization versus the costs of forgoing beneficial transactions foreshadows some of the issues that arise in the agency and transaction-cost literature.

In general, though, this literature, like the political science literature, has been more concerned with legislatures and voting than with public bureaucracy. There is, however, a line of public choice work specifically concerned with bureaucracy. This line traces back to William Niskanen's (1971, 1975) theory of the budget-maximizing bureaucrat, which is by now well established in the public finance literature. Niskanen's model was a major advance over the then-prevailing (perhaps still-prevailing) assumption implicit in most public finance literature that a benevolent government could costlessly remedy all sorts of market failures. Niskanen sharpened the general public choice point that we need to look at the incentives of individuals in the public sector as much as in the private sector.

A Niskanen-type approach, however, is limited by its high level of abstraction—we have "bureaucrats" and "legislators" playing a very stylized budget game. Models that consider other players as well (for example, Fred Thompson and L. R. Jones [1986]) may yield quite different conclusions about likely outcomes. Moreover, in Niskanen's framework, only one type of agency problem, the misrepresentation of budgetary needs, is assumed to exist. But this is by no means the only agency problem in bureaucracies, nor even obviously the most significant one.

Consider, for example, the question of policy implementation. In the classical agency model, as we saw, "effort" is anything that increases output but has a negative effect on utility. If output is the degree of implementation of policy, it is not hard to see that "effort" could be, for instance, a bureaucrat's degree of compliance with a policy with which she disagrees. Failure to appreciate this point has led some political scientists to assert that agency models are inapplicable to the public sector.[2]

6. The New Institutional Economics and Policy Analysis

What, then, do policy analysts have to learn from the new institutional economics? Certainly, an agency approach to public policy includes issues already familiar from other conceptual frameworks, such as the literature on "accountability." Accountability, however, captures only half the story—the half that in agency theory would be called "monitoring." The other half is incentives. A new institutional focus, unlike an accountability focus, highlights the fact that how much monitoring one needs depends on how well incentives are aligned in the first place.

One area where a new institutional approach seems particularly promising is the analysis of public-private interactions—privatization and government contracting. The non-economic work in this area tends to make appeals to ineffable qualities of communal action that are lost by going from public to private. Although there are certainly areas where this is a legitimate concern—the criminal justice system, for instance—the difficulty seems greatly overstated for workaday services such as garbage collection or electricity.

Among economists, on the other hand, the theoretical and empirical work on private versus public provision generally relies on an extremely simple property rights schema: Private providers have the right to capture efficiency gains; public providers don't; so private providers should be more efficient than public providers. Like the Niskanen bureaucrat, this idea was at one time a major advance over the conventional public finance view of a neutral and benevolent government efficiently curing market failures, but it is no longer sufficient.

A more sophisticated approach would begin by recognizing that the issue of privatization is, to a first approximation, simply the issue of vertical integration: Should a service be "made" or "bought"? And the issue of vertical integration is, as we have seen, the issue of firm versus market that is so central in the transaction cost literature. Viewed in this light, the issue becomes whether the possible efficiency gains from a market transaction outweigh the increased risk of opportunism.

The answer will depend on characteristics of the transaction, such as ease of monitoring and asset specificity. When complete contracts are very difficult to write because outcomes are difficult to define, or when one side must make a substantial advance commitment, the possibilities for opportunism increase: Even if a private provider is more efficient, the efficiency gains will not necessarily be passed on to the public. Moe (1984) sketches out the basic theory of an incomplete-contracts approach to privatization, but to my knowledge John Donahue (1989) is the first author actually to apply such an approach to a study of a variety of public services.[3] Donahue does not engage in formal modeling, but he identifies salient features of programs that would make them more amenable or less amenable to market provision, and uses this framework to explain outcomes. This is a promising area for more research.

Even this approach can be criticized as insufficiently "discriminating," to use Williamson's word. For the framework here is still the simple property-rights dichotomy between the private entrepreneurial firm and the public bureaucracy. As Burton Weisbrod (1989: 541) remarks dryly, "Other institutional forms exist." For example, a substantial amount of government contracting, particularly in the human services area, is done with nonprofits. One would expect that problems of opportunism might be substantially different when contracting with nonprofits than when contracting with for-profits (and that the contractor's incentive for efficiency might be substantially different as well). Yet until very recently there has been little explicit consideration of this possibility. Weisbrod notes that a 1987 issue of the *Journal of Policy Analysis and Management* devoted entirely to privatization contained only passing mention of the existence of the private nonprofit sector. There is increasing academic interest in this area, of such recent vintage that much of the work is not yet published.

Similarly, the basic property-rights hypothesis about relative public and private efficiency has often been tested by comparing public and private utilities. This research tends to find no effect from the difference in ownership, or even an advantage to public provision. On the other hand, studies of such services as garbage collection have found that private provision is significantly cheaper. One possible explanation is that in monopoly contexts regulation of private providers may have its own intrinsic inefficiencies, such as the Averch-Johnson (1962) effect.

But there is another factor worthy of consideration: Many public utilities are not government bureaus but independent public corporations or authorities.[4] Such organizations have governance structures—and, in a certain sense, property-rights structures—quite different from those of bureaus. One might suspect, then, that their efficiency properties would be quite different. Yet researchers studying public utilities have not distinguished between these two types of organizations. (Admittedly, the task would be time-consuming because most data sources do not make the distinction.) Would the generally negative findings of researchers looking for superior efficiency from private sector utilities be different if the comparison group were bureaus rather than all public agencies? We do not know.

This brings us to another area where the need for contact between institutional economists and policy analysts is pressing: quite simply, the development of a more nuanced understanding of the differences among different types of not-for-profit organizations and how those differences affect policy outcomes.

In the case of private nonprofits, the situation is relatively good. As already noted, until recently the empirical research in public policy gave rather little thought to the nonprofit alternative (an exception being in health care, where the co-existence of public, private nonprofit, and private for-profit institutions is so strikingly apparent). But theory building toward an economics of nonprofit institutions is well underway. Henry Hansmann (1980) pioneered the application of new institutional economics to private nonprofits.[5] He noted that what distinguished nonprofits was a "nondistribution constraint"—not that nonprofits could not earn profits, but that there were severe restrictions on the distribution of those profits to individuals. He argued that where monitoring of output (specifically, quality of output) was difficult, the nondistribution constraint might make customers more confident. Note the similarity to a Williamson-style argument for an intraorganizational rather than a market transaction. Spurred on by Hansmann, as well as the forceful advocacy of Weisbrod (1977), research interest in nonprofits has surged.

The picture is less sanguine when it comes to understanding the different sorts of *public* institutions. Ideas from agency theory and transaction-cost economics have begun to diffuse into the study of the public sector, but one is hard-pressed to find the sort of differentiation among different public organizational forms that one finds for the private sector in, say, Fama and Jensen. With the possible exception of the considerable literature on state-owned enterprises, there has been little effort among economists (as opposed to political scientists) to consider the policy impacts of alternative forms of public organization. I have examined two such questions (Frant, 1989). First, does a city's choice of governance structure—elected mayor or city manager—by creating different incentives, affect its degree of bureaucratization? This question has considerable importance for public management, and there is indeed evidence of such an effect. Second, can we explain the fact that agencies organized as public authorities seem at times to perform better than government bureaus in maintaining infrastructure, and at other times to perform worse? This question is relevant to a variety of policy fields: transportation, water resources, housing, and so on. It appears that predictable differences in the ability and incentive to monitor different types of services may help account for differences in performance.

Considerable work remains to be done on these two research questions, and many more suggest themselves as well: Does an agency whose budget comes from an enterprise fund more nearly resemble a bureau (which it resembles in terms of "control") or an authority (which it resembles in terms of "ownership")? Can we gain any insight into the effects of pure "publicness" by comparing policy outcomes in intermediate public and private organizational forms, such as private nonprofits versus public authorities? To what extent do public for-profit corporations in the United States (Comsat, Amtrak) differ from state-owned enterprises in other countries? Does the strength of the link between employee compensation and performance in public agencies vary with the monitoring or contracting characteristics of the output?

Asking such questions requires some changes in our thinking. We are used to viewing a variety of policy variables—taxes, subsidies, regulations, budgets—as determining policy outcomes within the boundaries of a set of fixed parameters: the intrinsic natures of the private and public sectors. Now we need to consider that those apparently fixed parameters may in fact be policy variables as well. Institutional structure is a dimension of policy choice, one that may be critical to understanding a policy's success or failure.

Notes

1. In one sense, it is almost tautological to say that rational individuals will seek the efficient outcome, since to do otherwise would potentially make them worse off. In this sense one could say that monopoly pricing is efficient because there is no way to make both sides better off given the monopolist's inability to price discriminate. But this is not what people generally mean when they speak of efficiency.

2. This point is, as noted earlier, often misunderstood. See, for instance, the exchange between Cook and Wood (1989) about political control of the EPA. Wood asserts (and Cook implicitly agrees) that "principal-agent models assume bureaucrats are passive, lazy, and calculating only to the extent they want to avoid work." Wood goes on, "EPA bureaucrats engaged in strategic manipulation at crucial times to move outputs in unexpected directions. They acted independently and sometimes in opposition to political principals to maintain established policy" (p. 971). What Wood takes to be a refutation of principal-agent models is of course a confirmation of them (and a refutation of, say, a Weberian model).

3. John Vickers and George Yarrow (1988) apply some formal modeling, including agency theory, to a study of British-style privatization (denationalization), but their approach is quite different from the incomplete-contracts approach of Donahue.

4. Similarly, Caves and Christensen's (1980) study of Canadian railroads involved a comparison of a private corporation with a Crown corporation.

5. Both Alchian and Demsetz and Fama and Jensen (1983b) discuss nonprofits, but in much less detail.

References

Alchian, Armen A., and Harold Demsetz, "Production, Information Costs, and Economic Organization," *American Economic Review* 62:5 (December 1972), 777–795.

Averch, H., and L. Johnson, "Behavior of the Firm Under Regulatory Constraints," *American Economic Review* 53:5 (December 1962), 1052–1069.

Buchanan, James M., and Gordon Tullock, *The Calculus of Consent: Logical Foundations of Constitutional Democracy* (Ann Arbor: University of Michigan Press, 1962).

Caves, D. W., and L. R. Christensen, "The Relative Efficiency of Public and Private Firms in a Competitive Environment: The Case of Canadian Railroads," *Journal of Political Economy* 88:5 (October 1980), 958–976.

Coase, Ronald H., "Notes on the Problem of Social Cost," in *The Firm, the Market, and the Law* (Chicago: University of Chicago Press, 1988).

——, "The Problem of Social Cost," *Journal of Law and Economics* 3 (October 1960), 1–44.

——, "The Nature of the Firm," *Economica* 4 N.S. (1937), 386–405.

Cook, Brian J., and B. Dan Wood, "Principal-Agent Models of Political Control of Bureaucracy," *American Political Science Review* 83:3 (September 1989), 965–978.

Demsetz, Harold, "Toward a Theory of Property Rights," *American Economic Review* 57:2 (May 1967), 347–359.

Donahue, John D., *The Privatization Decision: Public Ends, Private Means* (New York: Basic Books, 1989).

Fama, Eugene F., "Agency Problems and the Theory of the Firm," *Journal of Political Economy* 88:2 (April 1980) 288–307.

Fama, Eugene F., and Michael C. Jensen, "Separation of Ownership and Control," *Journal of Law and Economics* 26:2 (June 1983a), 301–325.

——, "Agency Problems and Residual Claims," *Journal of Law and Economics* 26:2 (June 1983b), 327–349.

Frant, Howard L., *Incentive and Structure: On the Control of Managerial Opportunism* (Ann Arbor: University Microfilms International, 1989).

Hansmann, Henry B., "The Role of Nonprofit Enterprise," *Yale Law Journal*, 89:5 (April 1980), 835–898, reprinted in Susan Rose-Ackerman, ed., *The Economics of Nonprofit Institutions: Studies in Structure and Policy* (New York: Oxford University Press, 1986).

Harris, Milton, and Artur Raviv, "Some Results on Incentive Contracts with Applications to Education and Employment, Health Insurance and Law Enforcement," *American Economic Review* 68:1 (March 1978), 20–30.

Holmstrom, Bengt, "Moral Hazard and Observability," *Bell Journal of Economics* 10:1 (Spring 1979), 74–91.

Jensen, Michael C., and William Meckling, "Theory of the Firm: Managerial Behavior, Agency Costs and Ownership Structure," *Journal of Financial Economics* 3:4 (October 1976), 305–360.

Miller, Gary J., and Terry M. Moe, "The Positive Theory of Hierarchies," in Herbert F. Weisberg, ed., *Political Science: The Science of Politics* (New York: Agathon Press, 1986).

Moe, Terry M., "The New Economics of Organization," *American Journal of Political Science* 28:4 (1984), 739–777.

Niskanen, William, "Bureaucrats and Politicians," *Journal of Law and Economics* 18:3 (December 1975), 617–644.

———, *Bureaucracy and Representative Government* (Chicago: Aldine Atherton, 1971).

Ordeshook, Peter C., *Game Theory and Political Theory: An Introduction* (Cambridge: Cambridge University Press, 1986).

Ross, Stephen A., "The Economic Theory of Agency: The Principal's Problem," *American Economic Review* 63:2 (May 1973), 134–139.

Shavell, Steven, "Risk Sharing and Incentives in the Principal and Agent Relationship," *Bell Journal of Economics* 10:1 (Spring 1979), 55–73.

Simon, Herbert A., *Administrative Behavior*, 2nd ed. (New York: Free Press, 1957).

Spence, Michael, and Richard Zeckhauser, "Insurance, Information, and Individual Action," *American Economic Review* 61:2 (May 1971), 380–387.

Thompson, Fred, and L. R. Jones, "Controllership in the Public Sector," *Journal of Policy Analysis and Management* 5:3 (Summer 1986), 547–571.

U.S. General Accounting Office, *Additional Federal Aid for Urban Water Systems Should Wait Until Needs Are Clearly Established*, Report #CED-81-17 (Washington, D.C.: U.S. General Accounting Office, 1980).

Vickers, John, and George Yarrow, *Privatization: An Economic Analysis* (Cambridge, Mass.: MIT Press, 1988).

Weisbrod, Burton A., "Rewarding Performance That Is Hard to Measure: The Private Nonprofit Sector," *Science* 244 (5 May 1989), 541–546.

———, *The Voluntary Nonprofit Sector: An Economic Analysis* (Lexington, Mass.: Lexington Books, 1977).

Williamson, Oliver E., "The Firm as a Nexus of Treaties: An Introduction," in Masahiko Aoki, Bo Gustafsson, and Oliver E. Williamson, eds., *The Firm as a Nexus of Treaties* (Beverly Hills: Sage, 1990).

———, *The Economic Institutions of Capitalism: Firm, Markets, Relational Contracting* (New York: Free Press, 1985).

———, *Markets and Hierarchies: Analysis and Antitrust Implications* (New York: Free Press, 1975).

Williamson, Oliver E., Michael L. Wachter, and Jeffrey E. Harris, "Understanding the Employment Relation: The Analysis of Idiosyncratic Exchange," *Bell Journal of Economics* 6:1 (Spring 1975), 250–280.

7 MACROECONOMICS AND MACROECONOMISTS AS INSTRUMENTS OF POLICY

George Horwich

1. Introduction

Macroeconomic theory has evolved for several centuries into a powerful tool for policy analysts who understand both its strengths and its limitations. Its strengths lie in its highly developed and more or less empirically validated logical framework. Besides a number of unresolved theoretical issues, its limitations involve the difficulty of applying the theory— determining the relevant time frame and level of aggregation, measuring accurately the underlying variables, and estimating the parameters and dynamic processes relevant to particular policy problems. The dynamic issues include the oft-mentioned leads and lags of policy interventions and the role of expectations.

This chapter summarizes the main features of modern macrotheory as they apply, and have been applied, to U.S. policy experience. The discussion begins with a brief survey of the monetary equation of exchange and the textbook aggregate supply and demand framework and then examines the major policy episodes since 1929. The chapter ends with a review of the episodes both as historical events and as objects of macroeconomic interpretation by professional economist-analysts and policy decision makers.

2. The Monetary Equation of Exchange

The earliest attempts at modeling the macroeconomy involve the aggregate exchange relationship between money and goods: Total money expenditures equal total receipts from the sale of goods and services. Dividing each side of the equation into two underlying components, we write

$$M \times V = P \times Q$$

where, on the expenditures or demand side, M is the total existing quantity of money and V is its velocity or rate of turnover; on the receipts or supply side, Q is the total quantity of output and P is its average price.

There are, of course, many alternative definitions of the four variables, depending on the purpose or data at hand. Generally, M is defined as the medium of exchange (currency plus demand deposits) held by the public, and Q is final output of goods and services or, simply, the real GNP.

As a simple statement equating expenditures and receipts, the equation of exchange (EOE) is an undeniable identity. The variables are subject, however, to numerous underlying behavioral hypotheses and statements of causality that have broad relevance to policy analysis. These relationships are derived in terms of traditional supply and demand microanalysis, as in the supply and demand for bank reserves (a determinant of M), the demand for money (a determinant of V), and the supply and demand for labor (a determinant of Q). One aggregate relationship that falls out of the equation is the causal connection between changes in the quantity of money and resulting changes in the price level—the so-called "quantity theory"—given fixed or otherwise explainable values of the other variables.

In skillful hands, the EOE is as useful today as it was before 1936, when Keynes published his *General Theory of Employment, Interest and Money*. The *General Theory*, however, opened the way to a more complex classification of expenditure and wealth variables beyond the quantity of money, the modern formulation of which—the "aggregate supply and demand" framework—is a durable bastion of macro understanding. Nevertheless, despite its detractors, including Keynes, the EOE stands as a useful summary statement of the monetary/price-level/aggregate-output relationships generated by the more complex Keynesian system. For example, in terms of EOE, a sudden reduction in the supply of output Q caused by a reduction of worldwide energy supplies must, ceteris paribus, cause the *general* price level P to rise. This rather straightforward link between the oil crises of the 1970s and the inflation rate was totally missed by early modelers of those events, including whole segments of the macropolicy fraternity.

3. Aggregate Supply and Demand

The Keynesian system divides money expenditures MV into consumption, investment, and government outlays, which sum to total money income or, equivalently, the value of output PQ. Tax revenues, and thus the government deficit, are also identified in the expenditure stream, as is saving, defined as the difference between disposable income (total income minus taxes) and consumption. The stock of money is treated as a form of wealth, the demand for which depends on income and the rate of interest.

This basic model, expressed in constant prices, formed the demand side of a general equilibrium framework that was gradually enlarged to include a labor market and an explicit production or supply sector. Keynes' original formulation was cast purely in terms of the expenditure or demand components; implicitly, supply was infinitely elastic and the price level was constant. Even the rate of interest was generally assumed fixed by depression circumstances. But Hicks (1937), in his famous *IS-LM* generalization, allowed the expenditure functions, in combination with the supply and demand for money, to determine the level of both national income and interest, both of which could vary. Marschak (1951), in his lectures, *Income, Employment, and the Price Level*, introduced the production side of the economy, which, together with expenditure equations, determined an explicit equilibrium price level.

In Marschak's model it is possible to derive two independent equilibrium relationships between total income or output and the general price level. One equilibrates the demand side (expenditure and tax functions and money market), and the other the supply side (labor market and production function), of the system. Plotted on a diagram with the price level P on the vertical axis and aggregate output Q on the horizontal, the resulting aggregate demand AD and aggregate supply AS curves bear an obvious and appealing parallel to the familiar demand and supply schedules of microanalysis.

Although the aggregate schedules look, and in many ways behave, like their micro counterparts, they are really quite different (see Barron, Loewenstein, and Lynch, 1989: chap. 7). They are not the simple sum of the micro demand and supply curves, which are related to indivdual relative prices and not to the general price level. In fact, the existence of a relationship between the general price level and the aggregate supply or demand for output is neither obvious nor inevitable. On the demand side, a rise in the price level reduces the real value of cash balances held in private portfolios. In the absence of offsetting responses by those to whom the balances are a liability (ultimately, on net, the government), consumption spending, which depends positively on wealth, will fall. If, at the same time, the demand for real balances varies inversely with the rate of interest, wealthholders will try to regain some portion of the lost balances by selling securities. This action will raise the rate of interest and reduce the level of investment spending. With both consumption and investment reduced, the level of income (the aggregate quantity of output "demanded") at which the expenditure components sum exactly to income is itself lower at the higher price level.

On the supply side, a positive relationship between the price level and output rests, for a given technology and productivity schedule of labor, on an incomplete response by labor to changes in real wages caused by changes in the price level. For a given money wage, a rise in the price level reduces the real wage, which will raise the quantity of labor demanded by firms. If, because it is in a state of excess supply, labor accepts the loss of real wages by allowing its money wage to remain fixed or to rise less than prices, the induced increase in labor demand will raise employment and output. Labor's acquiescence in its loss of real wages, sparked by the higher price level, thereby imparts an upward slope to aggregate supply in the $P-Q$ space. We assume, for simplicity, that all points along a given AS schedule are generated by a fixed money wage, as well as underlying productivity function. In the event that labor insists on a full adjustment of the money wage to the price level, real wages remaining constant, AS is simply a vertical line.

The aggregate supply and demand framework is easily enlarged to include a foreign sector—net exports balanced by a net capital flow of opposite sign. The foreign transactions will make aggregate demand a flatter schedule. A rise in the price level, for example, and the associated rise in the interest rate reduce not only the domestic spending components but net exports as well. Exports fall and imports rise both as a direct result of the higher domestic price level and as an indirect consequence of the higher domestic interest rate. The latter attracts foreign capital, which drives up the exchange rate.

Expectations of price level change or other shocks to the system can also be incorporated in one or more schedule shifts, which will be illustrated by applying the model to an examination of the major macropolicy issues that have arisen since 1929.

4. The Depression of the 1930s

More than 60 years after the event, there is still no consensus among economists as to the direct cause of the catastrophic downturn that began in September 1929. There is widespread agreement, however, that the failure of the Federal Reserve to maintain the money supply helped turn what might otherwise have been a severe, but normal, fluctuation into a macroeconomic disaster.

4.1. Monetary Policy: The Early Years

One can readily make the case that policy-makers and their advisers should have understood the importance of defending the money supply immediately against the forces reducing it.[1] The causative role of money in determining prices and output—including the havoc that a sudden contraction of money can wreak—was well understood by Hume (1955: 40) almost two centuries earlier. The quantity theory had, in fact, received its most detailed and elegant treatment at the hands of Keynes (1950) in his *Treatise on Money*. Though published in 1930, the ideas had been discussed and widely circulated in the 1920s. At the same time, Charles Hardy (1932), of the Brookings Institution, was only one of a number of American economists who thoroughly understood the nature of central bank operations. Another American, Chester Phillips (1921), had earlier produced the definitive statement on the relation between bank reserves and the money stock.

   Nevertheless, the Federal Reserve Board, distracted by alternative indicators and policy goals, permitted a currency drain and other forces to decimate bank reserves and the stock of money. For some decision makers, causality in the equation of exchange moved primarily from the right side of the equation to the left: The quantity of money was passively determined by the forces of commerce and the state of economic activity, as expressed in the demand for loanable funds. From this perspective, the adequacy of the money supply was gauged by its price, a low interest rate indicating that the supply, relative to demand, was ample. Because short-term rates dropped steadily despite the loss of reserves following the October 1929 stock market crash and the collapse of investment, one not inconsequential view was that the Federal Reserve needed to take no aggressive expansionary action. At the same time, monetary officials were eager to protect the gold reserve by preventing short-term rates from falling too low—a goal that aggressive monetary injections might defeat.

   The Federal Reserve eventually conducted open market purchases sufficient to create a net rise in Federal Reserve credit, but only after the economy had experienced a full two years of its steepest decline on record. At that point the ability of the central bank to create money was severely constrained by the unwillingness of banks or their customers to borrow.

4.2. Fiscal Policy

An alternative means of stimulating the economy was through Treasury fiscal policy, either by increased government spending, if one wanted to take that route, or via tax reduction. Both measures raise disposable incomes and create a deficit, which raises the quantity or velocity of money. But in 1930 that approach was still in its prenatal stage. It was, in fact, expecting too much of U.S. policy-makers to appreciate the value of fiscal deficits or to understand the utter perversity of the tax increase of 1932.[2] On the other hand, the Hoover administration in 1931 created a prototypical New Deal agency, the Reconstruction Finance Corporation, which extended loans to distressed state and local governments and private businesses.

Although much discussed and maligned by the media and social commentators, the federal government's deficit in the 1930s peaked at 5.4 percent of the GNP in 1934 and averaged only 2.9 percent for the remainder of the decade.[3] Although high by historical peacetime standards, the deficits were hardly adequate to the task of stimulating an economy whose output had dropped 30 percent between 1929 and 1933. By comparison, in 1983, in a much healthier economy, the federal deficit (based on a unified budget) was 6.8 percent of GNP. But it should be noted that that deficit was 21 percent of 1983's federal expenditures, whereas the deficits of the 1930s were often 40 or 50 percent of the total budget—as much, perhaps, as could reasonably be expected, given the limited understanding of fiscal policy as an economic stabilizer.

Between 1933 and 1937 the economy grew 46 percent, essentially restoring the 1929 level of output. Whereas 9 million jobs had been lost in the downturn, generating a 1933 unemployment rate of 24.9 percent, only 7.5 million were added in the upswing.[4] At the same time, the working-age population grew between 1929 and 1937, leaving 7.7 million, or 14.3 percent of the labor force, unemployed. The growth of real GNP during the upswing averaged 9.8 percent per year, a more rapid increase than had previously been seen in the recorded data for other than a single year. But as impressive as the recovery was, it was not sufficient to achieve full employment.

4.3. The Problem of Excess Bank Reserves

The monetary authorities, meanwhile, focused on the huge accumulation of excess reserves in the banking system, due mainly to the inflow of gold, whose price had almost doubled in 1934. By January 1936 the excess reserves had reached $3 billion—ten to fifteen times their normal level. The Board of Governors feared that these reserves placed the banking system outside their control; the banks might decide spontaneously to use the reserves to extend vast amounts of credit (Friedman and Schwartz, 1963: 520). The *economic* point of view held that the excess reserves were reflective of the increased demand for liquidity characteristic of all sectors in the low interest rate economy of the 1930s and that they would not be disgorged precipitously. One economic interpretation saw the banks' marginal propensity to invest reserves as low but positive; the excess reserves were desired and their removal by the Federal Reserve would force the banks to contract their earning assets and the money supply in an effort to replace them (Friedman and Schwartz, 1963: 527). An alternative (Keynesian) view held that the marginal propensity to invest reserves was zero (reserves and earning assets were perfect substitutes) and that only increased demands for funds by borrowers could activate them; removal of the excess reserves by the authorities would be passively accepted without affecting the banks' holdings of earning assets or the money supply (Horwich, 1963).

In no event was there empirical or theoretical evidence supporting the concerns of the Board of Governors. Nevertheless, between August 1936 and May 1937, the excess reserves were sharply lowered by a phased doubling of reserve requirements. During this period, but with a considerable lag behind the policy moves, the banks reduced their earning assets and the money supply. In May the economy entered a sharp decline. Though deep, the recession lasted only a year. Real GNP at the end of the decade (1939) was only slightly above its 1929 level, and the unemployment rate was a staggering 17.2 percent.

Whether the increase in reserve requirements precipitated the banks' response and triggered the recession or whether an independently declining external demand for loanable funds induced banks to liquidate their assets will never be known with certainty. There is evidence on both sides. In retrospect, it is probably fair to say that the Federal Reserve should have waited for the excess reserves to cause trouble, not anticipate that they might do so by taking an inherently risky neutralizing action.[5] In a decade plagued by insufficient aggregate demand and no *net* rise in the price level, fears of aggressive use by banks of their excess reserves seem grossly misplaced. Indeed, the reemergence of excess reserves in 1938–1941 to almost triple their mid-thirties levels further undercut the board's view that excess reserves in this period were nonfunctional and might be spontaneously drawn down.

4.4. The 1930s in Perspective

The 1930s, America's worst economic decade, suffered not only from the limitations of macrotheory—fiscal policy was only dimly understood during the downturn and later—but from a failure to act seriously on the theory that *was* known: the quantity theory of money. Similarly, one of the most egregious policy errors of the decade outside of pure macropolicy was the Smoot-Hawley tariff of 1930, which imposed tariffs equal to an average of 60 percent of the value of U.S. imports. There was never any doubt that the overwhelming majority of American economists understood this measure to be destructive of trade and welfare; 1,028 of them signed a petition to President Hoover urging him to veto it (Kindleberger, 1986: 124). The tariff predictably invited global retaliation and contributed to the two-thirds emasculation of world trade that occurred in 1929–1933 just when aggregate demand was most in need of shoring up.

Most of the subsequent New Deal measures had little to do with macropolicy and involved instead attempts to protect selected sectors by price supports or legalized cartelization. Their impact was relevant more to redistribution and perceived social equity than to economic efficiency or business (in particular, investment) confidence.

Today the continuing search for the causes of the depression is yielding new insights into the more microeconomic dimensions of the collapse. A recent contribution suggests that the 1930s ushered in an era of remarkably extensive and rapid change—from manufacturing to services, and within manufacturing, to larger scale and technologically innovative techniques of production (Bernstein, 1987). The extraordinary magnitude of the change in the optimal mix of output required an economic adjustment that would have been painful and prolonged even in the presence of sound monetary and fiscal policies and that was catastrophic in their absence.

In terms of the aggregate supply and demand framework, the new technology and character of output caused a temporary leftward shift of the aggregate supply schedule: Output fell in declining industries but could not rise much, if at all, in expanding industries until resources underwent the massive reallocation required of them. At any average level of prices, total output was thus less, implying a leftward shift of the entire AS schedule. In the 1930s this shift of AS was, of course, overwhelmed by an even greater leftward shift of AD, reflecting the contraction of money and resulting in a decline of both the general price level and aggregate output.

5. The 1940s: War and Peace

Both the conversion to a wartime economy in World War II and the return to civilian output after the war were unique, all-encompassing episodes in U.S. economic history. We examine some of their policy implications.

5.1. Mobilization[6]

Between 1939 and 1944 U.S. real GNP grew at a remarkable average rate of 11.2 percent per year, a cumulative increase of 70 percent. This increment, roughly equal to the additional output of war materiel and services, absorbed not only the remaining pool of unemployed workers but drew millions of additional workers, primarily women, into the work force.

The demand changes were thus government-driven, and the industrial response was also to a large extent mandated by centralized authorities. General price controls were imposed early in 1942, severely limiting free market activity. Nevertheless, price adjustments in response to market forces were occasionally made and a fair degree of wage flexibility was permitted to draw millions of workers to new and geographically disparate employments.

The price controls were widely accepted as an inevitable wartime measure, necessary to contain inflation. In an interesting reappraisal of this policy, Paul Evans (1982) finds that while the controls reduced the price level by 30 percent, they reduced aggregate output 7 percent and employment almost 12 percent. These reductions resulted from the inability of households to acquire additional goods with their increased incomes, thereby reducing their work incentives. As well as the wartime economy performed, it thus could have produced an even greater output (or, more importantly, the same output more rapidly) under free market prices and an accommodating monetary policy that permitted the same degree of measured inflation.

As a contribution to social harmony, particularly in a national emergency, a defense of controls can perhaps be made. But they are economically tolerable only for limited periods. If the war had lasted longer, the inefficiencies resulting from the absence of relative price signals would have cut deeper and deeper into aggregate output. Fortunately, as the war wound down in 1945, enforcement of the controls became increasingly lax. By September 1946 they were totally removed.

5.2. Demobilization

The freeing of prices set the stage for the most extensive restructuring of the economy to occur in any single year of U.S. history. In 1946 government defense spending fell by 80 percent, from 37 percent of 1945's GNP to 8 percent of 1946's GNP. Eight million people were released from the armed forces, and 2.5 million civilian jobs were added. The difference, equal to 5.6 million people, left the labor force or joined the unemployment rolls. As many as a third of the 65 million persons employed by the private or public sectors (including the military) changed jobs or returned to the household and nonprofit sector.

The real GNP (in 1947 prices) fell 11.1 percent in 1946, but unemployment rose by only 1.3 million from a wartime low of 1.9 percent to a sustainable 3.9 percent. Most remarkable is that all this occurred without a trace of centralized direction or control. The adjustment was a purely price-directed market phenomenon.

Many, if not most macroeconomists, however, were fearful that demobilization would ravage aggregate demand and result in a deep postwar depression (see Copeland, 1944; Hagen and Kirkpatrick, 1944). What they overlooked was the enormous sums of money in the hands of the public built up by wartime deficit spending and which the public, facing wartime shortages of goods, had retained (velocity had fallen sharply). This was the very opposite of the monetary situation in the early 1930s. Between 1939 and 1946, real M_1 balances (the public's currency plus demand deposits) rose 129 percent.[7] By comparison, real balances in World War I fell 8 percent, which may have contributed to the downturns of both 1918 and 1920.

American economists, like others, were not aware of the importance of real balances or, more generally, wealth as a determinant of expenditures. Nor were they likely to believe, after the 1930s, that a capitalist economy was capable of undergoing a vast peacetime transformation without a high degree of government planning or, at least, centralized coordination. Nineteen forty-six was instructive on both counts. That the demobilization proceeded in a postwar frenzy of laissez-faire without serious intervention by government or macroeconomists is one of those fortunate accidents of economic history.

6. 1950–1953: The Korean War

Before turning to the cyclical behavior of the postwar economy, the Korean War will be examined for its particular blend of macropolicies.

Prices rose almost immediately following the June 1950 outbreak of hostilities. The cause was an increase in expenditures—government outlays for war materiel and consumer spending in anticipation of higher prices. Both money and velocity rose, but the rise in velocity was especially pronounced, as might be expected in these circumstances.

A tax increase was quickly enacted, and the money supply gradually tightened. In January 1951 price controls were imposed. Unlike the price ceilings of World War II, the removal of the controls in 1953 was not followed by an increase of prices that had been only temporarily repressed. The Korean controls had not been binding. Nevertheless, they may have played a useful role in defusing inflationary expectations and imposing pricing discipline on the part of both suppliers and demanders in the context of general stabilizing policies. This, at least, is the econometric finding of George Perry (1973). Others, such as Herbert Stein (1984: 119–120), consider the monetary and fiscal measures to have been sufficient and the price controls superfluous.

Inflationary expectations shift aggregate demand upward (to the right) and aggregate supply upward (to the left). The supply shift is now characteristic of recessionary periods, as will be argued in the next section. In fact, it was the belief (though not articulated as such) that such a shift was taking place in the summer of 1971 that led in August to the only other postwar imposition of general wage and price controls. But the evidence for the gathering inflation was weak, and the controls proved to be binding and disruptive and positively disastrous when the oil price shocks occurred in the fall of 1973.

Still, the distinction is worth making between price controls of the World War II variety that serve only to repress inflation caused by underlying monetary or fiscal forces versus controls that defuse inflationary expectations that need not be realized and need not reappear at a later date. There is a difference, in principle, at least. In practice, recognizing perverse expectations, imposing controls in a timely and effective manner to neutralize them, and then removing the controls before their interference with relative prices causes too much damage is almost certainly undoable—both economically and politically—as the controls of 1971–1973 demonstrated. But there *is* a difference.

By contrast with 1950, policy-makers in 1971 focused on union–management negotiations and price indices whose trends bearing on inflation and inflationary expectations were not clear. The controls were binding from the start in that inflationary forces due not to expectations but to excessive growth of the money supply were at work. In the following two years the controls masked continued expansionary monetary and fiscal policies and were still in force in 1973 in the energy markets, when world oil markets erupted and imposed an economy wide reallocation of resources that the controls severely hampered (see Stein, 1984: chap. 5).

7. The Post-1949 Business Cycle

The first postwar recession occurred in 1948–1949 and, though a minor event by comparison, was like the downturn of 1929–1933 in that both output and the price level fell. In later recessions a new pattern was established in which output fell but prices rose. These subsequent fluctuations are described in terms of the aggregate supply and demand framework. What follows is schematic description of more or less ideal states, not necessarily a complete account of an actual sequence of events.

Starting at a trough of economic activity, recovery is characterized by a rightward shifting AD schedule in response to an accelerated growth of money or autonomous increases in the expenditure functions. AD initially shifts along a relatively flat AS schedule, with output rising relatively more than the price level. Two factors contribute to this pattern: To regain their jobs unemployed workers are willing to allow money wages to rise less than the price level, reducing the real wage; at the same time, productivity gains for labor are likely to be substantial in the earlier stages of recovery, so that even with an increase in real wages, marginal production costs do not necessarily rise or rise very much.[8] As full employment of resources is approached, continued increases in prices tend to evoke equiproportionate increases in money wages. Since AS is constructed on the assumption of a fixed money wage, the increase of money wages gradually pushes real wages above productivity and causes AS to shift leftward.

Eventually the excess supply of labor disappears and a point of full employment is reached in which output (relative to trend) is at capacity and can rise no more. AD continues shifting to the right, however, causing prices, wages, and other costs to rise equally. Accompanying every rightward (or, equivalently, upward) movement of AD is thus an equal leftward (or upward) movement of AS. Output is constant and prices continue to increase.

Although what constitutes an acceptable rate of inflation will differ in time and place, a continuing inflation will sooner or later become politically intolerable to the administration, whichever party is in power. The money supply is tightened and AD decelerates in its rightward shifts; relative to trend, or absolutely, it may cease shifting altogether. AS, possibly for a variety of reasons, fails to adapt to the change of policy and continues to shift upward along the relatively more stable AD schedule, causing prices to continue to rise but output to fall. In effect, the supply side of the economy prices its product (AS shifts upward) in anticipation of demand increases (upward shifts of AD) that fail to materialize. At the higher prices (traced along a given AD schedule), sales decline, as do output and employment. The economy is in a typical post-1949 recession.

The failure of aggregate supply to adapt to the deceleration of demand may result from an informational gap: suppliers and owners of resources do not immediately know what is happening to aggregate demand or, if they do, how it will affect their individual markets. Continuing supply-price increases may also reflect the skepticism of suppliers that the monetary authority has the will or the ability to pursue and successfully implement a policy of restraint.

The lack of coordination between demand and supply pricing will gradually correct itself, however, causing the upward shifts of AS to diminish. When they cease (generally after about 11 months),[9] the decline of output and employment ends, and the economy is poised for a renewed period of economic growth with little or no inflation.

Table 7–1 summarizes the price and output changes of eight postwar recessions and shows the net decline of demand of the 1948–1949 downturn occurring in the first two quarters of 1949 (that is, output and the price level simultaneously decline). In the last two quarters, output successively increased and then decreased while prices remained constant. We can infer that AS and AD shifted equally—to the right in 1949:3 (the third quarter of 1949) and to the left in 1949:4.

In the 1953–1954 recession, however, a net leftward shift of AD occurred only in 1953:4. In the other three quarters, output fell while prices rose by varying degrees, indicating that the inflation was supply induced in the sense that it was caused by a net leftward shift of AS. In 1957–1958 output declined sharply in two quarters, during which prices rose, though only moderately. A good guess would be that the upward movement of AS was being effectively restrained by significant decreases of AD, an expression of the anti-inflationary resolve of the monetary authority. Indeed, in the 1960–1961 recession prices were virtually flat, indicating that in the two quarters in which output fell, the inflationary tendency in supply (the leftward shift of AS) was only strong enough to neutralize the price effect of the decline (the leftward shift) of AD.

It is a plausible conclusion that three closely spaced Eisenhower recessions, all of which served to restrain inflation, laid the groundwork for the next nine years of steady growth at low rates of inflation. By the late 1960s, however, price increases were beginning to occur, and in those quarters of

Table 7–1.   Annual Percentage Changes in Real GNP (*Q*) and the GNP Deflator (*P*) in Eight Post–World War II Recessions.

11/48–10/49			7/53–5/54			8/57–4/58		
	P	*Q*		*P*	*Q*		*P*	*Q*
1948:4	−1.7	3.3	1953:3	1.5	−3.1	1957:3	4.2	2.3
1949:1	−3.4	−4.7	4	−3.1	−3.2	4	1.4	−6.2
2	−3.4	−2.3	1954:1	6.2	−5.6	1958:1	2.8	−8.1
3	0.0	3.0	2	1.5	−1.6	2	1.4	2.2
4	0.0	−3.9						

4/60–2/61			12/69–11/70			11/73–3/75		
	P	*Q*		*P*	*Q*		*P*	*Q*
1960:2	0.0	−1.1	1969:4	5.0	−1.6	1973:4	9.6	3.6
3	1.3	0.4	1970:1	6.9	−2.5	1974:1	5.5	−2.2
4	0.0	−3.4	2	5.8	−0.3	2	8.5	1.1
1961:1	0.0	4.1	3	2.9	4.9	3	13.6	−5.2
			4	4.7	−3.6	4	10.9	−3.5
						1975:1	9.9	−7.8

1/80–7/80			7/81–11/82		
	P	*Q*		*P*	*Q*
1980:1	8.4	4.0	1981:3	9.1	1.8
2	9.2	−9.5	4	7.6	−5.6
3	9.0	0.3	1982:1	6.2	−6.0
			2	4.9	1.2
			3	5.6	−3.2
			4	3.6	0.6

Note: 1948:4 denotes 1948, fourth quarter.

Source: Recessions and upswings are designated by the National Bureau of Economic Research as reported in the U.S. Department of Commerce periodical, *Business Conditions Digest* (January 1987: 104). All percentage changes are computed from data in U.S. Department of Commerce, Bureau of Economic Analysis (1986: 37–39 and 335–337).

the 1969–1970 downturn in which output fell, the inflation was pure supply-push (caused by a net leftward shift of *AS*), as table 7–1 indicates. A similar pattern appears in the recessions of 1973–1975, 1980, and 1981–1982, in which all reductions in output were accompanied by significant price increases, the result of leftward shifts of *AS*. As it happened, these shifts were exacerbated by the world oil disruptions then occurring. The oil price shocks will be discussed in a later section.

Like the 1960s, the postrecession 1980s experienced good growth at tolerable rates of inflation, inflationary expectations having been more or less wrung out of the economy in the Carter/Reagan recessions. The tax cuts of 1964 and 1981 also appear to have contributed to the prosperity, as did the absence of destabilizing shocks and a monetary policy that on hindsight was roughly stabilizing in the upswings of both decades.

As noted, the foregoing sketch of the postwar business cycle is schematic, not necessarily historical. The pattern of events was in fact irregular, an upswing sometimes being interrupted by a temporary faltering of the economy (1952: 2, 1962: 4, 1966: 2, 1968: 4), the recession perhaps ending with inflation above acceptable levels (1970: 4, 1975: 1), and the supply side shifting for reasons other than its delayed reaction to a policy-driven slowdown of demand (for example, as a result of the energy shocks).

8. The Phillips Curve

One of the empirical generalizations drawn from the postwar cyclical experience was the Phillips Curve, an inverse relation between the rate of change of money wages (or the price level) and unemployment (Phillips, 1958). The curve enjoyed considerable currency among macroeconomists and policy-makers in the 1960s and 1970s. In his 1967 presidential address, Milton Friedman (1968) questioned the basis for it, arguing that inflation could not lower real wages and unemployment below their "natural" level unless it was unexpected, and even then, only temporarily (see also Phelps, 1968).

In terms of our analysis, increases in the price level, whether anticipated or not, are effective in lowering unemployment when there is excess supply in the labor market. In that circumstance inflation may be the only way to bring about the reduction in real wages that will clear the market. But once the excess supply disappears, Friedman is surely correct that further increases in the price level will not permanently raise employment.

In general, both the labor market and financial markets appear to have seriously embraced inflationary expectations for the first time in American history in the late 1960s. Prior to that time U.S. markets seem to have regarded peacetime inflation as a rare, nonrepeatable event—which, in large measure, it was.

The anticyclical pattern of real wages implied by the Keynesian analysis of the labor market is often challenged by claims that real wages are in fact acyclical or even procyclical (Mankiw, 1988: 446). The total wage bill, however, as a percentage of GNP is markedly anticyclical in every cycle since 1929, with the possible exception of the 1937–1938 downturn.[10] This could indicate that changing technology and overall factor productivity alter the net burden of real wages—however they alone are changing—in a direction consistent with the Keynesian hypothesis.

9. The Oil Price Shocks

Macroeconomists had a difficult time interpreting the macro impacts of the world oil supply disruptions of 1973–1974 and 1979–1980. The ongoing postwar debates between Keynesians and monetarists focused on the superiority of one set of demand-side variables (Keynesian expenditure and asset-holding functions) over another (money and velocity). Neither camp was particularly adept at analyzing disruptions originating on the supply side of the system, although world food shortfalls due to weather and natural disturbances had occurred in the early 1970s.

9.1. The Oil Supply Disruption as a Macro Event

As noted earlier, the macroanalysis of the oil shocks is straightforward. The worldwide reduction in supply and increase in price of the most widely used energy resource raised the marginal cost of producing almost every component of the world's GNP. In response, every country's aggregate supply curve (including those of OPEC and other oil exporting countries) shifted up or to the left, reflecting those higher costs and, simultaneously, lower factor productivities. The upward shift of AS along a given AD curve reduced output and raised the general price level.[11] In the equation of exchange, Q fell autonomously and P rose to balance it.

The large econometric models, such as the Data Resources Incorporated and the Wharton, were based on the Keynesian demand-side-only model of the 1930s and early 1940s. In the absence of an independent production sector, which, together with the demand equations determined output and the price level, there was no feasible way to introduce the oil shocks and come out with the correct answers. Manipulators of the models, knowing that the shocks entailed a loss of income, tended to treat *that* as the disturbance. Entering a reduced income into the model reduced consumption and, through various steps, investment. In effect, aggregate demand, rather than supply, shifted to the left. The impact on the price level was problematical and varied with the model and the operator. Usually prices rose at first but then, as might be expected in a demand-side shock, fell (see, for example, Curtis, 1979).

A number of government agencies, most notably the Department of Energy (DOE), relied on the big econometric models. DOE, under Secretary Schlesinger, mandated that all its departments use DRI for their analyses. But some agencies, such as the Council of Economic Advisers (CEA), had more flexibility and were able to employ a wider view of macroeconomic relationships. The policy analysis, however, was complicated by the fact that both oil price shocks of the 1970s occurred just as the economy was about to enter a downturn in which aggregate supply, driven by perverse inflationary expectations, was already drifting upward along a stalled (monetary-restricted) aggregate demand. The energy shocks accelerated the leftward movement of supply, intensifying the inflation and the decline of output and employment.

Few, if any, macroeconomists saw the first energy shock or the simultaneous cyclical downturn in these stark supply-demand terms. In their February 1974 report, the CEA, though recognizing that productive capacity might be reduced by the oil curtailments, felt that capacity was as yet unaffected (CEA, 1974: 24). They discussed the weaknesses in real income and demand, but without distinguishing between two possible causes: (1) an independent reduction of demand-side variables, such as the quantity of money, and (2) an independent reduction in aggregate supply, whether due to uncoordinated supply-side pricing or the energy shock. In the first case demand is weak in the sense of a leftward shift *of* the aggregate demand schedule due, in this instance, to a restrictive monetary policy. In the second case demand is weak because of an induced upward movement *along* aggregate demand. Only the latter, of course, explains the simultaneous reduction of real income and rise in the price level. The 1974 *Economic Report* explains the inflation by reference to the importance of energy and food prices in the overall inflation rate (CEA, 1974: 28). But this is tautologous: Any price index is an identity with respect to its components, none of which can themselves explain anything as to the index's overall level or underlying determinants—for example, whether the price changes originated in autonomous supply or demand forces.

In this connection a curious assertion, commonly made by monetarists but others as well, is that, in the absence of monetary accommodation, the rise in energy prices tends to be offset by an equal decline in other prices.[12] Herbert Stein, who was chairman of the CEA that produced the 1974 report but is not a monetarist, remarks in his recent policy book (1984: 185): "If demand had been rigorously controlled by tight fiscal and monetary policy, the rises of food and petroleum prices might have been absorbed by an offsetting decline of other prices." There is, however, no basis for this belief. It makes sense only if the increase in energy prices is purely a demand phenomenon resulting from a transfer of demand to energy from nonenergy markets. Moreover, in the context of the oil supply disruption and aggregate *supply* shift, with all the likely attendant controls and natural bottlenecks, it is doubtful that monetary or fiscal tightening would reduce absolute or relative prices very much. Most of the demand curtailment would fall on real output and employment.

In the second disruption, 1979–1980, the CEA did not offer a more logical or internally consistent macro interpretation of the events than the council had in 1974. The Carter CEA seemed equally and alternately concerned with restraining the inflationary impact of the oil shock and dealing with a possibly massive "oil price drag." The latter phenomenon is a deflationary decline (leftward shift) of aggregate demand owing to a diversion and piling up of funds in the hands of domestic and foreign oil producers. It could be a particular problem in oil markets because the short-run demand for oil and oil products is very inelastic—a rise in price causes a relatively much smaller reduction in consumption, resulting in an increase in the total dollar outlay on oil. In the 1970s, with crude oil prices first quintupling and then, later, more than doubling, the increased flow of funds to oil producers, domestic and foreign, was enormous. The possibility of drag was addressed with growing concern by the CEA's *Economic Report* of 1974 (p. 29), 1975 (pp. 30, 42), and 1980 (pp. 29, 51), all of which feared that the companies would be unable to recycle their receipts fast enough to avoid a serious loss of purchasing power from the economy at large. The empirical evidence, in this author's opinion, does not support their concern.[13]

9.2. The Macropolicy Response

Meanwhile, the 1980 report did not see the increase in oil prices as directly raising production costs or, in our terms, shifting AS to the left. Instead, it viewed the oil price hikes as contributing to general inflation and to heightened inflationary expectations, particularly by wage earners. The cure for this, it declared, was strong monetary and fiscal restraint (CEA, 1980: 79). But if the report had distinguished between leftward shifts of AS due to inflationary expectations and those caused by a shrinkage of capacity output due to higher oil prices, it could not have taken quite so unqualified a stand for demand tightening.

There is in fact little that macropolicy can do for an oil-constricted economy. Demand restraint, as noted, will likely reduce output much more than prices—to no apparent net gain. The rise in prices due to an oil shock is, moreover, a one-time effect, not a component of an ongoing inflation. Considering only the oil shock, some monetary or fiscal ease would be a far more appropriate policy response. It would facilitate the reallocation of resources dictated by the higher price of energy and it would counter any possible oil price drag. In the context of upward shifting *AS* schedules due to perverse inflationary expectations, macropolicy, which has directly triggered such supply behavior by restraining aggregate demand, might pursue a middle course—restraining demand less than if it had only the business cycle to deal with.

The monetary authorities, however, possessing even less sophistication than others as to aggregate supply, demand, and their interaction, treated the inflations of the 1970s as purely demand-driven and calling for unqualified restraint.[14] Though occurring on a much smaller scale, the situation in the 1970s was comparable to that of 1929, 1939, or 1946, when a huge adjustment in the composition of output loomed, and for which monetary ease and stability were necessary catalysts. Instead, as in 1929, the monetary response in the 1970s was contractionary and destabilizing.[15]

The central banks of all the countries of the Organization for Economic Cooperation and Development plunged ahead with monetary restriction whose harmful effects were magnified by the energy-induced leftward shifts of aggregate supply. Several researchers have argued that tight money, both in 1974 and 1979–1981, was responsible for a greater reduction in output and employment than was caused directly by the rise in oil prices (Bohi, 1989: chap. 7).

9.3. Policy with Respect to Oil Market Controls

If macropolicy cannot do much to protect or restore an oil-disrupted economy, particularly in the stagflation phase of the cycle, other varieties of public policy may be more helpful. The construction and drawdown of national petroleum stockpiles is an obvious direct offset to the loss of oil in the world economy (Horwich and Weimer, 1984: chap. 4; 1988: chaps. 5, 9). Public policy can make a further contribution to economic welfare by dismantling any prevailing oil price ceilings or mandatory fuel allocations, which almost invariably prevent resources from going to their most valued uses. The 1974 report gingerly suggested that higher prices might accomplish much of what needed to be done in energy markets; it did not criticize the controls or discuss their ability to damage the economy (CEA, 1974: 33). The 1975 report, after more than a full year's experience with controls, called forthrightly for their removal from oil and natural gas, for construction of a strategic petroleum reserve, and for general reliance on free market prices (CEA, 1975: 21, 30).

In June 1979 the oil decontrol process initiated by President Carter began, and the 1980 report endorsed it (CEA, 1980: 107–108). But its approval was qualified. While applauding more rational prices, it urged establishment of a standby fuel rationing plan and, by implication, price ceilings on gasoline, diesel fuel, and heating oil for use in a major disruption (p. 106). It warned that decontrol would bring producer windfalls that would do nothing to increase supplies and that decontrol generally would reduce the real incomes of consumers (p. 109). The latter assertion is diametrically at odds with the conventional demonstration of the gain of consumer surplus from removal of price ceilings (Arrow and Kalt, 1979; Ford Foundation, 1979: chap. 5). Price ceilings and product rationing make internal sense only if decontrol and free-market prices are seen as increasing consumer vulnerability to oil price drag: The ceilings may limit the drag by limiting the transfer from consumers to the oil industry.[16] But when one considers that U.S. controls, by discouraging production and subsidizing imports, resulted in increased world oil prices (Horwich and Weimer, 1984: 70, 72, 107), it is unclear that drag would be less under domestic controls than in uncontrolled markets.

10. The 1980s: The Fiscal Deficits

Macroeconomists frequently lament the absence of a systematic theory of the optimal mix of monetary and fiscal stimulus. An even larger problem, in this writer's opinion, is our inability to *know* what the deficit is. We do not have a widely accepted standard procedure for separating endogenous from exogenous components or for looking at the deficit as part of the government's total income and wealth position. The measurement of monetary stimulus suffers from the same failure to distinguish between the change in money that is endogenous from that which is exogenous—that is, attributable to the monetary authority. A measure of the exogenous money supply would certainly be worth having (see Hendershott, 1968). But it is less critical than for fiscal policy because money is more easily and readily altered and more subject to government control than are the federal budget and its determinants.

In the 1980s, as the measured deficit reached historic peacetime highs even as the economy flourished, the criticism of established government accounting practice mounted. The complaints came from an unusual mixture of ideological voices in the economics profession, all in agreement that to continue lumping everything government does into a single current consumption account was highly misleading (Eisner and Pieper, 1985; Darby, 1987). The inability of recent econometric studies to find a correlation between the deficit and interest rates (Bailey et al., 1984; Evans, 1985) suggests at least the possibility that the measured deficit is not a very meaningful magnitude.

In retrospect, we should have realized the inadequacy of the conventional measure. Some of the simplest suggested adjustments make for enormous changes in the deficit:

1. The observed deficit as a fraction of the GNP is a scale adjustment that obviously should be, and in fact usually is, made routinely.
2. The high-employment deficit, a measure of the exogenous (noncyclical) component, is often significantly different from the observed deficit even on the basis of a small difference between the prevailing and an assumed full-employment level of unemployment. John Tatom (1984) reports on the Commerce Department high-employment deficit series, which is based on a 5 percent level of frictional unemployment. Expressing the Commerce series as a fraction of GNP reduces the relatively traumatic deficits of 1958:2 and 1958:3 (they "curled" the hair of Treasury Secretary Humphrey) from almost 3 percent observed to 0.0 percent and 0.5 percent adjusted, respectively; the 1975:2 deficit from 6.5 percent observed to 3.5 percent adjusted; the 1982:2 deficit from almost 4 percent observed to 0.2 percent adjusted; and the 1982:4 deficit from almost 7 percent observed to 2 percent adjusted. On this procedure alone, there do not appear to be any really serious deficits after World War II and before 1975 and the mid-1980s. All the pre-1970s deficits and most of those of the 1970s reflected the operation of the automatic stabilizers and little else.
3. If one takes the first step in a total balance sheet approach to the government's fiscal position and adjusts the current account for the change in the inflation-adjusted value of outstanding liabilities (the federal debt), the effect on the current deficit can be overwhelming. The public holds over $2 trillion in government bonds; a 5 percent inflation reduces their value more than $100 billion,

which, when subtracted from recent deficits, reduces them by half or more. Increases in interest rates can also lower the value of outstanding debt and current deficits significantly. From a policy perspective, these adjustments for the change in the real value of debt are especially important. There are both theoretical and empirical reasons for believing that the interest-rate inflation premium on government bonds compensates the public for losses of its government-bond portfolio due to inflation (Cagan, 1981: 3). The public makes up these losses by applying revenues from the inflation premium to the purchase of an equal additional amount of government bonds. To that extent, the current deficit is neutral in its impact on the capital market.

4. So-called Ricardian equivalence, whereby the public increases its saving in anticipation of future tax liabilities, amplifies the reaction described in item 3. A long-held belief, first voiced (but not endorsed) by Ricardo, is that households will save more in response to increased government deficits in anticipation of taxes that must be levied to pay the interest on the debt (Bailey, 1962: 71–80; 1971: chap.9; Barro, 1974). There are some dramatic examples of this possible tendency, such as the 50 percent and 79 percent increases in the ratio of saving to GNP in World Wars I and II, respectively (Horwich and Bjornstad, 1991). A government capital account would help, of course, to distinguish between government expenditures that are pure consumption and those that add to social capital. The latter will provide its own saving and funding to pay the interest on the debt (Kormendi, 1983: 1005–1007).

The larger step of classifying government expenditures into consumption and investment categories is more difficult. But the political thicket this effort would encounter should not preclude such an attempt. It could be done to a limited degree (as other countries do), including in government investment, at an initial stage, only physical assets such as buildings, roads, and dams. Almost certainly the general task should be delegated to a private nonprofit agency, such as the National Bureau of Economic Research (which is also the organization that determines the business cycle turning points).

Alternative measures of the deficit, including various degrees of consolidation with state and local government (which ran enormous surpluses in the 1980s) and various degrees of disaggregation with respect to the Social Security and other pension funds, would also be useful.

11. Summary and Conclusion: The Major Policy Issues

During most of the period covered by this survey, macrotheory focused on demand-side variables, moving from the relatively simple world of money and its demand (or velocity) to the more complex Keynesian expenditure models. By the end of World War II, the convulsive economic events of the 1930s and 1940s, including the phenomenal wartime expansion, had made Keynesianism the preeminent doctrine among macroeconomists. A large government fiscal presence, particularly on the side of spending, was widely regarded as necessary to compensate for the weakness of private investment in a mature economy. At the same time an automatic counter-cyclical role was created by the increased level and progressivity of income taxes and various government social programs enacted in the 1930s and 1940s.

Although Keynesianism was the predominant macro framework, it was not ensconced in the highest policy circles until Walter Heller became chairman of the Council of Economic Advisers in 1961. And while the early Keynesians had emphasized government spending as the primary stabilizer, a change in tax rates was used effectively in the 1960s in the celebrated tax cut of 1964. The use of a surcharge to contain Vietnam-era spending in 1968 was widely judged to be ineffective because the public viewed the policy as only temporary, which it was.

11.1. The Revival of Money

Independent monetary policy suffered doctrinal eclipse following its failure in the 1929–1933 downturn and its de facto paralysis under the 1941 Federal Reserve commitment to support interest rates at designated low levels. At the same time Keynesians had undermined the theoretical underpinnings of monetary policy by arguing that, in any case, it was ineffective in the low interest rate, low investment world that had emerged from the 1930s and 1940s.

As observed earlier, the successful World War II demobilization and peacetime conversion lent renewed credence to the importance of real balances—the centrality of money—in economic activity. But it was not until April 1951 that the Federal Reserve–Treasury Accord freed the Federal Reserve from its hand-tying policy of automatically supporting interest rates at low levels. As we saw, three recessions followed in the next nine years, all preceded by monetary restraint of one degree or another.

But the restraint was compatible with overall GNP growth in the 1950s that was quite satisfactory (3.3 percent compounded annually) and, as noted, created a noninflationary environment for the long upswing of the 1960s.

11.2. Aggregate Supply

Serious macroeconomic attention to the production or supply side of the system did not appear until the 1960s, when it surfaced as discussion of the Phillips Curve. This inverse relationship between the rate of change of money wages or the inflation rate and unemployment was one of the implications of the upward-sloping aggregate supply curve—an increase in the price level evokes an increase in employment and a decrease in unemployment. According to the Keynesian interpretation of the labor market, employment rises only if the real wage falls; thus the accompanying rise in money wages cannot be as great as the inflation rate. This remains the most widely accepted explanation of labor market behavior, but it has not been verified empirically. Rather than moving countercyclically, as the theory predicts, real wages tend to be procyclical or even acyclical. An internally consistent, fully empirically validated explanation of the aggregate supply/price level relationship remains elusive.

Meanwhile, the Phillips Curve came under attack by those who claimed that, in general, workers would not allow inflation to reduce their real wages unless it was unexpected, and even then only temporarily. But the Phillips Curve and the aggregate supply curve that underlies it are valid if there is excess supply in the labor market; that is, unemployment is above the natural or frictional level. As inflation gradually rose in the late 1960s and in the upswing of the late 1970s, plots of the Phillips relation indeed kept shifting to the right, suggesting that workers were not allowing inflation to reduce their real wages very much and that the positive response of employment to inflation was growing weaker.

Some of the rightward shifts, notably in 1970, were so great as to trace a positive inflation/unemployment path. This was the Phillips counterpart to the upward shifting aggregate supply schedules as they lagged the deceleration of upward shifting aggregate demand, catapulting the economy into a typical post-1949 inflationary recession. Adding to the upward shifts of aggregate supply (and the rightward shifts of the Phillips Curve) were, of course, the oil price shocks, which increased inflation by decreasing productive capacity.

11.3. The Decline of Countercyclical Fiscal Policy

The United States enters the 1990s with monetary policy as the single flexible tool of demand management. The only certain role of fiscal policy in the short term is the operation of the automatic stabilizers. In the 1980s a tax cut (1981) and reduction of marginal rates (1986) provided short-term and, in the latter case, longer-term stimulus, but such measures are extremely cumbersome politically and cannot be counted on for routine countercyclical duty. Moreover, the measured deficit component of the budget has been criticized for (1) being a meaningless end product of the crude and unsatisfactory way in which government keeps its accounts— everything goes into a current statement (there is no capital account); and (2) the very real possibility that the economic impact of the deficit may be partially or totally offset by increases in household saving that anticipate the future taxes required to service the additional debt. At this moment, fiscal policy as a short-term tool is in a highly unsettled state: in particular, the deficit, accurately measured, is probably neither as large nor as harmful as popularly supposed.

11.4. A Monetary Rule?

A useful way to conclude this chapter would be to enunciate a policy rule for the stock of money or the monetary base. In his historical survey, Stein (1984) described the failures of policies that, at various times, focused on narrow targets: unemployment, always a sluggish *indicator* of the state of the economy; the price level, as often as not poorly measured by the various indices; the market rate of interest, determined by many forces, many of them international, and thereby an unreliable target of stabilization without detailed knowledge of other variables. To this list we can add the exchange rate, which, like the interest rate, is too endogenous to be manipulated by the authorities with impunity.

It is tempting to entertain the use of a monetary policy rule, such as constant growth of the monetary base. Such a rule might at least have avoided the monetary debacles of the 1930s. It might also have provided greater stability and softened the recessions of 1948–1949, the 1950s, 1960–1961, and 1969–1970, none of which were associated with a severe nonmonetary shock. In the face of such shocks, it is probably neither realistic nor desirable to adhere rigidly to any rule. For wars such as World

War II, in which government defense spending rose from 1.4 percent of GNP in 1939 to 42.8 percent in 1944, it is unrealistic and almost certainly suboptimal not to allow additional money and some inflation to reduce the necessary increases in taxes and real interest rates. But even for smaller mobilizations, an increased monetary or fiscal stimulus may be desirable. For supply-side shocks, such as the adjustments imposed by the energy disturbances of the 1970s and 1990 or, even more, the vast transformation required of the 1930s, as described by Bernstein (1987), it is unlikely that a fixed rule would or should be tolerated.

None of the preceding, however, should be construed as a case for fine tuning if by that we mean the mindless, almost automatic support of interest rates—a policy we have grown accustomed to; the response to changes in price indices before a trend has been established; or the focus on unemployment rates that may contain a large structural—in addition to a cyclical—component.

Finally, we need to underscore the fact that monetary policy is not a panacea. If monetary restraint has triggered the usual inflationary recession, the only effective response may be resolute determination by the authorities to stay the course, thereby defusing the public's inflationary expectations. In future upswings the Federal Reserve may want to exercise tighter control of money to limit the need for later reversal. In response to supply-side shocks, monetary policy should avoid compounding the adjustment with a monetary shock. In these cases the most useful policy moves are likely to lie outside the macro realm—the drawdown of strategic stockpiles and the removal of price ceilings, mandatory allocations, and other impediments to the free operation of markets. Although price controls make no economic sense as a response to supply shocks, they may, in principle, be imposed effectively to dampen general inflationary expectations triggered by demand forces. In practice, however, they are unlikely to be used expeditiously—they are the ultimate in fine tuning. The worst part of the 1970 recession was the impatience with the subsequent recovery and the decision to impose price controls soon after it began.

11.5. Beyond Supply and Demand?

This chapter concludes by repeating the claim that aggregate supply and demand is a trustworthy tool for understanding what macro–policy-makers need to know. Although it is a barebones model and needs constant refinement and elaboration, it is a great organizer. At the same time, new theoretical developments lie ahead, including the exciting possibilities of rational expectations.[17] When and if they reach the policy stage, however, they will not render supply and demand, whether micro or macro, obsolete. On the contrary, one would expect to know more at that point about the aggregate schedules and how and where they will shift in response to policy initiatives. Properly armed, macroeconomists can thereby play a meaningful role in the effort to mitigate the impact of future disturbances.

Acknowledgment

For many helpful comments and criticisms, I thank John Carlson, Stan Engerman, Glenn Hueckel, Dan Kovenock, and Steve Sullivan.

Notes

1. See the exhaustive and scholarly treatment of the monetary events of the 1930s in Friedman and Schwartz (1963), chapter 7.

2. See Stein (1984) for a definitive treatment of this and other central episodes in post–World War II macroeconomic policy. On the material in this paragraph, see p. 33.

3. National income and government expenditure and receipts data throughout this study are taken from various issues of CEA, *Economic Report of the President* and U.S. Department of Commerce (1975, 1986).

4. Michael Darby (1976) discovered that the official employment statistics of the 1930s counted as unemployed some 3.5 million workers employed in various government work programs: the Civilian Conservation Corps, the Works Progress Administration, and the Public Works Administration. Counting these individuals as employed would reduce the official unemployment rate by over 6 percentage points.

5. This was the view expressed by William McChesney Martin of the St. Louis Federal Reserve Bank, as reported in Friedman and Schwartz (1963: 522).

6. This and the section on demobilization draw on Horwich and Bjornstad (1991).

7. By mid-1946 prices were essentially free of controls and reflected with reasonable accuracy the real costs of goods and services. The 1946 level of real balances can therefore also be regarded as accurately measured.

8. Firms, of course, make substantial investments in the training of their personnel and often find that it pays to retain workers throughout the business cycle, avoiding the costs of rehiring and retraining. In view of this, measured productivity per worker will tend to fall with the decline of output in downturns, when the work force is above the short-run optimum, and rise in the subsequent upswing when output expands. On long-term contracts and labor "stockpiling," see Samuel Morley (1979: 45–59).

9. This is the average length of recessions in the post–World War II period. See U.S. Department of Commerce (1987: 104).

10. Author's worksheets are available on request. The relevant time series can also be expressed as the ratio of real wages to average labor productivity: letting w be the money wage rate and N the level of employment, the ratio of real wages (w/P) to average labor productivity (Q/N) reduces to wN/PQ, which is labor's share of the national product.

11. The earliest clear statement of the supply-side nature of an oil-supply disruption is by Phelps (1975: 53). See also Phelps (1978.) It is possible, and indeed probable, that the oil shocks will cause investment to decline in the sense of a schedule shift. In response, AD itself would shift to the left. There is no indication, however, that any such shift of AD, which exerts downward pressure on the price level, was as great as the leftward shift of AS, which raises prices and was unquestionably the dominant shift in 1973–1974 and 1979–1980.

12. Phelps (1975: 52) also criticizes the assertion.

13. The Carter CEA (CEA, 1980: 65) defined gross oil price drag as the "gross value of changes in cost [exceeding the rate of inflation] that users of oil and refined products must pay." Net drag was obtained by subtracting from gross drag expenditures of oil producers on goods in U.S. markets in the same year: an assumed 30 percent of after-tax revenues by domestic producers and 20 percent by foreign producers (spent on U.S. exports). On this procedure, the CEA estimated drag for 1979 at 2.1 percent of GNP and projected it at 3 percent for 1980. An alternative measurement of drag based on the actual balance sheets and income statements of U.S. oil companies, and the assumption, following the CEA, that foreign oil companies spend only 20 percent of their receipts on U.S. exports of goods in the current year, yielded much lower estimates for 1973, 1974, 1979, and 1980: 0.83, 1.86, 1.39, and 0.45 percent of GNP. See Horwich and Weimer (1984: 29–30, 152–165, 200–13).

14. Simulations by John Tatom (1981) of the St. Louis Federal Reserve Bank and Mork and Hall (1980), employing versions of the aggregate supply-demand framework, attribute one-fifth to one-fourth of the measured inflations to the rise in energy prices. But that fraction does not necessarily capture the full extent of the resource reallocation ultimately imposed by the oil shocks.

15. The 1970s and the early 1930s are alike in that both experienced leftward drifting AS schedules—the 1970s because of the oil shocks and the 1930s probably as a result of the adjustments described by Bernstein (1987). Both decades also suffered policy-induced leftward shifts of demand, which, in the 1930s but not the 1970s, were dominant. The Carter CEA, however, fully expected oil price drag to mushroom and create a deficiency of demand that would be the major consequence of the oil shocks. See the next section.

16. The desire to retain or impose oil price ceilings in a disruption in order to stave off oil price drag is made explicit in numerous contemporaneous CEA memoranda and correspondence. For example, a memorandum of April 21, 1980, from George Eads, a member of the CEA, to various OMB, DOE, and White House staff personnel asserts: "the potential for oil price drag would be reduced with coupons" (p. 14), "Using a new currency [i.e., rationing coupons] automatically neutralizes much of the effect of potential oil price drag" (p. 20).

17. One possible way to anticipate the impact of expectations on macro behavior is to employ techniques of experimental economics (Smith, 1980), feeding subjects realistic (that is, not necessarily perfectly adjusted) measures of macroeconomic variables such as the federal deficit, the price level, the stock of money, the rate of unemployment, and the Commerce Department's index of leading indicators. There is, moreover, no reason to limit the analysis of macropolicies to the aggregate supply and demand framework. Growth models, for example, may be more appropriate for analyzing longer-run phenomena, such as the rate of saving or the ultimate impact of a merchandise trade deficit (see Gordon, 1990).

References

Arrow, K. J., and J. P. Kalt, *Petroleum Price Regulation: Should We Decontrol?* (Washington, D.C.: American Enterprise Institute, 1979).

Bailey, M. J., *National Income and the Price Level* (New York: McGraw-Hill, 1962, 1971).

Bailey, M. J., G. P. Balabanis, G. Tavlas, and M. Ulan, "U.S. Deficits and Interest Rates," manuscript, U.S. Department of State, Office of the Under Secretary of State for Economic Affairs (May 11, 1984).

Barro, R.J., "Are Government Bonds Net Wealth?" *Journal of Political Economy* 82:6 (November–December 1974), 1095–1117.

Barron, J. M., M. A. Loewenstein, and G. J. Lynch, *Macroeconomics* (Reading, Mass.: Addison-Wesley, 1989).

Bernstein, M. A., *The Great Depression* (Cambridge: Cambridge University Press, 1987).

Bohi, D. R., *Energy Price Shocks and Macroeconomic Performance* (Washington, D.C.: Resources for the Future, 1989).

Cagan, P., "The Real Federal Deficit and Financial Markets," *The AEI Economist* (November, 1981).

Copeland, M. A., "How [to] Achieve Full and Stable Employment," *American Economic Review* 34:1 Supplement, Part 2 (March 1944), 134–147.

Council of Economic Advisers, *Economic Report of the President* (Washington, D.C.: Superintendent of Documents, 1974, 1975, 1980).

Curtis, W., *Analysis Memorandum: Macroeconomic Effects of Petroleum Supply Interruptions*, vol. I (DOE/EIA-0102/48/1) (March 1979).

Darby, M. R., "Accounting for the Deficit: An Analysis of Sources of Change in the Federal and Total Government Deficits," Research Paper No. 8704, U.S. Department of Commerce (October 2, 1987).

———, "Three-and-a-Half Million U.S. Employees Have Been Mislaid: Or an Explanation of Unemployment," *Journal of Political Economy* 84:1 (February 1976), 1–16.

Eisner, R., and P. J. Pieper, "How to Make Sense of the Federal Deficit," *The Public Interest* 78 (Winter 1985), 101–118.

Evans, P., "Do Large Deficits Produce High Interest Rates?" *American Economic Review* 75:1 (March 1985), 68–87.

———, "The Effects of General Price Controls in the United States During World War II," *Journal of Political Economy* 90:5 (October 1982), 944–966.

Ford Foundation, *Energy: The Next Twenty Years* (Cambridge, Mass: Balinger, 1979).

Friedman, M., "The Role of Monetary Policy," *American Economic Review* 58:1 (March 1968), 1–17.

Friedman, M., and A. J. Schwartz, *A Monetary History of the United States* (Princeton: Princeton University Press, 1963).

Gordon, R. J., "The Gordon Update," Supplemental Newsletter for Use with Gordon's *Macroeconomics*, Fifth Edition (Spring, 1990).

Hagen, E. E., and N. B. Kirkpatrick, "The National Output at Full Employment in 1950," *American Economic Review* 34:1 (September 1944), 472–500.

Hardy, Charles O., *Credit Policies of the Federal Reserve System* (Washington, D.C.: The Brookings Institution, 1932).

Hendershott, P. H., *The Neutralized Money Stock* (Homewood, Ill.: Richard D. Irwin, Inc., 1968).

Hicks, J. R., "Mr. Keynes and the 'Classics'; A Suggested Interpretation," *Econometrica* 5:2 (April 1937), 147–59.

Horwich, G., "Effective Reserves, Credit, and Causality in the Banking System of the Thirties," in D. Carson (ed.), *Banking and Monetary Studies* (Homewood, Ill.: Richard D. Irwin, Inc., 1963).

────── and D. J. Bjornstad, "Spending and Manpower in Four U.S. Mobilizations—A Macro/Policy Perspective," *Journal of Policy History* 3:2 (Spring 1971), 173–202.

────── and D. L. Weimer, eds. *Responding to International Oil Crises* (Washington, D.C.: American Enterprise Institute, 1988).

──────, *Oil Price Shocks, Market Response, and Contingency Planning* (Washington, D.C.: American Enterprise Institute, 1984).

Hume, D., *Writings on Economics*, ed. E. Rotwein (Madison: University of Wisconsin Press, 1955).

Keynes, J. M., *A Treatise on Money*, vols. I and II (London: Macmillan & Co., Ltd., 1950).

──────, *The General Theory of Employment, Interest and Money* (New York: Harcourt, Brace & Co., 1936).

Kindleberger, C. P., *The World in Depression* (Berkeley: University of California Press, 1986).

Kormendi, R. C., "Government Debt, Government Spending, and Private Sector Behavior," *American Economic Review* 73:5 (December 1983), 994–1010.

Mankiw, N. G., "Recent Developments in Macroeconomics: A Very Quick Refresher Course," *Journal of Money, Credit, and Banking* 20:3 Part II (August 1988), 436–449.

Marschak, J., *Income, Employment, and the Price Level* (New York: Augustus M. Kelley, Inc., 1951).

Mork, K. A., and R. E. Hall, "Energy Prices, Inflation, and Recession, 1974–75," *The Energy Journal* 1:3 (July 1980), 31–63.

Morley, S. A., *Inflation and Unemployment* (Hinsdale, Ill.: Dryden Press, 1979).

Perry, G. L., "The Success of Anti-Inflation Policies in the United States," *Journal of Money, Credit, and Banking* 5:1 Part II (February 1973), 569–593.

Phelps, E. S., "Commodity-Supply Shock and Full-Employment Monetary Policy," *Journal of Money, Credit, and Banking* 10:2 (May 1978), 206–221.

──────, "Stopover Monetarism: Supply and Demand Factors in the 1972–74 Inflation," *The Japan-U.S. Assembly* (Washington, D.C.: American Enterprise Institute, 1975), pp. 51–68.

──────, "Money Wage Dynamics and Labor Market Equilibrium," *Journal of Political Economy* 76:4 (August 1968), 687–711.

Phillips, A. W., "The Relation Between Unemployment and the Rate of Change of Money Wage Rates in the U.K., 1861–1957," *Economica* 25 N.S. (November 1958), 283–299.

Phillips, C. A., *Bank Credit* (New York: Macmillan and Co, 1921).

Smith, V. L., "Relevance of Laboratory Experiments to Testing Resource Allocation Theory," in J. Kmenta and J. Ramsey, eds., *Evaluating Econometric Models* (New York: Academic Press, 1980).

Stein, H., *Presidential Economics* (New York: Simon and Schuster, 1984).

Tatom, J. A., "A Perspective on the Federal Deficit Problem," *Federal Reserve Bank of St. Louis Review* (June–July 1984), 5–17.

————, "Energy Prices and Short-Run Economic Performance," *Federal Reserve Bank of St. Louis Review* (January 1981), 3–17.

U.S. Department of Commerce, Bureau of the Census, *Historical Statistics of the United States: Colonial Times to 1970*, Part I (Washington, D.C.: Superintendent of Documents, 1975).

U.S. Department of Commerce, Bureau of Economic Analysis, *The National Income and Product Accounts 1929–82. Statistical Tables* (Washington, D.C.: Superintendent of Documents, 1986).

U.S. Department of Commerce, Bureau of Economic Analysis, *Business Conditions Digest* (Washington, D.C.: Superintendent of Documents, January 1987).

8 THE NEW TRADE THEORY: IMPLICATIONS FOR POLICY ANALYSIS

John Pomery

1. Overview

Changes in the way economists perceive international trade have led to a greater variety of trade policy prescriptions, each given with muted confidence. A selective sample gives some hint of the diversity. Paul Krugman (1987: 132) puts the case for free trade:

> free trade is not passé, but it is an idea which has irretrievably lost its innocence. Its status has shifted from optimum to reasonable rule of thumb. There is still a case for free trade as a good policy, and as a useful target in the practical world of politics, but it can never again be asserted as the policy that economic theory tells us is always right.

Reviewing a book by Elhanan Helpman and Krugman (1989), Robert Lucas (1990: 666–667) questions the value of this "rule of thumb":

> Helpman and Krugman seem not so much to be defending the validity of what they call the "central economic tenet" of free trade as trying to avoid the blame for being the first to expose its emptiness!

Lucas then goes on to assert that

theory does not provide us a blanket vindication of any single, universally applicable policy conclusion, but it does provide a coherent framework for examining specific policy interventions on their merits, case by case. I think it is a mistake to ask more than this from policy analysis.

Later Lucas concludes, concerning some of the "surprising implications" emerging from the "Smithian" models in the Helpman-Krugman monograph, "They are, I think, outstanding illustrations of why we work to construct useful, explicit theories rather than being content with good rules of thumb."

Robert Baldwin (1989: 132–133) expresses a concern for understanding the political process within which trade policy decisions are made:

> If economists wish their advice to carry more weight in the political process, they must be more willing to examine the influences of institutions and procedures on policies.... If they are to make policy recommendations, economists need better empirical and experimental studies of the economic and political feasibility of well-known policy measures.

Later, in the spirit of Krugman's position, Baldwin remarks:

> Even if further research ... confirms that there are some real world situations where protection would be the best available measure for maximizing social welfare, economists should be very cautious about surrendering the efficiency argument for free trade.

Judith Goldstein and Stephen Krasner (1984: 284–285) have a different emphasis again, focusing on the possibility of using strategic policies to induce greater cooperation among national governments:

> The United States is in an ideal position to play Tit for Tat because of its large domestic market, provided that both parties are clear about the values in the matrix and the classification of behaviour as cooperation (fair) and defection (unfair).... The defense of liberalism by the most liberal solution to trade distortions has not worked in practice for it does not work in theory. The United States should meet protectionism in kind. We *cannot* defend liberalism unilaterally; without pressure, our trading partners *will not* act in accordance with GATT norms. [Emphasis in original.]

Goldstein and Krasner's focus on repeated games echoes a criticism of Lucas (1990: 666) concerning Helpman and Krugman's narrow concern with static, noncooperative models of interaction. Going further into the "political" dimension of the debate, Robert Gilpin (1987: 44–5) asserts:

> As a means to understand society and especially its dynamics, economics is limited; it cannot serve as a comprehensive approach to political economy. ... The first of these limitations is that economics artificially separates the

economy from other aspects of society and accepts the existing sociopolitical framework as given, including the distribution of power and property rights; resource and other endowments of individuals, groups, and national societies; and the framework of social, political, and cultural institutions. The liberal world is viewed as one of homogeneous, rational, and equal individuals living in a world free from political boundaries and social constraints.

Jagdish Bhagwati (1988: 17), almost anticipating a Gilpin-style criticism, adopts a broader view (for most economists) of the policy arena:

> Profound commitments to policies are generally due to a mix of ideological factors (in the form of ideas and example), interests (as defined by politics and economics), and institutions (as they shape constraints and opportunities).

Bhagwati (1988: xiii), perhaps even more so than Baldwin or Krugman, has no doubt as to where the enemy is:

> To assist the hand of history, so that it does not falter, we will have to reform and strengthen the institutional framework, national and international, to harness these pro-trade interests and contain the forces of protectionism more effectively.

These quotes are selective but not unrepresentative of differing perspectives found in the literature. This chapter will argue that the heterogeneous views of economists concerning the appropriate trade policy are not, to any significant extent, empirical issues or normative issues. Rather they reflect more basic opinions about the interaction of theory, empirics, and policy. In a way, the difficulty arises from our tendency to seek unambiguous policy conclusions from economic science. Such unambiguity would seem to require a strong form of "foundationalism," but the message from philosophers for the past half-century has been that we cannot locate a satisfactory foundationalist philosophy. For this reason, the ambivalence about trade policy, which Lucas so keenly identifies, holds not only between economists but seems to have a hold on many individuals. There is a temptation to be pulled a little way toward each of the views already outlined. The goal here is not to resolve the debate concerning trade policy but instead to argue that much of the discussion is at cross purposes and that the attempt to resolve the debate is in itself partially misconceived.

The ambivalence in the policy debate can be summarized in simple fashion, as partially captured by the previous quotes. A large number, possibly the majority, of economists seem committed to the view that free trade is the desired policy stance, at least as a "rule of thumb." Recent advances in trade theory, incorporating models of imperfect competition, have cast increased doubt as to the relevance of such a rule of thumb.

Many of the models of imperfect competition of the last decade do not invite a laissez-faire approach to trade policy. Furthermore, the properties of these models tend to be very sensitive to apparently minor changes in specification, thus raising a suspicion that there can be no general "rule of thumb" for trade policy in an imperfectly competitive environment.

The situation is further clouded by the parallel development of classes of models, involving (for example) strategic policy interaction between national governments or explicit roles for domestic interest groups, where the model *endogenously* predicts trade policy for each country. In such models it is not clear where an *exogenous* policy recommendation gains its leverage to alter behavior. In a related, but always interconnected literature, specialists in political and economic dimensions of international relations use a different language, not immediately commensurate with that of many economists.

To these concerns should be added the observation that, despite the persistence of academic advocacy of free trade, the level of trade barriers (particularly nontariff barriers) seems to remain obstinately high. Also add considerable debate as to the appropriate way to compare and interpret, for example, the recent histories of the U.S. and Japanese economies: Is the more rapid Japanese growth sustainable? Does it constitute a case for more active industrial policy? And, if so, can the experience be translated to the United States? The comparison with Japan has to be melded with interpretation of recent experiences in Eastern Europe, and of the comparative track records of export-oriented newly industrialized countries compared to other developing countries. These latter data can be interpreted as offering presumptive evidence of the value of liberal, market-oriented policies with respect to trade and other aspects of resource allocation.

With all this as background, even the staunchest advocates of free trade are not completely confident, nor in unity, about the basis for, or the extent of relevance of, their advocacy. A significant minority in the debate wonder whether it is time to abandon the traditional loyalty to free trade once and for all.

2. The Nature of the Dominant Belief in Free Trade

For many years, mainstream economists in the United States have had a strong tendency to be advocates of free trade (at minimum, as a good "rule of thumb"!). Even in the past there have been reservations about the justification of this position in the literature. The impact of the "New

Trade Theory" has been to alter the grounds, and to amplify the extent, of this ambivalence. A discussion of the impact of the New Trade Theory on policy debates should consider the reasons for the earlier ambivalence and the ways in which recent theoretical developments have altered the situation.

The case for free trade originates with the study of the international economy as a system of perfectly competitive markets. The simple text-book versions of traditional models of international trade (such as the basic Ricardian or Heckscher-Ohlin models) assume price-taking behavior by the private sector, free entry and exit, constant returns to scale in pro-duction, fixed supplies of "nation-specific" factors of production, no nonpecuniary externalities (that is, complete markets), no uncertainty, no intertemporal effects, no transportation costs, and more. In this environ-ment, free trade is efficient for the world as a whole (relative to the assumption of nation-specific factors) and leaves each country being at least as well off as it would be under autarky (the absence of international trade).

That the country as a whole benefits from trade does not imply that everyone in the country will be better off from free trade than from autarky. As relative prices alter in the move between autarky and free trade, income redistributes between the net buyers and the net sellers of a good within a country. In particular there is a presumption that the net sellers of goods (or factors of production), which become less scarce as a result of the opportunity to trade in international markets, will be hurt by the change in relative prices. What might be termed "the surplus revenue result" says that, given a world price different from national autarkic price and given the ability to substitute in production or consumption, it is possible at world prices under free trade to allocate each individual in a nation enough revenue to leave him or her as well off as at autarky, and for the nation to have additional revenue left over (Alan Woodland, 1982: sec. 9.2; Wilfred Ethier, 1988: app. J). In this sense, the winners in the move from autarky to free trade are capable of compensating the losers so that everyone is better off than at autarky—although whether such compensa-tion takes place is another matter.

There are two traditional qualifications to the argument for free trade. First, the *optimal tariff argument* is basically an argument for exertion of market power by the tariff-imposing country (John Pomery, 1987). From the *national* viewpoint, an optimizing country should equalize its trade-off in consumption (the marginal rate of substitution in consumption), in production (the marginal rate of product transformation), and in trade. The world price represents the *average* rate of transformation through trade and is not equal to the *marginal* rate[1] unless the country has no power to influence price in world markets. If it does possess such power, and if it can assume that the rest of the world will not retaliate, the marginal rate of transformation through trade is given by the slope of the foreign offer curve. The optimal tariff requires the country to reduce its own volume of trade (in response to the tariff) so that the market-clearing equilibrium shifts around the rest of the world's offer curve until that offer curve is just tangent to the highest attainable trade indifference curve for the tariff-imposing country.

Second, an argument for trade intervention arises in the case of *domestic market distortions*. For example, suppose there is a minimum wage constraint in a Heckscher-Ohlin economy, such that a low relative price of the labor-intensive good triggers the minimum wage constraint and leads to unemployment. Autarky can occur at full employment while free trade leads to a fall in the price of the labor-intensive good and to a dramatic surge in unemployment. In this case, autarky could be better than free trade for the nation as a whole, and a prohibitive tariff, which takes the country back to autarky, would be better than free trade (Brecher, 1974). With such claims of distortions in domestic resource allocation, it is desirable to counter the distortion as close to the source as possible. A wage subsidy would put the country back on its undistorted production possibility frontier and lead to free trade which is superior to autarky. Thus for policy recommendations it is important to identify which policy alternatives are feasible and, among those, which works most directly at the source of distortion. (At an even more basic level, our underlying philosophy of science may influence what is to count as a "genuine" externality.)

Nevertheless, the traditional advocacy of free trade had an apparently strong foundation arising from the efficiency properties of free trade in a world of perfectly competitive markets. Perfect competition had an entrenched "benchmark" status for empirics, theory, and policy, although qualifications to the intuition of a world of a complete set of perfectly competitive markets were clearly understood.[2] For example, economists were well aware of the optimum tariff argument, but they tended to view it as of limited importance because of its implications for global efficiency, the likelihood of retaliation, and even its lack of an appropriate moral commitment. Economists were also aware of the central implication of second-best theory, namely, that first-best policies may not be optimal in the presence of existing distortions (Bhagwati, 1971). The possibility that certain interest groups, such as labor or capital, might prefer restricted trade to free trade was firmly emphasized by Wolfgang Stolper and Paul Samuelson (1941).[3] Harry Johnson (1953–54) had shown that it was possible for one country to benefit from a tariff war.

Advocacy of free trade was not predicated on ignorance of possible counterexamples nor on a presupposition that free trade reflected the narrow self-interests of all participants in the global economy. Rather, it seemed to arise from a combination of beliefs that it was appropriate, as a first approximation descriptively, to treat the world economy as a system of perfectly competitive markets and that the goal of free trade, with its efficiency properties given the perfectly competitive description of the world, was, normatively, an appropriate ideal.[4]

There was also the ever-present concern among those interested in policy that any admission that free trade was not the appropriate policy would be seized by special interests or the economically illiterate and used to subvert the efficiency of global resource allocation. The knowledge that trade taxes or subsidies were often not the most appropriate form of intervention, and the prominence of "fallacious arguments" for trade barriers, gave added strength to this concern.

3. Newer Perspectives on Trade

The results and implications outlined in the previous section were largely understood 20 or 30 years ago (although the depth of our understanding or the manner of presenting results often has been modified by subsequent developments). There is some ambiguity over the extent of the more recent changes. One possible interpretation of the significance of the changes in the perspectives of international economists is that the profession is on the brink of totally abandoning the perfectly competitive view of international trade. A more conservative interpretation treats the recent developments as leading to greatly increased emphasis on the exceptions and qualifications of the free trade argument while still preserving the central insights of the perfectly-competitive view. Thus the changes can be viewed *either* as fairly revolutionary *or* as a significant shift in emphasis while conserving the original framework. At the same time, sensitivity to the potential endogeneity of policy decisions, and to the conspicuous failure of policy-makers to follow the advice of economists, reinforces the suggestion of an urgent need for a greater attempt to describe the political process.

It is not possible here to give an exhaustive list of topics and models that have influenced the way the international economy is viewed, but it is worth touching on some examples. The coverage here is selective; see Ethier (1987) for a more extended treatment.

Consideration of *national* economies of scale (that is, economies of scale determined by the level of output of the national industry and affecting costs only for firms in that nation's industry) introduces the possibility that a country that is led to abandon an industry with increasing returns under free trade can be worse off at free trade than at autarky (Helpman, 1984; Ethier, 1979). If industries with strong national economies of scale are associated with positive economic rents, each national government has an incentive to try to preempt the pattern of world production by subsidizing its own industry. A parallel result is to be expected if there are dynamic learning effects that are specific at the national level.

Consideration of *international* economies of scale (where scale effects depend on the level of world output for the industry and affect costs in all firms in the industry worldwide) gives a different intuition, namely, that countries will receive all the standard gains from trade plus an additional benefit arising from pooling all production in an international industry that creates the scale economies. Though the case of international scale economies is less destructive to the intuitions of traditional trade theory than the case of national scale economies, it does suggest that the international coordination problem is more complicated than envisaged by the models of perfect competition under constant returns to scale.

Models of imperfect competition, and particularly of international oligopolies, also undercut any narrow intuition from perfect competition. Cournot oligopolists fail to set price equal to marginal cost (except in the limit), and so introduce a domestic distortion. They also achieve economic rents in foreign markets. The poor coordination aspects of Cournot oligopolists allow such "strange" phenomena as two-way trade in the same physical commodity, even in the presence of nonzero transportation costs (James Brander, 1981). Moreover, the presence of rents creates a case for increasing national welfare by shifting profits from foreign firms. In an example that has become a standard in the literature (Brander and Spencer, 1985), if two Cournot duopolists from different countries sell in a third country, an export subsidy by the government of one of the firms can lead to capture of profits (in excess of the amount of the subsidy) at the expense of the foreign firm. In traditional perfectly competitive trade theory, export subsidies, when viewed as a potential first-best instrument, tend to expand trade beyond the optimal volume while creating excess supply of the exportable good in the world market. Given the lack of convincing explanation within the perfectly competitive framework about the prevalence of export subsidies, this type of result contributed to increased interest in models of imperfect competition.

The results under imperfect competition have to be used with caution due to lack of robustness of conclusions. For example, the conclusion that adopting export subsidies is in the national interest has to be significantly modified if the producing country whose government intervenes also consumes the good, or if there is more than one producer in that country, or if the duopolists interact through prices rather than quantities (Eaton and Grossman, 1986), or if there are several such duopolistic industries with all the domestic firms drawing on the same fixed pool of factors of production (Dixit and Grossman, 1986). (All this without even considering the impact of repetition, retaliation, or the implications for global efficiency.) In general, situations of imperfect competition may lead to behavior that may look paradoxical to an intuition honed on models of perfect competition (Helpman and Krugman, 1989; Richardson, 1989; Grossman and Richardson, 1985). Trade barriers may lead a "domestic monopolist" to produce more output *or* less output for the domestic market; trade intervention may or may not preempt entry into a global market by foreign rivals; trade intervention may increase or decrease tacit collusion between domestic and foreign firms.

Other areas of economic theory also complicate the possibilities for international trade policy. For example, if the theory of search is applied to national labor markets, another source of externalities is introduced (Davidson, Martin, and Matusz, 1988). The presence of an additional participant on either side of the labor market alters the probabilities of a match, and hence the incentive for search, by all participants. The presence of uncertainly with incomplete markets can also generate externalities (Newbery and Stiglitz, 1981; Grinols, 1987; Dixit, 1987). Such externalities again may give rise to justification for intervention (although not necessarily trade intervention as a first-best policy).

Policy issues have also become hemmed in by the tendency to endogenize the political decision-making process. One of the first hints of the potential importance of this development was given by Anne Krueger's (1974) application of the concept of rent seeking to developing countries. In Krueger's model the presence of an import quota created economic rents; resources shifted from agricultural production to compete for the fixed number of jobs in the distributional sector, generating unemployment such that the expected wage in distribution is equalized to the certain wage in agriculture. Whereas the natural policy recommendation might be to avoid import quotas in the first place (and particularly for a small country), the Krueger application emphasized the possible implications of applying the paradigm of narrow self-interest to political aspects of resource allocation.

Significant work by authors such as Bhagwati (1982) (summarized in the notion of DUP, or directly unproductive profit-seeking activities), Ronald Findlay and Stanislaw Wellisz (1982), Stephen Magee, William Brock, and Leslie Young (1989) (using game-theoretic models of interest groups), and of Wolfgang Mayer (1984) (applying median voter theory) suggested that self-centered actions can lead to socially unfavorable outcomes. It is important to note that these political forms of intervention and redistribution are typically not "first-best" ways to redistribute income. This raises questions about the appropriate policy instruments to model as vehicles for DUP-style activities, and also about the level of "social rationality" that can be expected from the combination of political and economic interaction. (Baldwin, 1989, provides an introduction to a much wider literature concerning government behavior.)

Another strand of endogenization of trade policy arises from treating governments as actors in a game between governments (McMillan, 1986; Bagwell and Staiger, 1990). Typically, each government is assumed to act as representative of national interests (appropriately aggregated) and to optimize given its perception of the intergovernmental game being played (examples include Marie Thursby and Richard Jensen, 1983; Dan Bernhardt and Alice Enders, 1989; John Kennan and Raymond Riezman, 1988). Such models are sensitive to the solution concept used and to the way that perceptions feed into reputations. Equally important, the fact that policies are endogenously determined suggests that any policy recommendation may be irrelevant. (If not, policy advocacy would seem to change the structure of the game.) Policy analysis becomes essentially descriptive.

These game-theoretic models overlap with the literature on international relations. Some of the concepts in the latter literature have natural interpretations in the economists' conversation; for example, "hegemony" has a natural, albeit partial, analog in the familiar concepts of the dominant firm of industrial organization, or the dominant contributor to a public good. On the other hand, discussion of national goals and considerations, such as stability, security, identity, power, or growth (Krasner, 1976; Gilpin, 1987; Rangarajan, 1984), sometimes involves a flavor of "group identity" or "group preferences" or of perceptual relationships that are less individualistic than traditional fare for economists.

4. Changing Perceptions of the International Economy

Over the past two or three decades, many things have changed concerning the international economy. Certainly, the global economy itself has changed in many ways, with increased openness of most economies, decolonialization, lowered real costs of transportation, communication and information processing, areas of deregulation, increased internationalization of financial markets and of the banking system, changes in exchange rate regimes, increased literacy, and more. Economists' knowledge of the international economy has increased: The presence of intraindustry trade, the presence of scale economies, the presence of imperfect competition, the sensitivity of neo-factoral explanations of trade to the description and level of disaggregation of factors are all better understood.

Yet an even more important change has come in how economists tend to perceive perfect competition in relation to other forms of social interaction. The roles of game theory (and certain very special examples such as the one-shot Prisoner's Dilemma), and of applications of game theory to industrial organization and to political behavior that influences the economic system, have altered the way economists think about international trade.

As we have seen, these changes create an awkward situation. Game theoretic models—with oligopolistic firms interacting at the private level, or national governments interacting strategically at the level of trade intervention, or interest groups interacting strategically to influence national governments—seldom led to an unambiguous conclusion that free trade is both attainable and in the best interests of either global efficiency or national welfare. Thus the policy advocacy of free trade is stripped of the implicit support arising from the presumption that the world is essentially a system of perfectly competitive markets.

The awkwardness runs even deeper than the possible failure of the "natural" policy prescription of free trade. In many cases, the answer to the question whether a trade tax or a trade subsidy is a better policy from the national viewpoint is acutely sensitive to the specification of the model. It is no longer obvious that there is any single best policy prescription; rather each situation may have to be evaluated in great detail before any recommendation can be made.

We have identified a third level of difficulty, which arises because models of strategic interactions between governments, or of endogenous optimizing choices by domestic interest groups, suggest that policy decisions are *not* unrestricted choice variables for the purposes of policy advocates but may already be determined by "rational" decisions in realms beyond the narrow market context.

Despite these difficulties, many (but not all) economists are reluctant to abandon the presumption that free trade is the recommendation of first resort. What has changed is less the policy prescription than the confidence with which the prescription is offered, and the grounds used to support the prescription.

Much of what has been said so far should be relatively uncontroversial, albeit highly selective and at times oversimplified. The potential for controversy arises in deriving implications from these changes in modeling the international economy for policy purposes. The range of views is fairly wide. Some economists see a justification for an actively interventionist policy, perhaps coupled with an explicit industrial policy (Brander, 1986). Others deplore the sense of confusion and reaffirm the dominant role of free trade as the preferred policy. Still others welcome the diversity of possibilities implicit in a more eclectic approach, viewing this diversity as a symptom of a richer understanding of the world and as a reflection of the limits of very sweeping policy recommendations, but they warn of the likely limited applicability of some of the less traditional implications of the new theory (Dixit, 1986). Several authors have tried to draw a set of principles out of the literature on imperfect competition, either with an eye to showing the feasibility of a carefully constructed trade policy or with an eye to showing how difficult to implement, and limited in scope, such a policy might be (Brander, 1986; Krugman, 1986: 15–20, give somewhat opposed conclusions). Often there is a plea to be cautious and to await further developments. Other economists suggest a need for increased research into the description of political decision making and the role of lobbies (Baldwin, 1989). At times there is a concern that any abandonment of advocacy of free trade may give comfort to special interest groups (Krugman, 1987; Bhagwati, 1988). There has been some attempt to get empirical estimates of the nature and importance of the various effects, although typically comparing free trade and autarky rather than comparing free trade with trade under selective interventions (Richardson, 1989).

From a more "management-oriented" perspective, the MIT Commission believes it found a role for a much more interventionist policy, based on some perceived successes of the Japanese economy and on some observations on productivity failings of many U.S. firms (Michael Dertouzos et al. 1989; also see William Baumol et al. 1989, where a more traditional perspective for economists is used to invite a less alarming conclusion). From another direction, discussions of international relations by authors with a background in political science seem to assume the almost-complete demise of the perfectly competitive view of international trade and the irrelevance of much of the perspective of liberal economists (Gilpin, 1987: 215).

It would be convenient at this point to pick one of the perspectives found in the literature and to declare it the winner. Such an approach would be satisfying since policy debates, being action-oriented, invite an unequivocal outcome. However, closer inspection suggests doubts whether it is reasonable to expect such a strong conclusion.

For example, if one looks at the defense of free trade as a "rule of thumb" (identified here with such authors as Krugman, Baldwin, and Helpman), it seems clear the there is a market for policy advice in terms of broad rules of thumb and that there is room for legitimate concern about the way interest groups selectively use ideas emanating from academia. At the same time, the extent to which research has drifted from the perfectly competitive paradigm raises doubts as to how weight can be put on such a rule of thumb.

Lucas's view, that we drop rules of thumb and turn to explicit, useful theories seems to be the most "rational" approach. However, as will be discussed later, underlying a Lucas-style position appears to be a commitment to a very heroic view of the philosophy of science.

As we move to broader views of the arena of policy debate, the implicit criticisms of the political economy models and of the multi-faceted views of Bhagwati (not to mention the explicit criticisms of authors such as Gilpin), the expanding domain of "positive" description seems to squeeze out an effective role for policy advocacy.

The remainder of this chapter will raise the following questions: Why are we driven so strongly to seek an unequivocal resolution of policy debates? What reasons are there for believing the policy debates are incapable of complete closure? How does our view of the underlying philosophy of science affect our stance in this policy debate? Why does the policy debate always appear to be pushed back by expanding domains of scientific description? How can we make something constructive out of policy debate that seems to fracture into sometimes overlapping, sometimes competing perspectives?

5. Policy Debate in an Intellectual Environment of Antifoundationalism

The way one describes the current situation in trade theory depends on the philosophy of science that one espouses. For many contemporary economists, it would be natural to consider the debate as a signal of an imminent paradigm shift. As will be explained later, this way of looking at things is probably of limited interest. Instead, the discussion is couched in terms of a clash between "foundationalism" and "antifoundationalism."

In a very crude form, the problem of foundationalism can be summarized as follows: (a) as practical beings, we need to make decisions (about beliefs, actions, values, et cetera); (b) we do not know how to make decisions without introducing "foundational" beliefs to underpin those decisions; (c) all attempts to build a credible position to justify those foundations, whether in mathematics, analytic philosophy, or science, appear to be seriously inadequate; (d) yet we have difficulty making sense of a pure "antifoundationalist" world.[5] The upshot, of about 60 years of debate since the crest of foundationalist thinking, is a curious milieu of foundationalist and antifoundationalist ideas.

As we evaluate alternative positions with respect to trade policy, part of the debate is over the role of scientific models. In turn, our differing conceptions of that role carry different levels of foundationalist presuppositions. One can see the way that an implicit philosophy of science directs our perception of policy issues. For example, writing almost two decades ago, Corden naturally follows a traditional distinction between positive and normative economics.[6]

Such a two-stage procedure suggests that, first, the world is described in a neutral, value-free manner (albeit, following Popper, in a fallible way); then, given the description, a value judgment is imposed as to how the world should be. But an adequate neutral, value-free scientific methodology is precisely what foundationalists have been unable to deliver in this area.[7]

The positive-normative distinction is often accompanied by an emphasis on critical empirical tests. Yet it is not clear whether it is more useful to think in terms of *competing* theories or of *complementary* perspectives. Even simple descriptions tend to be norm-driven. The competing-theories view seems to see the descriptive choice as analogous to choosing between the proposition "It is raining outside" and the proposition "It is not raining outside." Surely we simply look out the window and record the facts?[8] Contrast this decision with the question, "Is this table top flat?" From a very macro perspective, the table top may look smooth and level; within that perspective the table top can legitimately be described as flat. But from a more micro perspective, using say a high-powered microscrope, we would expect the table top to look extremely uneven; within that perspective, the table-top is clearly not flat. Worse still, if we talk to a particle physicist, we may learn that, when the table is conceived as a bunch of elementary particles, we have no way to describe the table top, and indeed there is a sense that, within this perspective, the table top does not exist.

If the question concerning the flatness of the table is a better analogy for policy-relevant descriptions than the question as to whether it is raining outside, description has to be evaluated relative to a perspective. Only if we can find a privileged perspective among the alternatives can we hope to resolve the policy debate unambiguously.[9] (Furthermore, results in social choice theory suggest that our tendency to equivocate over the use of concepts will only exacerbate any barrier to consensus. Consider Graciela

Chichilnisky and Geoffrey Heal [1983], for example, and their focus on the role of common regions of excluded preferences.)

Shifting to a policy prescription involves more than adding a value judgment to pure description; it implies the much stronger claim that the chosen perspective has a privileged status.

To give a simple example, if a particle physicist were to claim that the table is a bunch of neutrons and orbiting electrons such that the table top cannot be defined meaningfully, and *then* used that to conclude that one should not put books on the table, we would rightly regard him (or her) as very confused. The confusion arises because of moving from an assertion that is legitimate within a particular (scientific) perspective to a claim—in this case, an absurd claim—that this has implications outside that perspective. In the example of the table top, the foolishness of this leap is transparent. Yet there seem to be times when economists make an analogous jump without qualms. The moral is that *within*-perspective conclusions cannot automatically be assumed to carry over into the broader realm of policy.

If one drops the emphasis on science as neutral description, it appears more useful to consider the policy prescription process as involving four stages. The first stage is the choice of perspective. The second is a choice of description within that perspective. The third is an assertion of how the world *should* be, given the perspective-driven description. The fourth step, for effective policy prescription, is an assertion of how the world *could* be. Notice that whereas empirical testing occurs at the second stage, much of the policy thrust will come from the first stage; for economists with a strong foundationalist outlook, however, the two steps tend to be compressed into one. Under a simple positive-normative dichotomy, there are only two steps: the combined first step and the value judgment entering at stage three.

Even though there will always be a role for additional data, the issues involved in the current trade policy debate are less empirical or normative in the traditional sense. The disagreements come in terms of the significance of the observed data and of the various formal models, that is, a difference driven by choice of perspective, *and* (in part) by implications concerning the effectiveness of changing the system.[10]

6. Possible Ways Out?

The previous section, though necessarily briefly stated, should raise serious doubts about whether a closure of policy debates is possible. It was suggested that to think of the current debate as a potential paradigm shift is not very helpful. Not only does ambiguity over the scope of a paradigm leave the question hard to resolve, but the confusions in the current debate are not to be resolved simply by switching paradigms. From the point of view of a practitioner of normal science, the notion of paradigm is conservative and protective, even though for a "scientific revolutionary" it may appear to have radical connotations. The danger of characterizing the shift in the policy debate as a paradigm shift is that the "within-paradigm" myopia may simply reappear in a new context. The problem is not just *which* paradigm to use (however the boundaries of a paradigm are defined), but how to use information acquired within any given paradigm.

It seems that the problem of finding a balance between what lies within a perspective and what lies outside is at the heart of the policy debate. Before turning to that topic, the discussion turns to a line that may, in the long run, be a false avenue for resolving the policy debate.

There is a strong temptation to believe that expansion in the knowledge base of economists will, by increasing their power of description (and, hopefully, prediction), result in unambiguous policy conclusions. If the problem were simply one of inadequate description, this might work. Yet, to the extent that the difficulties arise from the constraints imposed by partially conflicting and partially overlapping perspectives, and to the extent that these are inevitable constraints in a process characterized by abstraction and conceptualization, descriptive progress within any given perspective will not be sufficient.

This issue, of the power of improved description to resolve policy disputes, is particularly important because of the role of repeated games in the current thinking of economists. Thus Lucas' (1990) querying of Helpman and Krugman's focus on static non-cooperative models of interaction seems to carry with it a suggestion that a broader approach, possibly allowing more cooperative outcomes, would be more insightful. Authors such as Goldstein and Krasner (1984) emphasize the role of repeated games, and of particular strategies within those games, to influence outcomes.

If there is any hope for a "better description" of the trade arena, it would seem to come from repeated games. There are a number of reasons for being extremely cautions in expecting unequivocal policy pronouncements from this kind of analysis. It is hard to know which game we should focus on or, more accurately, how we should abstract from the world to obtain a well-defined game. Do we focus on interactions between national governments? Do we include interactions between interest groups and governments? Do we include military-type links between countries that may influence the application of trade policies? Do we include the way that social factors, such as education, religious beliefs, family structure, and the like, feed into perceptions of how individuals fit into their economic and political system? Any notion that there is, out there in the "real world," *the* correct repeated game just waiting to be discovered seems a hopelessly heroic leap of faith.

Although repeated games promise to add major insights to the way economists interpret the world, they also have potential weaknesses. Within the perspective of repeated games, it is well known that "almost anything" can be a possible outcome and that attempts to refine solution concepts have not succeeded in clarifying the possibilities as unequivocally as might be hoped (Ledyard, 1986). "Outside" the perspective of repeated games seems to be a deeper problem, namely, whether situations can be constrained to be viewed as repeated games without any loss of generality. (One might note the "foundationalist" aspects of John Harsanyi's (1967–1968) ingenious, and path-breaking, method of dealing with this issue.) Thus one would expect to see weaknesses emerging in any "game-theoretic paradigm" (however defined), just as are found now in the "perfectly-competitive paradigm"; equivocation within the paradigm and inability to think of what may lie outside the paradigm may just reinstate confusion.

7. A Bottom Line?

Thus, while one might naturally hope that the ambivalence exhibited in the trade policy debate will be resolved by increased knowledge, to the extent that the ambivalence emanates in part from the process of conceptualization and abstraction, one is likely to be disappointed. Equivocal use of concepts, differing perspectives, and underlying that, different beliefs about the role of economic models, all should act as barriers to consensus.

Perhaps the best move, not to resolving the debate but to making it more productive, is to recognize the different presuppositions we bring to the debate—and the different conversations in which we think we are involved.[11] And a first step may be to discuss more carefully the distinction between what lies within a perspective and what lies outside it, and why this matters.

One place where the distinction plays a role is in a clear trend for a shift in focus for the "leverage" of policy. Twenty-five years ago the political system was viewed as essentially disjoint from economists' explanatory domain. Since then, economists have devoted much effort to bringing both the political system and aspects of information within the bounds of economic description. By endogenizing these channels for policy leverage, prescient authors, such as Bhagwati (1988), have been forced to bring into the discussion the notions of ideologies, ideas, and institutions.

Policy analysis suffers a parallel problem to that of philosophy. In philosophy, once an area becomes clarified and well defined, it is likely to be spun off into a separate discipline; as a consequence philosophy is left with its most intractable problems. In policy analysis, if a channel (such as the political system) is a particularly effective way to alter behavior, it is likely to be considered as another locus of optimizing behavior. But once the channel has been endogenized within a model, questions arise as to how, within the perspective of *that* model, it can be simultaneously assumed that policy advocacy can alter behavior through the channel. The move to endogenize both political behavior and information acquisition has indeed pushed potential policy "leverage points" to areas such as ideology, ideas, and institutions.

The tendency of economists to expand the domain of economics leaves some awkward questions. One might argue that the progress of natural science should not be viewed as one of unqualified expansion; though the natural sciences have tended to increase the number of applications and the extent of their "within-discipline" understanding, that progress has sometimes been accompanied by a narrowing of the goals of the discipline in terms of the questions the discipline views as within its purview. Thus while one would expect economists to find insightful things to say about what were once "noneconomic areas," such as political decisions or institutional design, progress in economics may also entail a narrowing of the objectives of the science. Any such narrowing clearly has implications for policy advocacy because it invites questions as to how the perspectives of economists fit with perspectives that lie outside the discipline. Moreover, the trend to moving potential policy channels within the domain of economics suggests a possible limiting outcome: If economics is the study of conditioned behavior (in terms of optimization subject to constraints and to the incentives implied by those constraints), the complete dominance of such economic analysis would imply the only way policy changes could be effected is by *unconditional* changes in people's beliefs, perceptions, preferences, or the like. We are reminded that, although within the perspective of such a science there would be no role for "moral (or unconditional) behavior," it could play a dominant role in policy debates.

Put another way, what is missing from a model, or theory, may be as important as what is included. Traditionally, the way to present a model is to list its assumptions. (What else can one do?) However, from a policy perspective this may be inadequate. It is impossible to understand the significance of assumptions without knowing not only what is assumed, but what is excluded. Indeed it is arguable that, from the point of view of a policy-maker, what the model cannot comprehend may be crucial in terms of evaluating the usefulness of the policy prescription.

All this suggests that we focus on what is inside each policy advocate's perspective, what is outside it, and how the advocate views the relation between the inside and the outside. Rather than view the foundationalist approach as an algorithm for rational decision making, it may be more helpful to view it as a way of understanding how stringent are the requirements for achieving consensus—even in the scientific arena. To bring some order to the debate, it is useful to recognize the nature of the conversation that each author is involved in. For example, Helpman and Krugman, along with many other economists, are involved in a conversation where it is accepted that policy pronouncements of economists are potential influences on special interest groups and that this is a relevant consideration. Underlying this is a view of the theory-empirics-policy nexus that assumes that, in order to discuss policy, one must move back somewhat from the narrow focus of the theory. (At the same time, they do not move back enough to introduce concerns about whether the presence of special interest groups may make moot the whole discussion of optimal policy, either at the national or the global level. They certainly do not go as "far back" as Bhagwati does in his monograph, nor as far back as some of the authors of the 1940s and early 1950s, who allowed themselves the luxury of talking of a moral dimension to trade policy.)

Lucas is clearly not in the same conversation. For example, for him, there is a strong distinction between what is learned from economic theory and personal stances about how one expresses one's opinions before the general public. There is no doubt that the difference between Lucas, on the one hand, and Helpman and Krugman, on the other, is driven largely by a different perception of the role of economic theory. Whether one could flesh out Lucas's view of science without resorting to "rules of thumb" is an open question. Moreover, with such a "hard-line" conception of economic theory, one wonders how policy analysis can (or is intended to) break free of mere description and what criterion is used to determine which theories are useful—and for what purposes. This view is so focused on being "inside" economics that there seems to be no place for policy to get leverage.

Baldwin, to take another example, seems to be advocating expanding the boundaries of economics to include modeling of the political system. Baldwin is more clearly trying to stand both inside the broader conception of economics (by modeling and testing political behavior in relation to trade policy) and outside economics (by asserting a role for policy advocacy despite this endogenization of the political mechanism). This seems again a different conversation from that of Helpman and Krugman (who do not focus on this dimension of decision making) and of Lucas (who seems determined to avoid acknowledging anything of value "outside" economics).

Goldstein and Krasner emphasize the lack of commitment to liberal trade policies among U.S. trading partners and the value of a U.S. strategy to induce more cooperative behavior by the rest of the world. Although the "inside" of their perspective seems broader in some ways than that of Helpman and Krugman or of Lucas, it carries the twin presumptions that liberal trade is the appropriate goal and that the U.S. internal political structure would permit a well-defined, and well-oriented, tit-for-tat policy. Again, a different conversation, and again a case where what is "outside" the perspective seems as important as what is inside.

One can read "moral crusades" in many of the writings. Both Helpman and Krugman and Baldwin, not to mention Bhagwati, are fighting to keep the faith in free trade as the presumptive, or default, policy. Lucas' implicit crusade seems to involve keeping the faith in a philosophy of science that allows theory to be given a privileged status, compared to mere personal stances and other subjective aspects of the policy-making environment. Crusades are usually about rules, about perceiving the world "in the right way." And rules are notoriously hard to evaluate, in part because of the difficulty of locating a correct perspective from which to do the evaluation.

One way to understand the wedge between Lucas on the one hand, and Helpman, Krugman, Baldwin, and Bhagwati on the other, is that Lucas conceives a world where each case can (costlessly, neutrally, and unambiguously) be evaluated on its merits, whereas the others have a picture of a more constrained situation. In other words, it is not (just) different perceptions of the international economy, but different perceptions of the way the international economy is evaluated, that are affecting the policy stances. Obtaining a consensus on policy involves not just an empirical and a normative consensus, but deeper levels of consensus too.

This chapter has argued that the absence of an adequate theory of empirical confirmation (or verification, or refutation), which allows us to get beyond the theory being tested, implies that policy debates are rarely going to be resolved purely by more information. Stepping back outside the theory can be done in a relative sense, but not (in an antifoundationalist world) to the point of allowing a neutral starting point. Leaving the debate to be characterized as a battle over a paradigm shift ignores the balance between the "inside" and the "outside" of alternative perspectives. Philosophers are seeking to develop a workable theory of ideas related to our notion of being inside versus outside a theory or a perspective; but it is unclear that there is a way to reconcile completely the conflicting demands on such a theory (Nicholas Rescher, 1985; Thomas Nagel, 1986; Hilary Putnam, 1987).

In a sense we have been exploring the bite of the conflict between a desire to be practical and effective and the desire to be neutral and free of cultural contingency. Policy needs pull us toward seeking an unambiguous policy stance. Practicality requires we adopt a particular position and hence (at least temporarily) ignore the unquestioned presuppositions. If we could find acceptable foundations in which to ground our knowledge, there would be no conflict between being practical and being neutral; unfortunately no one has a watertight foundationalist position, and even anti-foundationalists are unsure how to proceed without foundations. If we appeal to communal consensus as a substitute source of grounding, we need to be aware of the "bias" implicit in the presuppositions of the community.

It is often suggested that we can do no better than allow the experts to make the decisions. But if we look, for example, at the conflict between Lucas and Helpman and Krugman, both sides have claims to expert status. Neither empirical criteria, nor logical criteria, nor expertise may be sufficient to adjudicate between alternative policy recommendations. In addition, we should remember that expertise brings with it not only positive connotations of skills and communal respect but also negative connotations of self-interest and selective myopia. (For a gentle suggestion of such a role for self-interest, see Robert Solow [1988]; Rom Harré [1986] gives a very different emphasis. The potential ubiquity of network externalities in the market for ideas raises doubts about the efficacy of competitive forces as an antidote to self-interest; John Haltiwanger and Michael Waldman [1985] and Michael Katz and Carl Shapiro [1986].) There is also a suspicion that many policy pronouncements of economists reflect in significant part the presuppositions of their "world-view," while claiming the cloak of scientific respectability in terms of empirical accountability.

It would be nice to unveil a bottom line to the discussion. However, there should be enough evidence so far to suggest that the cost of achieving any bottom line is to ignore some potentially important aspects of the situation. There is no useful sense in which to talk about an unambiguous trade policy, and there are good reasons to expect failure of closure in such a debate. The trade policy debate seems to have some of the flavor of an argument, as to whether the table top is flat, between proponents of different perspectives. The stances in the debate are driven largely by differences in perspective, both immediate differences about how best to view the international economy and by more indirect differences about what we learn from economic models and how this learning feeds into policy discussion.

In essence, economists resolve the "foundationalist dilemma" by exiting with some, at least temporarily, unchallenged presupposition. But different economists choose different points of exit. Foundationalist issues occur at multiple levels: the basis for decisions of economic agents within the model; the basis for choosing one model over another; the basis for interpreting what we learn from the chosen model and how it is to be seen in the policy setting. Not surprisingly, it is hard to reach a consensus, and tendencies toward consensus seem to reflect common presuppositions above all else.

It may be time to recognize that trade policy operates in an environment that cannot usefully be comprehended within a single perspective. A broadly defined paradigm is likely to result in equivocal, and still blinkered, recommendations, whereas a narrowly defined paradigm seems certain to miss important dimensions of the situation. Our foundationalist heritage leaves us prone to two forms of questionable belief. One belief is that, if our descriptive abilities are refined enough, then the policy debate can be closed. The other belief is that, if we analyze our different presuppositions, we can fully understand each other and can agree to disagree. Both these beliefs, one is tempted to call them "mirages," seem to require stronger foundations than can reasonably be assumed. While we should continue to seek better descriptions (however we choose to define "better") and greater understanding of the presuppositions of various competing advocates, nevertheless the "trade policy conversation" is likely to go on, and on, and on . . .

Notes

1. As always, "marginal" is defined relative to the perceptions of the decision maker. If our philosophy of science allowed us to believe that we can describe the world objectively, that is, in some sense as it "really is," we would note that these perceptions may be mistaken. However, as will be argued later, it is not clear that we can achieve the required objectivity.

2. In this respect, Krugman's talk, of free trade having lost its innocence in the light of recent developments, seems a trifle heroic in its interpretation of the situation of the 1950s and 1960s. Max Corden (1974: 7–8) has a cautionary approach: "Theory is vital, but it is not enough. Theory does not 'say'—as is often asserted by the ill-informed or the badly taught—that 'free trade is best.' It says that, *given certain assumptions*, it is 'best.'" (Emphasis in original.)

3. The prepublication history of this article gives a fascinating insight into some of the norms of the profession 50 years ago.

4. These beliefs were probably reinforced by a number of considerations. The development of proofs of optimality and existence of abstract general equilibrium models of complete sets of perfectly competitive markets paralleled the growth of formal models of international trade and suggested the intellectual respectability of competitive models of trade. (See McKenzie, 1954, for example.) The central descriptive issue, the pattern of trade, appeared to be handled in a robust way by focusing on the role of competitive markets. Major alternatives to models of perfectly competitive markets were viewed at that time as either essentially disjoint approaches (as with Keynesian macroeconomic models) or as dominated by the capabilities of an ideal market system (as with centrally planned command economies).

5. See Evan Simpson (1987) for a good discussion of some of the current debate between "foundationalists" and "antifoundationalists". Richard Bernstein (1983) gives a flavor of the issues at stake, while Alfred MacKay (1980: 112–117) gives an account of the type of impossibility theorem that drives the problem.

6. See Corden (1974: 5–8). As noted in an earlier quote from this text, Corden rightly—given his positive-normative dichotomy—emphasizes the contingent nature of policy prescriptions.

7. Here we are talking not just of the rapid demise of verificationism, and the weaknesses of refutationism as emphasized by Thomas Kuhn (1970). Even one of the stronger hopes of the foundationalist tradition in the philosophy of science, namely the confirmation criterion espoused, for example, by Clark Glymour (1980), is still an incompletely developed theory of confirmation and, more importantly, aspires at best to provide a criterion of confirmation *within a theory*.

8. Even this example is not as simple as to looks. There should be little doubt that, had human physiology been different so that, for example, any contact between drops of rain and the human skin were fatal, our criterion for deciding whether it is, or is not, raining would be much different, and far more refined, than it is now.

9. This may explain some of the strong feelings concerning foundationalism in the economics profession. On a perspectival view, the assertion that there is a privileged, neutral description of the phenomena under observation amounts to a claim that there is only one "correct" perspective to adopt. How do we locate that correct perspective? Maybe from critical empirical tests that distinguish between competing hypotheses. But this is exactly what the foundationalists have failed to deliver in the philosophy of science, a criterion that discriminates between different perspectives in a neutral way. At best we can seek confirmation within a theory, not in any absolute sense. As a consequence, from a "nonfoundationalist" perspective, the committed foundationalist seems to have introduced a spurious sense of objectivity into the discussion, while to the committed foundationalist, his or her critics simply don't understand the nature of "good science."

10. A concern with a position such as that of Lucas (1990) would be whether one can flesh out the notion of "useful, explicit theories" (and other implicit commitments, concerning the philosophy of science, made by Lucas) in a way that meets criticisms from an antifoundationalist perspective. An instrumentalist interpretation would still leave a question as to *which* useful, explicit theories should be accessed for policy recommendations. On the other hand, turning to a strong critic of traditional Western philosophy such as Richard Rorty (1989) has its own set of problems; see, for example, the discussions of Rorty's position in Simpson (1987).

11. The (related) issues of incommensurability and of indeterminacy of translation have a major place in twentieth-century philosophy. Donald Davidson (1984) makes an argument that the notion of a conceptual scheme, so central to relativistic approaches, is incoherent because we do, in fact, communicate to some extent—and this would not be possible with

entirely distinct conceptual schemes. Nonetheless, given the fluidity of concepts envisaged in the later works of Ludwig Wittgenstein (1958), there seems little doubt we can get at cross purposes without always being aware of it. (The contrast between the later Wittgenstein and his earlier works [see Wittgenstein, 1974] seems to capture well the tension between anti-foundationalist and foundationalist views of philosophy.)

References

Bagwell, Kyle, and Robert W. Staiger, "A Theory of Managed Trade," *The American Economic Review*, 80:4 (September 1990), 779–795.

Baldwin, Robert E., "The Political Economy of Trade Protection," *The Journal of Economic Perspectives*, 3:4 (Fall 1989), 119–135.

Baumol, William J., Sue Anne Batey Blackman, and Edward N. Wolff, *Productivity and American Leadership: The Long View* (Cambridge, Mass.: The MIT Press, 1989).

Bernhardt, Dan, and Alice Enders, "Free Trade Equilibria to Multi-Country Quota Games," *Journal of International Economics* 27:3/4 (November 1989), 319–333.

Bernstein, Richard J., *Beyond Objectivism and Relativism* (Philadelphia: University of Pennsylvania Press, 1983).

Bhagwati, Jagdish, *Protectionism* (Cambridge, Mass.: The MIT Press, 1988).

———, "Directly Unproductive, Profit-Seeking (DUP) Activities," *Journal of Political Economy* 90:5 (October 1982), 988–1002.

———, "The Generalized Theory of Distortions and Welfare," in Jagdish N. Bhagwati, Ronald W. Jones, Robert A. Mundell, and Jaroslav Vanek, eds., *Trade, Balance of Payments, and Growth: Papers in International Economics in Honor of Charles P. Kindleberger* (Amsterdam: North-Holland Publishing Co., 1971).

Brander, James A., "Rationales for Strategic Trade and Industrial Policy," in Paul R. Krugman, ed., *Strategic Trade Policy and the New International Economics* (Cambridge Mass.: The MIT Press, 1986).

Brander, James A., "Intra-industry Trade in Identical Commodities," *Journal of International Economics* 11:1 (February 1981), 1–14.

Brander, James A., and Barbara J. Spencer, "Export Subsidies and International Market Rivalry," *Journal of International Economics* 18:1/2 (February 1985), 83–100.

Brecher, Richard A., "Minimum Wage Rates and the Pure Theory of International Trade," *The Quarterly Journal of Economics* 88:1 (February 1974), 98–116.

Chichilnisky, Graciela, and Geoffrey Heal, "Necessary and Sufficient Conditions for a Resolution of the Social Choice Paradox," *Journal of Economic Theory* 31:3 (October 1983), 68–87.

Corden, W. M., *Trade Policy and Economic Welfare* (Oxford: Clarendon Press, 1974).

Davidson, Carl, Lawrence Martin and Steven Matusz, "The Structure of Simple

General Equilibrium Models with Frictional Unemployment," *Journal of Political Economy* 96:6 (December 1988), 1267–1293.

Davidson, Donald, "On the Very Idea of a Conceptual Scheme," reprinted as Essay 13 of *Inquiries into Truth and Interpretation*, D. Davidson (Oxford: Oxford University Press, 1984).

Dertouzos, Michael L., Richard K. Lester, Robert M. Solow and The MIT Commission on Industrial Productivity, *Made in America* (Cambridge Mass.: The MIT Press, 1989).

Dixit, Avinash, "Trade and Insurance with Moral Hazard," *Journal of International Econmics* 23:3/4 (November 1987), 201–220.

———, "Trade Policy: An Agenda for Research" in Paul R. Krugman, ed., *Strategic Trade Policy and the New International Economics* (Cambridge, Mass.: The MIT Press, 1986).

Dixit, Avinash K., and Gene M. Grossman, "Targeted Export Promotion with Several Oligopolistic Industries," *Journal of International Economics* 21:3/4 (November 1986), 233–250.

Eaton, Jonathan, and Gene M., Grossman "Optimal Trade and Industrial Policy Under Oligopoly," *The Quarterly Journal Of Economics* 101:2 (May 1986), 383–406.

Ethier, Wilfred J., *Modern International Economics*, 2nd. Edition (New York: W. W. Norton, 1988).

———, "The Theory of International Trade," in L. H. Officer, ed., *International Economics* (Boston: Kluwer Academic Publishers, 1987).

———, "Internationally Decreasing Costs and World Trade," *Journal of International Economics* 9:1 (February 1979), 1–24.

Findlay, Ronald, and Stanislaw Wellisz, "Endogenous Tariffs, the Political Economy of Trade Restrictions, and Welfare," in J. N. Bhagwati, ed., *Import Competition and Response* (Chicago: University of Chicago Press, 1982).

Gilpin, Robert, *The Political Economy of International Relations* (Princeton: Princeton University Press, 1987).

Glymour, Clark, *Theory and Evidence* (Princeton: Princeton University Press, 1980).

Goldstein, Judith L., and Stephen D. Krasner, "Unfair Trade Practices: The Case for a Differential Response," *The American Economic Review, Papers and Proceedings* 74:2 (May 1984), 282–287.

Grinols, Earl L, *Uncertainty and the Theory of International Trade* (Chur, Switzerland: Harwood Academic Publishers, 1987).

Grossman, Gene M., and J. David Richardson, *Strategic Trade Policy: A Survey of Issues and Early Analysis*, Special Papers in International Economics, No. 15 (April 1985).

Haltiwanger, John, and Michael Waldman, "Rational Expectations and the Limits of Optimality," *The American Economic Review* 75:3 (June 1985), 326–340.

Harré, Rom, *The Varieties of Realism: A Rationale for the Natural Sciences* (Oxford: Blackwell, 1986).

Harsanyi, John C., "Games with Incomplete Information Played by 'Bayesian'

Players, I–III," *Management Science* 14:3, 5, 7 (November 1967, January and March 1968), 159–182, 320–334, 486–502.

Helpman, Elhanan, "Increasing Returns, Imperfect Markets, and Trade Theory," Ronald W. Jones and Peter B. Kenen, eds., *Handbook of International Economics, volume I*, (Amsterdam: North-Holland, 1984).

Helpman, Elhanan, and Paul R. Krugman, *Trade Policy and Market Structure* (Cambridge, Mass.: The MIT Press, 1989).

Johnson, Harry G., "Optimum Tariffs and Retaliation," *The Review of Economic Studies* 21:2 (1953–4), 142–153.

Katz, Michael L., and Carl Shapiro, "Technology Adoption in the Presence of Network Externalities," *Journal of Political Economy* 94:4 (August 1986), 822–841.

Kennan, John, and Raymond Riezman, "Do Big Countries Win Tariff Wars?" *International Economic Review* 29:1 (February 1988), 81–85.

Krasner, Stephen D., "State Power and the Structure of International Trade," *World Politics* 28:3 (April 1976), 317–47.

Kreuger, Anne O., "The Political Economy of the Rent-Seeking Society," *The American Economic Review* 64:3 (June 1974), 291–303.

Krugman, Paul R., "Is Free Trade Passé?" *The Journal of Economic Perspectives* 1:2 (Fall 1987), 131–144.

———, "Introduction: New Thinking About Trade Policy," in Paul R. Krugman, ed., *Strategic Trade Policy and the New International Economics* (Cambridge, Mass.: The MIT Press, 1986).

Kuhn, Thomas S., *The Structure of Scientific Revolutions*, 2nd ed., enlarged, International Encyclopedia of Unified Science, Foundations of the Unity of Science, Volume II, Number 2, (Chicago: University of Chicago Press, 1970).

Ledyard, John O., "The Scope of the Hypothesis of Bayesian Equilibrium," *Journal of Economic Theory* 39:1 (June 1986), 59–82.

Lucas, Robert E., Jr., "Book Review of 'Trade Policy and Market Structure," by Elhanan Helpman and Paul R. Krugman" *Journal of Political Economy* 98:3 (June 1990), 664–667.

MacKay, Alfred F., *Arrow's Theorem: The Paradox of Social Choice* (New Haven: Yale University Press, 1980).

McKenzie, Lionel, "On Equilibrium in Graham's Model of World Trade and Other Competitive Systems," *Econometrica* 22:2 (April 1954), 147–161.

McMillan, John, *Game Theory in International Economics* (Chur, Switzerland: Harwood Academic Publishers, 1986).

Magee, Stephen P., William A. Brock, and Leslie Young, *Black Hole Tariffs and Endogenous Policy Theory* (Cambridge: Cambridge University Press, 1989).

Mayer, Wolfgang, "Endogenous Tariff Formation," *The American Economic Review*, 74:5 (December 1984), 970–985.

Nagel, Thomas, *The View from Nowhere* (New York: Oxford University Press, 1986).

Newbery, David M. G. and Joseph E. Stiglitz, *The Theory of Commodity Price Stabilization* (Oxford: Oxford University Press, 1981).

Pomery, John, "Optimal Tariffs," in John Eatwell, Murray Milgate, and Peter Newman eds., *The New Palgrave* (London: The MacMillan Press Ltd, 1987).

Putnam, Hilary, *The Many Faces of Realism* (LaSalle IL: Open Court Publishing Co., 1987).

Rangarajan, L., "The Politics of International Trade," in Susan Strange, ed., *Paths to International Political Economy* (London: George Allen and Unwin, 1984).

Rescher, Nicholas, *The Strife of Systems* (Pittsburgh: University of Pittsburgh Press, 1985).

Richardson, J. David, "Empirical Research on Trade Liberalization with Imperfect Competition: A Survey," *OECD Economic Studies* (Spring 1989), 7–50.

Rorty, Richard, *Contingency, Irony, and Solidarity* (Cambridge: Cambridge University Press, 1989).

Simpson, Evan, ed., *Anti-foundationalism and Practical Reasoning: Conversations between Hermeneutics and Analysis* (Edmonton, AB: Academic Print. & Pub., 1987).

Solow, Robert M., "Comments from Inside Economics," Chapter 3 of Arjo Klamer, Donald N. McCloskey, and Robert M. Solow, eds., *The Consequences of Economic Rhetoric* (Cambridge: Cambridge University Press, 1988).

Stolper, Wolfgang F., and Paul A. Samuelson, "Protection and Real Wages," *The Review of Economic Studies* 9:1 (November 1941), 58–73.

Thursby, Marie, and Richard Jensen, "A Conjectural Variation Approach to Strategic Tariff Equilibria," *Journal of International Economics*, 14:1/2 (February 1983), 145–161.

Wittgenstein, Ludwig, *Tractatus Logico-Philosophicus*, trans. D. F. Pears and B. F. McGuiness, with introduction by Bertrand Russell (London: Routledge & Kegan Paul, 1974).

———, *Philosophical Investigations*, the English text of the third edition, trans. G. E. M. Anscombe (New York: MacMillan, 1958).

Woodland, A. D., *International Trade and Resource Allocation* (Amsterdam: North-Holland Publishing Co., 1982).

9 POLICY RESEARCH: A WITHERING BRANCH OF ECONOMICS?

W. Lee Hansen

1. Introduction

What are the prospects that policy research will remain an important preoccupation of economists and that new economics Ph.D.s will continue to be trained for, interested in, and rewarded for doing policy research? This question is timely as policy schools and economics departments reexamine their respective missions and clarify their goals and objectives. Debate within public policy and public administration schools continues over the relative emphasis they should place on policy research and analysis versus public administration or management (Wildavsky, 1985; Kettl, 1990).

Meanwhile, the American Economic Association, responding to criticism about the profession's increasingly narrow focus, has undertaken a major study of how new Ph.D.s are educated and how their education shapes the direction of future research in economics (Hansen, 1990; Hansen, 1991; and Commission on Graduate Education in Economics, 1991). The implications of this study are important for both fields because economics and economists play a central role in public policy programs, and public policy issues have important dimensions that require the expertise of economists.

This chapter explores the linkages between economics and policy research, beginning with a brief review of the changing relationships between economics and policy research. The chapter will then examine the nature of the knowledge and skills required to do policy research, the extent to which economics graduate students are acquiring such knowledge and skills, and the implications of these findings for the linkages between economics and policy research.

Before proceeding, readers should realize that because the distinctions between policy research and policy analysis are blurred, these terms will be used interchangeably. In principle, they are separable, with policy analysis being more specifically client oriented (Weimer and Vining, 1989). As a consequence, academics doing policy research are less likely to be involved in policy analysis than their nonacademic colleagues who, even if they describe themselves as policy researchers, are typically more heavily engaged in policy analysis. The focus of the comments here is on this author's area of specialty in policy research, on human resource issues such as those in the areas of labor and welfare, as contrasted to health and the environment where conditions may be somewhat different.

2. The Setting

Understanding the linkages between economics and policy research is complicated by several developments. These developments include: the economic profession's apparently declining interest in, and attention to, public policy concerns; the current disillusionment of economists with policy analysis and its accomplishments; the weakening of interest in, and funding of, policy-oriented research; the growing presence of policy analysts in government; and finally the emergence of public policy schools which seek to educate and train policy researchers and analysts.

The waning of interest in policy issues among younger academic economists has raised concern about the scope and content of graduate training. Such training, it is argued, has become ever more narrowly focused on theoretical and technical matters, and gives less attention to empirical and problem-oriented research questions and to policy issues (Leonticf, 1982; Morgan, 1988; Colander and Klamer, 1987). There seems to be a growing belief that talented undergraduates interested in a more policy-oriented approach to economics are discouraged from beginning graduate study in this subject (Kasper, 1991). Those students who do retain strong policy-oriented interests must either put them aside while doing graduate work in economics or try to satisfy them by moving into some related graduate program, such as a public policy school, an agricultural economics department, industrial relations institute, or a business school. Of course, many economics graduate students still concentrate on policy research, but there is a sense that opportunities to build on these interests are eroding. In any case, because the training provided in graduate programs outside economics is by definition different, it remains unclear whether the existing stock of expertise in policy research and policy analysis, which has come to be dominated by economists, can continue to reproduce itself.

Traditionally, economists have demonstrated a keen interest in policy issues. Indeed, as the federal government broadened the scope of its activities, and particularly its social programs in the 1960s and the early 1970s, it relied increasingly on economists. They were called to offer advice on programs, to analyze program effectiveness and in some cases to help operate these programs. Substantial numbers of academic economists were attracted to the policy field because of its challenges, the availability of substantial funding to carry out research, and the possibility of having some effect on public policy (Nelson, 1987). Moreover, in the 1970s many new Ph.D.s in economics took positions in government agencies and policy research organizations to apply their knowledge and skills by carrying out policy research and analysis and by helping to formulate and implement policy.

As time passed, economists began to look back in an effort to assess their role in the arena of public policy. Early indications of the disillusionment about the prospects for policy research and analysis emerge from Henry Aaron's influential book, *Politics and The Professors: The Great Society in Perspective* (Aaron, 1978). In a wide-ranging analysis of the Great Society programs of the 1960s and early 1970s, he concludes that social science research on these programs, much of it undertaken by economists, often did not, and could not, answer the questions that needed to be answered. Even when it did, their results did not necessarily influence decision makers. And because many of these social programs were attacking complex problems, the results fell short of earlier expectations, as demonstrated by social science research. Aaron's sobering critique no doubt dampened the enthusiasm of economists for the future of policy research and analysis.

It is not clear that matters have improved as we enter the 1990s. Nothing demonstrates this more clearly than a recent discussion of social science research in the *Journal of Human Resources* (1990). The occasion was a broad-based review of two recent books by economists on policy research and analysis: Robert H. Haveman's *Poverty Policy and Poverty Research: The Great Society and the Social Sciences* and Richard P. Nathan's *Social Science in Government: Uses and Misuses*. Haveman and Nathan offer their assessments of the state of social science research in poverty and in the evaluation of employment and training programs. Both indicate that important progress has been made in policy analysis and evaluation research while at the same time they highlight continuing problems. After reading these volumes, one comes away with a more hopeful view than that expressed by Aaron.

Aaron, who participated in the *JHR* discussion, states his views even more bluntly, noting that economists have too often proposed policies that, though designed to improve welfare, gave far too little attention to whether such policies can be implemented and sustained. He suggests the existence of an inherent conflict between the values of the academic and policy worlds, where "the former praises technical virtuosity and elegance and rewards analytical innovation" and "the latter insists on simplicity and transparency and is indifferent to analytical innovation" (Aaron, 1990; 279).[1]

Another veteran policy researcher and analyst, Edward M. Gramlich, highlights the different incentives driving academics and policy-makers. As a result, policy-makers are often confused by policy research because "academic researchers do not exactly speak with one voice" (Gramlich, 1990: 288). Indeed, he goes on to question why politicians listen to researchers at all.

Eric A. Hanushek offers a different perspective, arguing that greater emphasis is needed on disciplinary research that is "motivated by the challenges perceived within the separate disciplines" (Hanushek, 1990: 291). Such research in economics, for example, may address some issues relating to public policy, but that is not the central purpose of disciplinary research. The objective of policy research, by contrast, is "to produce policy implications that have some hope or expectation of being taken seriously" (Hanushek, 1990: 291). Policy research differs from policy analysis, the latter being highly specific, client-oriented, and with a short time horizon. Based on his review, Hanushek suggests that resources should be concentrated on disciplinary research because such an allocation will have a stronger and more definite impact, including important effects on the beliefs of future generations of policy makers.

A harsher view is expressed by James J. Heckman who, focusing on the low level of existing social science knowledge, argues that the "pretence to knowledge undermines the acquisition of knowledge" (Heckman, 1990: 303). He goes on to say that "the failure of speculative social science theory and policy advocacy research has hurt empirical social science" (Heckman, 1990: 303) and accounts for diminished funding for all social science research. He laments the low quality of empirical advocacy research, which he asserts has harmed the academic credability of all empirical research.[2] Unfortunately, Heckman does not amplify on these intriguing and provocative comments, thus leaving readers to elaborate for themselves.

Though it might be argued that these economists do not constitute a fair sampling of the economics profession, they are nevertheless an influential group whose judgments about the relationships between disciplinary research, policy research, and policy analysis cannot easily be dismissed. None of the four reviewers express much optimism about the likelihood that policy research can have strong positive effects. Without saying so directly, though Hanushek and Heckman come closest, they suggest that the "real pay dirt" lies in disciplinary research.

The decline of interest and certainly funding of policy research in the labor-welfare area is quite apparent to economists even though comprehensive supporting data are not readily available. It is true that research funding grew rapidly from the mid-1960s to the late 1970s. Since then, real levels of funding for research on employment and training programs have plummeted, as have those for poverty research. The declining availability of federal research funds has been even more pervasive, with federal obligations for basic and applied research in economics falling by more than 40 percent from 1977 to 1986.[3] These declines are reflected in reduced research output. Haveman documents the falling number of published papers on poverty and poverty-related research that began in the late 1970s. Casual inspection of the journals indicates a similar decline in published papers in the human resources field.

Perhaps associated with declining funding are the sharply diminished opportunities for academic economists to gain policy experience. Unlike the situation in the early 1960s when the number of doctoral economists in government was minuscule, government agencies now support substantial staffs of economists as a result of being able for more than a decade to hire capable Ph.D. economists in permanent positions. The presence of staff economists in key agencies reduces, if not eliminates, the need for short-term expertise of the kind academics could and did provide; it seems that fewer young academic economists go off to work for the federal government in Washington, D.C., either during the summer or on academic year leaves. It is possible, of course, that government agencies have discovered that academics who might be interested in temporary employment in Washington would be of only marginal value because of the nature of their training and the requirements of the available jobs.

Meanwhile, a wide array of private for profit and nonprofit organizations employ Ph.D. economists to carry out research studies that academic economists might have done in the 1960s and early 1970s. These developments mean that fewer young academic economists have direct policy experience, and as a consequence they are less well equipped to convey what policy research and analysis means to their students.

The rise of public policy schools and the expansion of graduate programs in related fields are also causing some uneasiness. With the help of Ford Foundation funds, a number of public policy schools expanded in the 1970s, and they continue to be vigorous and productive. Whether their limited numbers of Ph.D. graduates and M.A. recipients can compete with Ph.D. economists is not clear. It is quite apparent that their production of Ph.D.s never was large, and it shows little or no change in recent years. These schools have produced a steady flow of master's degree students who may be at least partial substitutes for economics Ph.D.s in policy analysis. On the other hand, the market for public policy analysts, whether they hold master's or doctorate degrees, did not grow as rapidly in the 1980s as had been expected (Conant, 1991).

Less can be said about the production of policy researchers and analysts in economics because few if any graduate departments offer a special track in policy research and analysis. Nor is there a research field with such a designation. Rather, there are ten major fields, divided along traditional lines: economic theory, public finance, labor, international, and so on. Within these fields there is no easy way of knowing the methodological orientation of published research, that is, whether it is theoretical, empirical, institutional, or policy oriented.[4]

How the relative attractiveness of economics and public policy programs will change in the 1990s remains unclear. Much depends on what happens within the two fields and how the labor market evaluates the products of programs in these two fields.

3. What It Takes To Do Policy Research and Analysis

What is it that distinguishes the training of policy researchers and policy analysts? Several attempts have been made to describe the kinds of knowledge and skills required in these positions. Weimer and Vining (1989) list five areas of preparation: basic information-acquiring skills, a framework for considering the appropriateness of public policy interventions, the technical skills acquired through disciplinary study in fields such as economics and statistics, an understanding of political and organizational behavior, and some ethical framework for dealing with clients. Patton and Sawicki (1986) list three broad goals: learning to apply basic methods of analysis quickly and appropriately as the situation demands, becoming competent in using the methods of analysis and designing approaches to policy issues, and communicating the results. They also list 12 practical principles, ranging from learning how to focus quickly on the central features of the problem, to deciding how much time and effort to devote to a problem.

Nelson (1987) offers the fullest description of what it takes for an economist to participate effectively in the making of public policy. The knowledge and skills Nelson distills from his research are best summarized in his own words:

> Many economists would need to invest greater effort in improving writing skills, facility in reasoning by analogy, command of institutional details, knowledge of legal processes and reasoning, and political awareness and savvy. They might need to devote more time and effort to investigations of history, law, politics, and institutions, and their bearing on the economic topics of policy concern. Advocates of economic policies would need to tailor their policy proposals to reflect an accurate understanding of how these policies will be publicly perceived—in terms of social equity, the public sense of "fairness," impact on personal liberties, infringements on private property rights and other such public concerns. Proponents of economic policies need to be able to defend these policies, not only on narrow technical grounds, but also in broader ideological and philosophical terms. Sensitivity and knowledge in these areas are needed to establish one's standing and influence with policy makers, as well as to shape persuasive policy arguments. Understanding that reaches beyond the confines of economics is also likely to yield more promising economic policy proposals in the first place.
>
> To be more effective policy advocates, many economists would generally need to give more attention to "big-picture" skills. The ability to "tell a story" that makes sense, to "paint a picture," is at a premium in government. Top policy makers are often confronted with overwhelming amounts of information and data. Their greatest concern is to organize this diverse material in some meaningful way. The biggest asset of economists is the conceptual equipment that enables them to impose sense and order on an immensely confusing world of employment, industry, commerce, finance, and administration. Within the recently established profession of public policy analysis, a number of its members have described the practice of policy analysis as more an "art" than a "science" (Wildavsky, 1979). The skills of the "craftsman," rather than the "scientist," are most in demand in professional roles in government [P. 86]

The knowledge and skills used in policy research and analysis, as already described, appear to differ from the knowledge and skills of current mainline economists. Aside from differences in the substance of their interests, there appear to be important differences in the relative emphasis given to various types of knowledge and skills. To understand the commonalities and differences between economists and people in the policy field, it is essential to identify the special knowledge and skills possessed by economists as a result of their education and subsequent experience.

4. The Knowledge and Skills Taught to Economists

What knowledge and skills are being imparted to new economics Ph.D.s through their graduate training that might equip them to do policy research and analysis? An important source of information is the research undertaken for the American Economic Association's Commission on Graduate Education in Economics (COGEE), which recently completed a major examination of graduate education. That study focused on the structure and content of graduate training, in the realization that how new economists are trained helps shape the direction of the profession's future research. Based on this research and its deliberations, the commission recently issued its recommendations (Commission on Graduate Education in Economics, 1991). The presentation that follows draws on selected results from the COGEE study (Hansen, 1990; Hansen, 1991), principally surveys of faculty members and recent Ph.D.s.[5]

Before proceeding, it may be helpful to point out that no formal statement exists describing the knowledge and skills that are required of, or used by, economists. In an effort to capture what seem to be the distinguishing differences among economists, a classification of knowledge and skills was devised for use in the surveys. Interestingly, the survey responses of faculty members and graduate students about which knowledge and skills are being taught and which should be taught proved to be amazingly similar. Moreover, the responses were surprisingly similar among programs of different reputation (e.g., the top six ranked departments, the next nine ranked departments). These similarities no doubt reflect the socialization process that occurs in graduate training; students with different views either do not enter economics Ph.D. programs or they leave for other pursuits.

Knowledge.   To find out what graduate students are learning, faculty (and also graduate students) were asked to rank the relative importance now given, and that should be given, to each of six types of knowledge:

Table 9–1.   Ranking of Skills and Knowledge of Ph.D. Graduates, Based on Faculty Responses

Panel A: Ranking of Emphasis on Different Types of Knowledge That Is and Should Be Given in Graduate Education

Ranking	Currently Emphasized	Should Be Emphasized
1st	Theory	Theory
2nd	Econometrics	Econometrics
3rd	Empirical	Empirical
4th	Applications	Applications
5th	Institutions	Institutions
6th	Literature	Literature

Panel B: Ranking of Importance That Is and Should Be Given to Different Skills in Graduate Education

Ranking	Currently Important	Should Be Important
1st	Analytics	Analytics
2nd	Mathematics	Creativity
3rd	Critical judgment	Critical judgment
4th	Applications	Applications
5th	Computation	Communication
6th	Creativity	Mathematics
7th	Communication	Computation

Source: Hansen (1991).

economic theory, econometrics, institutions and history, literature, applications, and empirical economics.[6]

The results in table 9–1, panel A, indicate general satisfaction of faculty members with the current emphasis in graduate training, as evidenced by the similar rankings for "what is"and "what should be." The order of the rankings of knowledge is about what most economists would have expected. Economic theory leads the way, followed by econometrics; well behind come empirial economics, and applications, institutions, and literature are at the bottom. These results suggest that faculty members at Ph.D. granting departments see nothing seriously wrong with the relative emphasis given to the six different types of knowledge.

Skills.   Graduate education also imparts special skills utilized by economists. Thus respondents were asked to rank the importance that is given and should be given to seven different skills: analytics, mathematics, critical judgment, applications, computation, creativity, and communications.[7]

As shown in panel B of table 9–1, faculty members indicate that analytics and mathematics are the most important skills, with creativity and communication at the bottom of the list and critical judgment, applications, and computation ranking in the middle. The rankings change considerably when the focus is on which skills should be important. While analytics remains at the top the list, creativity vaults to second place, and communication moves up several notches. Meanwhile, mathematics and computation decline sharply in importance, moving to the bottom of the list of skills. Interestingly, the skill of application remains in the middle.

Summary.   Several conclusions emerge. First, there appears to be general agreement about what knowledge is, and what knowledge should be, emphasized in graduate education. Second, there is considerable divergence between the importance that is, and should be, given in graduate training to the various skills required of economists. Third, the differences in the skill rankings support the popular view that mathematics is overemphasized and creativity is undervalued in graduate education in economics.

5. The Knowledge and Skills Required in Public Policy

Because policy researchers and policy analysts could not be identified in the COGEE surveys, there was no direct way of finding out what knowledge and skills they thought were, and should be, emphasized. Nor was there time to survey public policy professionals to find out what knowledge and skills they gained in their graduate education and later used in their jobs. It might be possible to divine this from a detailed examination of the already-cited works by Weimer and Vining, Patton and Sawicki, and Nelson. In principle, they are all describing the relative importance of which knowledge and skills are learned, which should be learned, and which are used in practice.

A next best alternative is to examine what knowledge and skills recent economics Ph.D.s say they use in their jobs, with particular attention to nonacademic economists who are most heavily involved in policy research and analysis. The results presented here are for 1977–1978 economics Ph.D.s who by 1989 had extensive and varied experience on the job and knew what their work required.

Knowledge.   While recent Ph.D.s ranked the emphasis given to the six types of knowledge in their own graduate training quite similarly to the rankings of current faculty members, their rankings based on what they use in their current jobs proved to be quite different, as shown in table 9–2, panel A. Recent Ph.D.s ranked applications and empirical economics first and second by a wide margin, with theory and econometrics lagging behind and institutions and literature at the bottom. This emphasis given to applications and empirical economics contrasts sharply with what goes on in graduate school, where emphasis is given to economic theory and econometrics.

It is important to separate recent Ph.D.s by type of employment. Those in nonacademic jobs rate applications first and as strongly as they rated theory in their own Ph.D. training, with empirical economics a close second. These rankings are not much different from those for recent Ph.D.s employed in departments that educate graduate students.

Skills. The rankings of skills used on the job by recent Ph.D.s also differ considerably from those of current faculty members, being closer to the skills faculty members thought should be important relative to the skills faculty members thought actually were important in graduate training. Topping the rankings of skills used on the job (table 9–2, panel B) was communication, followed by critical judgment. Applications, analytics, and creativity were closely ranked; computation and mathematics trailed at the bottom of the rankings. These results indicate that the skills used by, and hence needed by, nonacademics differ considerably from what is emphasized in graduate education. These skills also differ from those used by recent Ph.D.s who are in Ph.D.-granting departments. They give first place to creativity, with communication, analytics, applications, and critical judgment ranked closely behind, followed by computation and mathematics at the bottom. Thus, the rankings of skills provided in graduate training differ considerably both for academic researchers at Ph.D.-granting institutions and for practicing economists in the non-academic sector who most closely approximate policy researchers and analysts.

Summary.   To the extent the rankings of the knowledge and skills used by recent Ph.D.s in nonacademic jobs can be taken as a reflection of the knowledge and skills used by policy researchers-analysts, the emphasis and importance given to the different types of knowledge and skills in graduate training differ markedly from what policy researchers-analysts use on the job.

6. Confirming Evidence from Economics Faculty

What do faculty members have to say about the capacity of graduate students to use their knowledge and skills? How proficient are they as future economists, not necessarily as policy researchers or analysts?

Table 9–2. Ranking of Knowledge and Skills of Recent Ph.D. Graduates, Based on Their Own Responses

Panel A: Emphasis Given to Different Types of Knowledge in Own Ph.D. Education, in Current Job, and in Current Nonacademic Job

Ranking	In Own Ph.D. Education	In Current Job	
		All Jobs	Nonacademic Jobs
1st	Theory	Application-Policy	Application-Policy
2nd	Econometrics	Empirical	Empirical
3rd	Empirical	Theory	Theory
4th	Application-Policy	Econometrics	Econometrics
5th	Literature	Literature	Institutions-History
6th	Institutions-History	Institutions-History	Literature

Panel B: Importance Given to Different Skills in Own Ph.D. Training, in Current Job, and in Current Nonacademic Job

Ranking	In Own Ph.D. Education	In Current Job	
		All Jobs	Nonacademic Jobs
1st	Analytics	Communication	Communication
2nd	Mathematics	Critical judgment	Critical judgment
3rd	Critical judgment	Applications	Analytics
4th	Applications	Analytics	Applications
5th	Creativity	Creativity	Creativity
6th	Computation	Computation	Computation
7th	Communication	Mathematics	Mathematics

Source: Hansen (1991).

Faculty members indicated that by the time of their comprehensive examinations many graduate students had not gained proficiency in using the knowledge and skills developed in their course work. At the high extreme, 58 percent of faculty members indicated that all or most students (as compared with "some" and "few or none") were well-grounded in economic theory. In sharp contrast, only 14 percent of faculty members could say that by the time students completed their comprehensive examinations most or all of them were good at using theory in empirical applications or at applying theory to the real world.

Nor is the quality of Ph.D. dissertations viewed as particularly impres-

sive by faculty dissertation supervisors. Asked to characterize the dissertations they had recently supervised, 68 percent of faculty members agreed
that most or all dissertations were good training instruments. No more than
half thought that all or most dissertations applied economics to real-world
problems or were well-grounded in economic theory, and only 40 percent
could say that most or all dissertations offered good empirical evidence to
support economic theory. Finally, less than a third of the faculty supervisors indicated that all or most dissertations were well written.

The importance of these selected findings should be apparent. To the
extent that economists have long played a major role in public policy
programs, it would appear that the training currently provided in graduate
programs may limit the interest and ability of new Ph.D.s to do public
policy research and to engage in public policy analysis. In the absence of
comparable data from an earlier period, however, this conclusion rests on
the assumption that the rankings of knowledge and skills from a decade or
two ago would have been different. Unfortunately, this possibility cannot
be checked because no comparable information is available, either for the
1970s when policy research and analysis received greater attention or for
the early 1960s when policy research and analysis had not yet taken shape
as a special area of expertise.

7. Economists and Public Policy

In light of these findings, what is the likely future role of economics in the
policy research and analysis? It is clear that currently economists play a
major role, with substantial numbers of faculty in public policy schools
holding doctorates in economics (Friedman, 1991). Though exact numbers
are difficult to obtain, the preponderance of economists emerge from
examining the membership list of the Association for Public Policy Analysis and Management. Thus, it is not surprising to learn that public policy
programs give extensive attention to economics in their master's and Ph.D.
curricula. Even a cursory acquaintance with policy analysis in federal
government agencies suggests that economists play a major role in carrying
out public policy research and in shaping public policy analysis.

The commanding position of economists in the public policy arena
is hardly surprising. Each year, approximately 40 percent of new Ph.D.s
enter nonacademic jobs, with most of them (about two thirds) going into
government positions, many of which involve policy research and analysis.
This is an underestimate because other new Ph.D.s who initially opt for
academic positions eventually gravitate to the nonacademic sector, where
they utilize their knowledge and skills in ways demanded by their positions
rather than by their graduate education. What is perhaps surprising is that

graduate training does not seem to serve well the educational needs of this large fraction of graduates.

Of those economics Ph.D.s who take academic jobs, a considerable number will require, because of the orientation of their own research, teaching, and professional interests, the mix of knowledge and skills that public policy programs seek to develop even though these academic Ph.D.s may not be labeled as policy researchers and analysts. Some will work in these areas in parallel with their disciplinary research. Others will utilize this intellectual equipment in their daily lives as teachers and members of their departments and university communities. Though not engaged in policy research or analysis, they will be discussing policy issues in their courses and demonstrating to their students how such issues are examined. In addition, developing new course materials, supervising student projects, and participating in study groups and university administrative activities all require expertise in the five areas of preparation mentioned by Weimer and Vining, in practicing the 12 principles presented by Patton and Sawicki, and in following the multifaceted approach described by Nelson. The many new Ph.D. economists who do not take academic jobs will benefit even more directly because of the nature of the work they perform.

8. Implications for Economics and for Public Policy Programs

What are the implications of the results presented here? Several emerge. In economics, graduate training is not well structured to prepare new Ph.D.s for the range of work that they will do, particularly for those graduate students interested in policy research and policy analysis. This development may indicate a turning away by the economics profession from its long-standing interest in economic policy issues. As a result, we can expect to find a diminishing proportion of economists with active interest in policy research and analysis.

It is conceivable that these patterns will be reversed. The creation of the AEA Commission may signal the end of a more than decade-long phase in economics that has emphasized abstract and technical issues to the exclusion of real-world, empirical policy issues. If so, possibilities are stronger that the Commission's findings and recommendations may produce changes in how graduate students are educated and in that sense gradually redirect the profession's interests. Whether the combined effects of these two forces can accelerate the pace of change and help policy research regain its position in economics is uncertain.

Should economics move away from policy research and analysis, an opportunity will arise for public policy schools to expand to fill the void. Whether public policy schools will be able to, or choose to, do so remains unclear. They labor under several constraints, one being the move to place greater emphasis on public management. This move appears to be motivated by the view that producing better managers is socially more important, particularly when neither the supply of students nor the demand for graduates can support large programs with a heavy emphasis on policy analysis. Even if there is no redirection of these programs toward public management, public policy schools may not be able to recruit talented young economists to their faculties. This difficulty may not be serious if public policy schools seek out experienced economists who have made their mark in policy research and analysis. On the other hand, if the number of new economists interested in, and prepared to move into, policy research and analysis does decline, the supply of eligible economists will be smaller than it has been in the past.

These developments suggest that public policy schools may want to think about "training their own" faculty members while at the same time attempting to meet the presumably growing nonacademic demand for their graduates, including the demand from employers who in the past may have hired economists. The major difficulty with this approach is the matter of scale. Gearing up to produce any appreciable number of Ph.D.s in public policy is both a formidable and costly undertaking. Moreover, such an approach could end up producing lower-quality substitutes whose presence would undermine the long-run prospects for the success of public policy programs. A further difficulty is that the demand for public policy Ph.D.s is apparently not that strong right now; certainly the flow of Ph.D.s is still quite small. And if interest in public policy is reversed in economics, public policy schools might see their Ph.D. market evaporate.

Whatever happens, it is apparent that the role of economics and economists in public policy research and analysis helps to bridge the gap between disciplinary research and the need by policy-makers for improved knowledge, specific studies of policy issues, and policy advice. Let us hope that economists will renew their interest and commitment to policy research and analysis, particularly in graduate economics but also in public policy schools. Let us hope that in doing so they can also be responsive to what has been learned in the past decade about how policy research and analysis can be strengthened and how the capacity of new economics Ph.D.s to contribute to the study of policy issues can be enhanced.

Acknowledgments

The author appreciates the comments and suggestions of Edward Bird, James Conant, Robert Haveman, and Robert Lampman. The author is indebted to the Andrew W. Mellon Foundation, the Alfred P. Sloan Foundation, and the National Science Foundation for its funding of the work of the American Economic Association's Commission on Graduate Education in Economics, from which this chapter is derived. The author also thanks Edward Bird, Thomas Buchmueller, and Jeffrey Dominitz for their research assistance. Suzanne Vinmans for her secretarial support, and Elaine Moran for her editorial advice.

Notes

1. Another statement of Aaron's current views is contained in his recent Ely Lecture to the American Economic Association (Aaron, 1989).

2. In a throw-away line, Heckman notes that "it is easier to prove theorems than to establish enduring facts."

3. Based on data for federal obligations for basic and applied research, deflated by the GNP deflator; see National Science Foundation, *Profiles–Economics: Human Resources and Funding*, Special Report NSF 88–333, table 31 and 33.

4. It might be useful for more fields to adopt key word identifiers to be supplied with paper abstracts, thereby permitting identification of papers by both subject and methodological orientation.

5. The samples of faculty members, graduate students, and recent Ph.D.s were drawn from a sample of 91 economics departments whose graduate programs were among those ranked in the 1982 study by the National Academy of Sciences (Jones, Lindzey, and Coggeshall, 1982). Further details on the surveys and other work for the Commission will be available in forthcoming publications by the author, who served as Executive Secretary of the Commission.

6. The knowledge categories reflect an effort to classify the major types of knowledge that are used by economists in their work and are taught to graduate students as part of their preparation as economists. Six categories or types of knowledge emerged:

   a. Economic theory (e.g., assumptions and theorems of economic behavior).
   b. Econometrics (e.g., statistical theorems in economics, properties of models, and distribution theory).
   c. Economic institutions and history (e.g., forms of economic association, historical economic forces).
   d. Economic literature (e.g., recent or comprehensive histories of economic ideas and approaches).
   e. Economic applications and policy issues (e.g., current topics of concern in business, government, and society).
   f. Empirical economics (e.g., testing implications of theoretical models, estimating behavioral responses, practical analysis of data, experience with economic databases).

7. The seven categories of skill used follow:

a. Critical judgment (e.g., analyzing ideas, reviewing literature, formulating pertinent comments).
b. Analytics (e.g., understanding and solving problems, making and analyzing logical arguments).
c. Applications (e.g., seeing practical implications of abstract ideas, analyzing real-world policies and processes).
d. Mathematics (e.g., constructing and analyzing proofs, manipulating mathematical abstractions).
e. Computation (e.g., effectively and quickly finding and manipulating relevant data sources, translating statistical theory into functioning programs).
f. Communication (e.g., speaking and writting effectively and with good style, quickly understanding spoken and written ideas of others).
g. Creativity (e.g., conceiving interesting research questions, finding new ways of analyzing topics).

References

Aaron, Henry, "Social Science Research and Policy: Review Essay," *Journal of Human Resources* 25 (Spring 1990), 276–280.

————, "Politics and the Professors Revisited," Richard T. Ely Lecture, in *American Economic Association: Papers and Proceedings* 79 (May 1989), 1–15.

————, *Politics and the Professors: The Great Society in Perspective* (Washington, D.C.: Brookings Institution, 1978).

Aaron, Henry, et al., "Review Essays of *Poverty Policy and Policy Research* by Robert Haveman and *Social Science Research in Government: Uses and Misuses* by Richard Nathan," *Journal of Human Resources* 25 (Spring 1990), 275–311.

Colander, David, and Arjo Klamer, "The Making of an Economist," *Journal of Economic Perspectives* 1 (Fall 1987), 95–112.

Commission on Graduate Education in Economics, "Report of the Commission on Graduate Education in Economics," *Journal of Economic Literature* (Forthcoming September 1991).

Conant, James, "The Enrollment Crash in Schools of Public Affairs and Administration—And the Aftermath: A Search for Winners and Losers," Robert M. La Follette Institute of Public Affairs, University of Wisconsin—Madison, 1991, 18 pp. mimeo., plus tables and appendices.

Jones, Lyle V., Gardner Lindzey, and Porter E. Coggeshall, editors, *An Assessment of Research-Doctorate Programs in the United States: Social and Behavioral Sciences* (Washington, D.C.: National Academy Press, 1982).

Friedman, Lee S., "Economists and Public Policy Programs," *Journal of Policy Analysis and Management* 10 (Spring 1991), 343–359.

Gramlich, Edward M., "Social Science Research and Policy: Review Essay," *Journal of Human Resources* 25 (Spring 1990), 281–289.

Hansen, W. Lee, "Educating and Training New Economics Ph.D.s: How Good a Job Are We Doing? *American Economic Review: Papers and Proceedings* 80

(May 1990), 437–444; and the related " Discussion" by Alan S. Blinder, Claudia Goldin, T. Paul Schultz, and Robert M. Solow, 445–450.

————, "The Education and Training of Economics Doctorates: Major Findings of the Executive Secretary of the American Economic Association's Commission on Graduate Education in Economics," *Journal of Economic Literature* (Forthcoming, September 1991).

Hanushek, Eric A., "Social Science Research and Policy: Review Essay," *Journal of Human Resources* 25 (Spring 1990), 290–295.

Haveman, Robert H., *Poverty Policy and Poverty Research: The Great Society and the Social Sciences* (Madison: University of Wisconsin Press, 1987).

Heckman, James J., "Social Science Research and Policy: Review Essay," *Journal of Human Resources* 25 (Spring 1990), 297–304.

Kasper, Hirschel, "The Education of Economists, From Undergraduate to Graduate Study: A Report of the Committee of College Faculty," *Journal of Economic Literature* (Forthcoming, September 1991).

Kettl, Donald F., "The Perils—and Prospects—of Public Administration,' 50 *PAR* (July/August 1990), 411–419.

Leontief, Wassily, "Academic Economics," *Science* 217 (2 July 1982), 106–107.

Morgan, Theodore, "Theory Versus Empiricism in Academic Economics: Update and Comparisons," *Journal of Economic Perspectives* 2 (Fall 1988), 159–164.

Nathan, Richard P., *Social Science in Government: Uses and Misuses* (New York: Basic Books, Inc., 1988).

National Science Foundation, *Profiles—Economics: Human Resources and Funding*, Special Report NSF 88–333, 1989.

Nelson, Robert H., "The Economics Profession and the Making of Economic Policy," *Journal of Economic Literature* 25 (March 1987), 49–91.

Patton, Carl V., and David S. Sawicki, *Basic Methods of Policy Analysis and Planning* (New York: Pentice-Hall, 1986).

Wildavsky, Aaron, "Social Science Research and Policy: Review Essay," *Journal of Human Resources* 25 (Spring 1979), 305–311.

————, "The Once and Future School of Public Policy," *The Public Interest* 79 (Spring 1985), 25–41.

Weimer, David L., and Aidan R. Vining, *Policy Analysis: Concepts and Practice* (Englewood Cliffs, N.J.: Prentice-Hall, 1989).

Index